Intermediate-Size Cities
as Growth Centers

Niles M. Hansen

The Praeger Special Studies program—utilizing the most modern and efficient book production techniques and a selective worldwide distribution network—makes available to the academic, government, and business communities significant, timely research in U.S. and international economic, social, and political development.

Intermediate-Size Cities as Growth Centers

Applications for Kentucky, the Piedmont Crescent, the Ozarks, and Texas

PRAEGER SPECIAL STUDIES IN U.S. ECONOMIC AND SOCIAL DEVELOPMENT

Praeger Publishers   New York   Washington   London

PRAEGER PUBLISHERS
111 Fourth Avenue, New York, N.Y. 10003, U.S.A.
5, Cromwell Place, London S.W.7, England

Published in the United States of America in 1971
by Praeger Publishers, Inc.

© 1971 by Praeger Publishers, Inc.

Library of Congress Catalog Card Number: 72-150709

Printed in the United States of America

This book is devoted to a consideration of growth center policy within the context of the United States. Although it shares a great deal in common with my *Rural Poverty and the Urban Crisis*, its emphases are quite different. For example, in contrast to the earlier work this book gives considerable attention to growth center theory and to growth center policies that have been introduced in other countries. Criteria for growth center policy also receive much more attention here. *Rural Poverty and the Urban Crisis* contained proposals for a growth center strategy based on intermediate-size cities, but few specific cases were cited. The present study devotes four chapters to detailed case studies of growth centers with relevance to lagging areas. There also is a chapter on the problems which are most likely to arise in attempts to implement the proposed growth center measures.

This study was made possible by the financial assistance of the Office of Economic Research, Economic Development Administration, U.S. Department of Commerce. It was carried out at the University of Kentucky and at the Center for Economic Development of the University of Texas under its Program on the Role of Growth Centers in Regional Development. Of course, the views presented do not necessarily reflect those of the agency. I have benefitted from the technical and moral support of many persons within the Economic Development Administration, particularly Gerald Duskin, whose initiative led to this undertaking, John Kaler, Roger Prior, and Samuel Rosenblatt. I have also learned a great deal from faculty colleagues and students at the University of Kentucky and the University of Texas. My coworker N. Dann Milne has been especially helpful during our association at both universities. I am grateful to Michael Curley for his work on South Texas and to William Gruben for his valuable assistance in the South Texas survey; to Eldon J. Nosari for his work on the Ozarks region; to Jean Shackelford for her investigations of self-sustained growth thresholds; to Alan Winger and Gary Mammel for their studies on the housing problem; and to Richard YuKhin for his important contributions to the section on Eastern Kentucky. Thanks are due to David Hirschberg and Gay Irwin for help on migration analyses. The invaluable administrative support of Charles Haywood and F. Ray Marshall must also be acknowledged. My contacts with colleagues from other countries through the United Nations Research Institute for Social Development in Geneva, Switzerland, have also proven very valuable. I finally would like to thank Pamela Pate for her able cartographic and secretarial assistance.

I wish to thank a number of sources for permission to use materials published elsewhere. The section on the French School of growth pole theory in Chapter 2 is adapted from my *French Regional Planning* (Bloomington: Indiana University Press, 1968). A portion of Chapter 3 appeared in modified form in *The Journal of the American Institute of Planners,* Vol. 35, No. 6 (November, 1969). The section on locational preferences in Chapter 5 is based on an article coauthored with Richard YuKhin and published in *The Journal of Human Resources*, Vol. 5, No. 3 (Summer, 1970). Part of Chapter 6 appeared in *The Review of Regional Studies*, Vol. 1, No. 1.

The introductory chapter presents the broad national setting for the subsequent chapters on growth centers. Chapter 2 deals with growth center theory as it has been developed first in France and then in other countries. Applications of growth center policies are discussed in the following chapter, which examines foreign experiences as well as those of the Economic Development Administration and the Appalachian Regional Commission in the United States. Criteria for a growth center policy for the United States are examined in Chapter 4 in the light of both empirical and theoretical considerations. In the next four chapters these criteria are applied to four areas: Kentucky, the Carolinas, the Ozarks, and Texas. Chapter 9 suggests some measures that might be taken to deal with problems that may arise in the implementation of growth center policies. The final chapter summarizes the findings of the previous chapters and suggests how growth center policy might be integrated with proposals now being made to decentralize federal programs.

Although the growth center concept has enjoyed considerable attention in recent years, this is the first book-length exploration of its relevance to urban and regional policy in the United States. Hopefully it may contribute to the work of scholars, government officials, and others concerned with the issues raised here, and hopefully they may be prompted to improve on its deficiencies; admittedly a great deal of exciting work on growth center theory and policy and their interrelations is yet to be done.

CONTENTS

LIST OF TABLES

TABLES IN THE APPENDIX

LIST OF MAPS

1

PROBLEMS OF
METROPOLITAN
GROWTH

In the years since World War II most European nations—both Western and Eastern—and many of the newly developing countries have adopted strategies to influence the spatial distribution of people and economic activity. The United States, with its historic tendency to place relatively great explicit and implicit reliance on market mechanisms, has been a latecomer in this area. However, the recent dramatic upsurge of concern about the ravages that have been wrought on the environment by laissez-faire attitudes has led to increased interest in, if not agreement on, policies to guide rural and urban development. Thus, as Lloyd Rodwin has pointed out,

> the conviction that urban growth does not take place the way it should is no longer the view of merely a few sensitive intellectuals and professional urbanists. It has become one of the dominant beliefs of the age. If somehow we could determine the best locations for urban growth, and could steer economic activities and families into those areas and away from less desirable ones, we would have powerful weapons for changing our environment. Instead of being stricken or overwhelmed by movements of population and economic activity, we could help communities and regions adjust more effectively to these changes.[1]

Of course, we do have federal agencies whose mission is to attract economic activity to lagging areas. The Appalachian Regional Commission, created by the Appalachian Regional Development Act of 1965, and the Economic Development Administration, created by the Public Works and Economic Development Act of 1965, are the most notable. Nevertheless, we still do not have programs to provide comprehensive assistance to workers who wish to move from areas of low income and high unemployment to areas where there are better opportunities. We also lack a national urban policy, though, as Wilbur Thompson has suggested, "when the federal government actively promotes policies which discourage the out-migration of the unemployed in the Detroit or Pittsburgh metropolitan areas, or implicitly approves the continued growth of New York and Chicago by not moving to contain their further growth, the national position can be read that we anticipate and approve of the growth of our metropolitan areas at an overall rate equal to their natural rates of increase plus the current rate of net in-migration."[2]

It should be emphasized that we are not primarily concerned here with farm-to-city migration, which now plays a relatively minor role in metropolitan growth. The shift from farms to cities began in earnest about 1940, when 30.5 million Americans lived on farms. By 1960, about 10.7 million persons fourteen years old and older lived on farms. The comparable figure for 1967 was 7.8 million, and that for 1968, 7.5 million. However, a relative stabilization of the farm population is indicated by the fact that the 1969 figure was also 7.5 million. Total farm population is now estimated at about 10 million, or about 5 per cent of total national population. Between 1959 and 1969 more than a million farms disappeared. The 3 million that remain have an average size of 377 acres, 30 per cent larger than the average farm in 1959. The great majority of remaining marginal farms are owned by farmers in late middle age or older; and, of course, when these farms cease to operate as their owners retire or die, there will not be any increase in migration to the city. There will be some exceptions—primarily in the South and particularly in tobacco-growing areas, where mechanization has yet to make its impact—but the last great surge of migration has probably already taken place.[3]

However, the decline in farm-to-city migration should not obscure problems related to the sizable rural nonfarm population and population shifts within the urban hierarchy. For example, the data in Table 1 indicate that although all categories of rural population declined between 1950 and 1960, about 33.3 per cent of the total population was still rural in 1960. Moreover, another 28.2 per cent (excluding the 5.5 per cent living in unincorporated parts of urbanized areas) lived in urban places with fewer than 50,000 persons.

These figures take on vital significance in the light of Brian J. L. Berry's analysis of the commuting behavior of the American population in 1960.[4] Berry found that all but 5 per cent of the country's population lives within the daily commuting field of metropolitan centers. These fields spread over the entire country except where population densities are less than two persons per square mile or where there are national parks and Indian reservations. Degree of metropolitan labor market participation was found to be the key variable in the "regional welfare syndrome," an index of the pattern of urban influence on the surrounding hinterlands' level of economic well-being as measured by such factors as income and employment. In general, degree of labor market participation (daily commuting to employment in the central city) declines with increasing distance from the city, as do the average values of farm land and buildings, median family income, median school years completed, rate of population increase (which is negative in the peripheries), and population gain through migration (which also becomes negative in the more outlying areas). Proportion of families with annual incomes less than $3,000 and the

TABLE 1

Urban and Rural Population by Size of Place, 1950 and 1960

Class and Size	Population (thousands)		Percentage of Total Population	
	1950	1960	1950	1960
URBAN	96,468	125,269	64.0	69.9
1,000,000 or more	17,404	17,484	11.5	9.8
500,000-1,000,000	9,187	11,111	6.1	6.2
250,000-500,000	8,242	10,766	5.5	6.0
100,000-250,000	9,479	11,652	6.3	6.5
50,000-100,000	8,931	13,836	5.9	7.7
25,000-50,000	8,808	14,951	5.8	8.3
10,000-25,000	11,867	17,568	7.9	9.8
5,000-10,000	8,139	9,780	5.4	5.5
2,500-5,000	6,490	7,580	4.3	4.2
Under 2,500	578	690	0.4	0.4
Unincorporated Parts of Urbanized Areas	7,344	9,851	4.9	5.5
RURAL	54,230	54,054	36.0	30.1
1,000-2,500	6,473	6,497	4.3	3.6
Under 1,000	4,031	3,894	2.7	2.2
Other Rural	43,725	43,664	29.0	24.3
UNITED STATES	150,697	179,323	100.0	100.0

Source: U.S. Bureau of the Census, *Statistical Abstract of the United States, 1969* (Washington, D.C.: Government Printing Office, 1969), p. 16.

unemployment rate are both directly related to distance from the central city. Thus, the lowest levels of welfare are at the edges of metropolitan fields, and especially in the nonurban interstices between them. When closely spaced metropolitan centers have overlapping labor markets, so that the population of one center can take advantage of employment opportunities in another, the decline in welfare levels with distance from the centers is reduced or eliminated. In contrast, the wider the centers are spread, the lower are the levels to which regional welfare measures fall. Berry found that, in general, "labor markets appear to need to be of greater than 250,000 population to be viable parts of the urban system"[5] and that "very few cities of less than 50,000 population appear to have any impact on the regional welfare syndrome."[6]

Between 1950 and 1960, urban places in the 50,000-100,000 range had the highest rate of population growth, but the 25,000-50,000 and 10,000-25,000 groups had the next highest rates. Though these data seem to contradict Berry's findings, it should be pointed out that most of the fast-growing cities in the middle-size group are close to a large city or parts of an urban complex, rather than independent cities dominating their own hinterlands. Indeed, although cities with over 1,000,000 persons grew only slightly between 1950 and 1960 (see Table 1), urban complexes grew rapidly. The data in Table 2 show that whereas the population of the United States grew at an annual rate of 1.7 per cent during the 1950's, the population in standard-metropolitan statistical areas (SMSA) grew by 2.4 per cent and the population in suburbs by 4.0 per cent. Between 1960 and 1968, the national population grew at an annual rate of 1.3 per cent, while the comparable SMSA and suburban values were 1.5 and 2.8, respectively.

Projections of future urban growth vary widely. The U.S. Bureau of the Census has made several estimates based on varying assumptions regarding fertility rates. Assuming a continuance of rates corresponding to the peak postwar years, the population of the country would double between 1960 and 2000. The Bureau's lowest-fertility projections, which correspond to the present rates, indicate a gain of about 100 million by 2000. Anthony Downs, on the assumption that fertility rates will continue to fall, believes that a figure of around 70 million is more probable. If metropolitan areas continue to account for about 80 per cent of total population growth, as they have over the past two decades, then metropolitan areas would grow by 80 million persons between 1960 and 2000 under the Bureau's lowest-fertility projections, or by 55 million using Downs's estimate. In any event, as Downs himself remarks, "future urban growth will hardly be trivial. A gain of 55 million people in metropolitan areas is just about *double* the gain experienced from 1950 to 1960—the great decade of suburbanization, and future growth after the year 2000 will probably make even the [Census Bureau's highest-fertility] projections for 2000 come true several decades later."[7] It is no wonder, therefore, that President Nixon, in his State of the Union address delivered in January, 1970, called for a national growth policy aimed at diverting population away from crowded big cities toward more habitable centers. Even though his suggestion that the federal government aid in creating "a balanced growth for America" carried no specific proposals, it at least indicated recognition of the need for more effort to influence consciously the location of population and economic activity.

TABLE 2

Metropolitan and Nonmetropolitan Population of the United States, 1950 to 1968

Residence	Population (thousands)		1968		Average Annual Percentage Change	
	1950[a]	1960[a]	Total	Percentage	1950-60	1960-68
Standard Metropolitan Statistical Areas[b]	89,162	112,900	127,477	64.3	2.4	1.5
Central Cities	52,190	57,790	58,373	29.4	1.0	0.1
Outside Central Cities	36,972	55,111	69,104	34.9	4.0	2.8
Nonmetropolitan	61,365	65,558	70,754	35.7	0.7	1.0
TOTAL	150,527	178,458	198,234	100.0	1.7	1.3

[a]For comparability with data from the Current Population Survey, figures have been adjusted to exclude members of the Armed Forces living in barracks and similar types of quarters.

[b]Data cover 212 areas as defined in 1960.

Source: U.S. Bureau of the Census, *Statistical Abstract of the United States, 1969* (Washington, D.C.: Government Printing Office, 1969), p. 18.

Policy decisions affecting spatial resource allocation inevitably must confront the potential conflict between national efficiency and interregional equity. At one extreme, it has been argued that more resources should be devoted to attracting firms to Indian reservations, remote mountain areas, and similar lagging areas because it is socially desirable, even though these same resources would yield a greater economic product in alternative locations. In contrast, there is evidence that regional disparities decline over time in relatively developed countries,[8] so that, in the long run, efficiency and equity goals would be reconciled. Thus, William Alonso argues that while account must be taken of political pressures and altruistic motives for hastening equalization, "it is tempting to conclude that national policies need not concern themselves with fighting further urbanization in the principal cities or with regional balance as such and that developing nations should concentrate on speeding the growth of national product."[9]

In the present study, it will be argued, on the grounds of economic efficiency and to a lesser extent on limited evidence concerning public locational preferences, that it is usually neither efficient nor effective to attempt to force feed economic growth in large, lagging regions and, that our big cities probably are too big. Furthermore, it is recognized that because rural problems and urban problems are interrelated, they cannot be dealt with in isolation. It is probable that changing technology and tastes will alleviate the need to unify metropolitan core areas and their peripheries within a single matrix, "the urban field."[10] However, there does not yet appear to be evidence that "the present dominance of the metropolitan core will become attenuated as economic activities are decentralized to smaller cities within the field or into the open country" or that "as the periphery becomes absorbed into the urban field, it will be eliminated as a distinctive problem area."[11] For example, recent American and foreign evidence indicates that growth in total national employment has been accounted for primarily by expanding tertiary activities (trade, finance, insurance, real estate, government, and personal, professional, business, and repair services), which have been located, for the most part, in metropolitan areas. Those firms that have tended to leave metropolitan areas have been characterized by relative stagnation or decline; they frequently seek cheap labor in areas with surplus agricultural populations. Rapidly expanding sectors, on the other hand, have favored metropolitan areas because of their external economies of agglomeration.[12] While there is less differentiation in economic and social structure among broad regions, there is increasing differentiation among large and small centers within the urban hierarchy. In other words, the location of economic activity is freer with respect to major regions but less free with respect to size of community.[13] Therefore, what this study proposes is a growth center policy of decentralized concentration,[14] a policy which, in the short run, will provoke intraregional disequilibrium and migration as the most effective means to mitigate in the long run the low income and high unemployment of lagging areas, as well as the external diseconomies of congestion in large metropolitan areas.

NOTES

1. Lloyd Rodwin, *Nations and Cities* (Boston: Houghton Mifflin, 1970), p. 3.

2. Wilbur R. Thompson, *A Preface to Urban Economics* (Baltimore: The Johns Hopkins Press, 1965), p. 190.

3. Data supplied by Calvin Beale, chief population specialist with the Department of Agriculture. See also William K. Stevens, "Farm-to-City Migration is Nearing End in U.S.," *New York Times* (March 23, 1969), pp. 1, 66.

4. Brian J. L. Berry, "Spatial Organization and Levels of Welfare: Degree of Metropolitan Labor Market Participation as a Variable in Economic Development" (paper presented to the Economic Development Administration Research Conference, Washington, D.C., October 9-13, 1967).

5. *Ibid.*, p. 14.

6. *Ibid.*, p. 19.

7. Anthony Downs, "Alternative Forms of Future Urban Growth in the United States," *Journal of the American Institute of Planners*, Vol. 36, No. 1 (January, 1970), 5.

8. See, for example, J. G. Williamson, "Regional Inequality and the Process of National Development: A Description of the Patterns," *Economic Development and Cultural Change*, Vol. 13, No. 4, Part II (July, 1965), 3-45; and George H. Borts and Jerome L. Stein, *Economic Growth in a Free Market* (New York: Columbia University Press, 1964).

9. William Alonso, "Urban and Regional Imbalances in Economic Development," *Economic Development and Cultural Change*, Vol. 17, No. 1 (October, 1968), 1-14.

10. John Friedmann and John Miller, "The Urban Field," *Journal of the American Institute of Planners*, Vol. 31, No. 4 (November, 1965), 312-20.

11. *Ibid.*, p. 315.

12. Erling Olsen, "Erhverslivets Lokalisering," *National-okonomisk Tidsskrift*, Nos. 1-2 (1965), 18-30; Wilbur R. Thompson, "Internal and External Factors in the Development of Urban Economies," in Harvey S. Perloff and Lowdon Wingo, Jr., eds., *Issues in Urban Economics* (Baltimore: The Johns Hopkins Press, 1968), pp. 43-62.

13. Edgar M. Hoover, "Some Old and New Issues in Regional Development," in E. A. G. Robinson, ed., *Backward Areas in Advanced Countries* (New York: St. Martin's Press, 1969), p. 356.

14. See Rodwin, *op. cit.*, pp. 4-8.

CHAPTER

2

GROWTH
CENTER
THEORY

The evolution of the growth center concept over the past fifteen years has been, in large measure, a reaction to more traditional tools of regional analysis that have failed to provide adequate means for dealing with problems of concern to regional policy. In France, for example, where the first attempts were made to formulate systematically a growth center theory, the prevalent point of view has been that the deductive models of classical location theory (Lösch, Weber, and others) are deficient in that their criteria for optimal spatial resource allocation are based only on the perspective of the firm. In addition, the classical approach assumes a homogeneous space within which private costs, particularly those related to transportation, are to be minimized. The homogeneity assumption ignores the social costs of agglomeration, which are not borne by the entrepreneur, and therefore fails to deal adequately with many issues of serious concern to French economists and planners, especially the issue of the congestion of the Paris region and policies to divert migration streams elsewhere.

Economic growth theory has been an equally common source of dissatisfaction. The theory of balanced growth and the steady growth theories of Hicks, Harrod, and Domar differ primarily in that the latter show how the dynamic equilibria of modern economies may be unstable. Both approaches, however, have proven generally unsatisfactory in explaining French regional or national experience. Although French thought has not denied the importance of some aspects emphasized in the more traditional theories, it nevertheless has been more oriented in recent years toward concepts which have been deemed more relevant as policy guides, and principally this orientation has been around the development pole (*pôle de croissance*) concept.[1]

The English-language literature has also tended to become increasingly critical of the relevance of many traditional tools to policy problems. Benjamin Higgins, in a recent survey of regional planning policies, notes that "the branch

11

of economic theory underlying regional planning (location theory) is in a particularly unsatisfactory state, providing only limited guidance for policy formation."[2] Eric Lampard similarly finds that, on operational grounds,

> the general theory of location and space economy is found wanting. . . . The theory is intended to determine locations in a framework of general equilibrium; it requires optimal behavior by producers and consumers throughout the system. But quite apart from the problem of handling so many complex interrelations, the outcome is still a static system that is not geared to the analysis of locational transformation. . . . The dependence of the general theory on what, in the last analysis is virtually a single-factor explanation, namely the systematically variable cost of surmounting distance under *ceteris paribus* conditions, renders its particular solutions of little more than formal interest to the student of historical development.[3]

E. A. G. Robinson, writing on location theory and regional economics, finds that as one attempts to relax the assumptions of Lösch and Weber, the results "become more and more unreal and inconsistent with one's analysis."[4] And Lloyd Rodwin argues that the limitations of location theory are best illustrated in the writings of Walter Isard, the most distinguished scholar in this field:

> In his major work on location theory [*Location and Space Economy*] he touches on the problem of determining "the optimal spatial distribution and hierarchy of cities of different size," and he specifically poses the question: "Given a network of cities and corresponding patterns of land use, along what channels should changes in the structure of this network and these patterns be fostered in order to attain a situation closer to optimum?" But, after a brief discussion of the agglomeration aspects of location theory, he concludes that there is "little to say beyond the obvious; units are attracted to or repelled from cities according to a simple comparison of advantages and disadvantages generated by these cities."[5]

In addition to location theory, many other widely used tools of spatial economic analysis also suffer from severe limitations. For example, many analyses of local and regional economies utilize the export base approach, which assumes that the total economic activity of a given area is a function of the region's output flowing outside the area. The principal difficulties with this approach include the definition and measurement of the economic base, the assumptions that the marginal propensity to export is stable and that the marginal and average propensities to export are the same, and the assumption that exports are independently and autonomously determined. In addition, the economic base approach has been shown empirically to be a poor predictor of urban growth.[6] It has even been argued that long-run urban growth is more a function of the service sector than of basic activities; because the economic base changes over time, a competitive service sector is necessary to replace stagnating basic activities with vigorous new ones.[7] Wilbur Thompson puts the matter in the following terms:

> The economic base of the larger metropolitan area is, then, the creativity of its universities and research parks, the sophistication of its engineering firms and financial institutions, the persuasiveness of its public relations and advertising agencies, the flexibility of its transportation networks and utility systems, and all the other dimensions of infrastructure that facilitate the quick and orderly transfer from old dying bases to new growing ones. A diversified set of current exports—"breadth"—softens the shock of exogenous change, while a rich infrastructure—"depth"—facilitates the adjustment to change by providing the socioeconomic institutions and physical facilities needed to initiate new enterprises, transfer capital from old to new forms, and retrain labor.[8]

Whether one wishes to maintain that service activities in the broadest sense are induced or inducing, or that basic and service activities are mutually interdependent and coequal in importance, it is still clear that analyses based on a distinction between basic and other activities or between service and other activities have not provided general explanations of why cities have grown the way they have. The determinants of urban growth are too complex to be handled within a framework which merely examines functional relationships between "basic" and "service" activities.

In general, the principal reason for which not only location theory and economic base analysis but also such traditional tools of regional analysis as input-output models, central place theory, urban hierarchy studies, industrial complex analysis, and gravity models have so often proven inadequate for policy purposes is that they have failed to take into account the changing nature of the actual determinants of location.[9] The emphasis given in classical location theory to minimizing transportation costs, for example, may be contrasted with the decline in importance of shipping costs of heavy and cumbersome goods. Long distance transfer costs have been significantly reduced, while the rapid movement of relatively light but highly elaborated products has increased in importance, as has the need to communicate information and intangible services. Moreover, whereas industrial location in the past was heavily influenced by factors such as energy sources, water, and transportation facilities, entrepreneurs today tend to be more attracted by external economies of agglomeration of the kind mentioned in the passage just quoted from Thompson. Economic activity also has become increasingly footloose. It has been estimated that today only about 7 per cent of the labor force needs to be located close to natural resources, whereas only thirty years ago 30 per cent were resource-bound. The trend is for the labor force to be potentially footloose and to locate in proximity to consumers, who themselves are relatively footloose. Economic opportunity therefore is increasingly associated with capital and human skill and not with land and natural resources.[10]

Among tertiary activities, the increasingly prominent place of amenities must be noted. The footloose nature of many activities is counterbalanced by noneconomic factors which enter into the choice of location of people and firms. Rising standards of living, more leisure, greater mobility, and better education make the quality of life a crucial factor in many location decisions. The quality of life offered by a locale is geared to the quality of its educational institutions, its climate, and its cultural and recreational opportunities, and except for climate, these are variables whose enhancement is "the result of community action and a will to attain high standards in the design of urban culture."[11]

Finally, a number of studies of the relative importance of various plant location factors from the viewpoint of industry have indicated the importance of markets.[12] This does not deny the importance of tertiary activities because market and tertiary factors are mutually reinforcing. Because they deal with such functions as communications, construction, trade, finance, government, the professions, and recreation, tertiary activities are, by and large, closely tied to markets.[13]

How then has growth center theory attempted to overcome the limitations of other analytic tools and in what ways has it been more relevant to the changing realities of location determination? No definitive answer can be given to this question because growth center theory has not yet reached a stage where there is general agreement on its most essential elements and their relation to one another. Moreover, in some of its variants it has not so much bypassed more traditional approaches as it has picked and chosen among them; it has not really integrated older approaches into a new synthesis. Yet, despite its imperfections, growth center theory at least does offer the possibility of a fresh approach to problems of urban and regional development (and stagnation), especially when it is integrated with such broader fields as manpower economics. Before elaborating further on these points it would be appropriate first to consider critically how growth center theory has developed, both in France, where it originated, and in other countries, where parallel movements have produced their own contributions.

THE FRENCH SCHOOL *

Perroux and Boudeville: The Theory of Development Poles

The theory of development poles was first propounded by François Perroux,[14] but it is prominent in the writings of most French regional

---

*The French School here includes the French language contributions of Belgian regional economists, who work closely with their French colleagues through the Association de Science Régionale de Langue Française.

economists. Unlike the balanced and steady growth theories, Perroux's approach holds that analysis of sustained growth of total production should concentrate on the process by which various activities appear, grow in importance, and in some cases disappear, and it emphasizes that growth rates vary considerably from sector to sector. Like Joseph Schumpeter, Perroux maintains that entrepreneurial innovation is a dominant factor in explaining the growth process, which takes the form of a succession of dynamic sectors, or poles, through time. A particularly regional flavor has been given to the pole concept by emphasizing that growth is concentrated in various spatial loci as well as in certain leading industrial branches.[15]

Another version of this theme, based largely on historic French experience, emphasizes that economic expansion generally follows a linear spatial path because of the influence of transportation routes which link important industrial centers. Pottier's findings indicate that in the last century the paths of these axes were influenced primarily by geographical considerations.[16] Growth of traffic along the original routes resulted in economies of scale and lower unit costs; new techniques could be more readily incorporated into the existing infrastructure because the volume of traffic guaranteed their "profitability." However, by lowering transport costs, the resultant increase in traffic volume created added demand for still newer improvements. This cumulative process tended to concentrate and juxtapose various modes of transportation along the original major routes. Population, industry, and commerce clustered along these axes, which constituted extended, easily accessible markets attractive to new economic activity. Even agriculture in close proximity to development axes benefitted relative to that in other areas because of its greater involvement in the dynamics of modernization and technological progress. These developments contributed to the economic expansion of the North, the East, and Paris, whereas the rest of the country remained relatively stagnant.[17] However, Pottier reflects prevalent French opinion when he states that "unlike the last century, it is now possible to create the bases for equilibrium growth throughout the country . . . by means of public intervention. Through its control or influence over public intervention. Through its control or influence over public overhead capital the modern State holds a decisive development control lever."[18]

It is necessary to emphasize that although the theory of development poles may be useful in analyzing and comparing the differing consequences of alternative choices of location, it is not in itself, strictly speaking, a theory of location. In Perroux's original article on the subject, he insisted that "growth does not appear everywhere at the same time; it shows itself in points or *pôles de croissance*, with variable intensities; it spreads by different channels and with variable final effects for the economy as a whole."[19] This should not be construed to mean, however, that a development pole is equivalent to a key industry, an economic base, an industrial zone, or even some geographically concentrated phenomenon. Rather, Perroux's concept should be interpreted in its essentially economic and functional sense.[20] To appreciate fully this perspective, it is necessary to place Perroux's article on development poles in the context of his somewhat earlier work on economic space.

Perroux's concept of economic space definitely is not to be confused with simple location as defined by geographical or political divisions. "A banal sense of space location creates the illusion of the coincidence of political space with economic and human space."[21] However, in reality there exist "as many spaces as there are structures of abstract relations which define an object. These *abstract spaces,* some of which are known to be extremely complicated, are sets of relations which respond to questions without involving directly the location of a point or a shape by two or three coordinates."[22] Thus, by distinguishing between Euclidean and abstract space, "we may distinguish in our discipline as many economic spaces as there are constituent structures of abstract relations which define each object of economic science."[23] For Perroux, there are three types of economic space: economic space as defined by a plan, economic space as a field of forces, and economic space as a homogeneous aggregate. The first of these spaces is defined by "the set of relations which exist between the firm and, on the one hand, the suppliers of input (raw materials, labor, power, capital) and, on the other hand, the buyers of the output (both intermediate and final)." Second, as "a field of forces, economic space consists of centres (or poles or foci) from which centrifugal forces emanate and to which centripetal forces are attracted. Each centre, being a centre of attraction and repulsion, has its proper field, which is set in the fields of other centres." Finally, the "firm has, or has not, a structure more or less homogeneous with those of other firms which are its neighbors topographically or economically—it belongs to a space where, roughly speaking, one price reigns."[24] It is quite clear, therefore, that Perroux's concept of economic spaces, in particular the second type, which is most relevant to the present discussion, is centered on complex economic relations, rather than on specifically geographical considerations.

In contrast to the approach of Perroux, that of Jacques Boudeville emphasizes the regional character of economic space. Following Perroux, Boudeville maintains that from an economic point of view, there are three types of space: homogeneous, polarized, and program, or planning, space. Thus, in the first place,

> the region can be characterized by its more or less pronounced uniformity: it is more or less homogeneous. In the second place, the region can be studied from the point of view of its more or less pronounced degree of coherence, that is to say, according to the interdependence of its diverse parts; it is more or less polarized. Finally, the region can be envisaged from the point of view of the goal that it pursues, of the program that it establishes; this is the program region or planning region.[25]

In Boudeville's thought, a homogeneous region corresponds to a continuous space wherein each of the constituent parts or zones has relevant characteristics as close as possible to those of the others. Thus, "from an economic viewpoint, Clermont, Lyon, Saint-Etienne, and Grenoble are equivalent to the North, that is to say, to the rich part of France."[26] The notion of polarized space, on the other hand, is closely related to that of a hierarchy of urban centers ranked according to the functions they perform; a polarized region is a heterogeneous space whose different parts complement and support one another and where these parts have more exchanges of goods and services with a dominant intraregional urban center, or pole, than with neighboring regions. In this sense, Lille would be the dominant pole for the North, and Lyon would have a similar role in the upper Rhone Valley. However, following Gunnar Alexandersson, Boudeville defines three types of polarization: national, regional, and local. This hierarchy corresponds to the hierarchy of specialized goods and services which are produced or furnished at these levels. Thus, national goods circulate throughout a given country, regional goods are characterized by a distribution network for the most part limited to the boundaries of a given region, and local goods are generally provided for only a small local market. A national center would, therefore, also be a regional and local center; it would perform the whole range of polarized functions. It is thus possible, given adequate data on the movement of goods, to classify the polarized regions of any given country.[27] Despite pronounced data inadequacies, Boudeville has made several studies which attempt to analyze regional polarization both within France as a whole and within certain of its broad subdivisions.[28]

Finally, the planning, or program, region "is a space whose various parts depend on the same decision"; in addition, it is "an instrument placed in the hands of an authority, whether or not localized in the region, to attain a given economic goal."[29]

To summarize briefly, it has been argued that a proper understanding of the development pole concept requires its consideration in the context of the related theory of economic spaces. The latter was originated by Perroux with an explicitly nongeographical orientation. However, Boudeville (and others), even though he borrows Perroux's terminology in toto, maintains that the theory of economic space "is the application of a mathematical space on or in a geographical space."[30] The question which must be posed, therefore, is whether or not it is possible to have a consistent theory of development poles without a correspondingly consistent theory of economic space. However, before taking up this problem, it is necessary to consider another aspect of the development pole theory, that relating to the concept of dominance.

The Concept of Dominance

The concept of dominance is yet another ubiquitous notion in French economic literature which owes its inception to Perroux, and along with the concept of development poles, it marks a key element in his general effort to provide a dynamic interpretation of economic activity. For Perroux, the effect of domination "consists of an irreversible or partially reversible influence exercised by one unit on another. An economic unit exercises this effect by reason of its dimension, its negotiating strength, the nature of its activity, or because it belongs to a zone of dominant activity."[31] The effect of domination has both a purely economic dimension, abstracted from any consideration of geographic space, and a spatial dimension. In addition, "as soon as any inequality among firms appears, the breach is opened by which the cumulative effect of domination insinuates itself."[32] Given these notions, it follows that the dominant, or propulsive, firm will generally be oligopolistic and large and will exert an important influence on the activities of suppliers and clients. Moreover, in terms of geographic space, dominant and propulsive industries make the cities in which they are located the poles of their regions.[33] This briefly outlined approach seems to have considerable validity when applied in abstraction from spatial considerations, but its significance in the latter regard is more ambiguous.

As to the first of these propositions, it is instructive to consider an input-output model proposed by H. Aujac, since it provides significant evidence that the concept of dominance does, in fact, have a corresponding empirical counterpart.[34] Aujac's model succeeds in ordering sectors in input-output form in such a manner that relatively large intermediate demands are situated below the principal diagonal, whereas those that are relatively weak are situated above it. This triangularization of the matrix is carried out on the basis of the "best customer." If A_{ij} represents sales from industry i to industry j and A_{ji} the converse, then j is said to dominate i if $(A_{ij}/P_i) > (A_{ji}/P_j)$, where P_i and P_j are, respectively, the total sales of i and j. On the basis of such calculations, a hierarchy is established in which each sector dominates the one which follows. Thus, changes in output in a given industry will affect industries coming after it in the hierarchy but will have only negligible effects on preceding industries, i.e., indirect effects do not travel up the triangular matrix and distort the hierarchy. The order of the hierarchy established by Aujac for France is as follows: construction and public works; diverse services; food and agricultural industries; agriculture; mechanical and electrical industries; textiles and leathers; wood, paper, and furniture; diverse industries; chemicals; steel; nonferrous metals; transportation and communications; energy; rubber; tenant farming.

It might be supposed that Aujac's model would provide a convenient tool of regional analysis even though it is not formally constructed in regional terms. If, for example, one wished to examine the direct and indirect effects of the transfer from Paris to the provinces of firms in various industries, it might be possible to calculate the importance and number of suppliers who would tend to follow one or another migrating industry. Similarly, the comparative effects of establishing different industries in a given region could be examined. To analyze the effects of introducing a steel complex, for example, it would only be necessary to calculate modifications in industries following steel in the matrix hierarchy. However, the difficulties involved in any straightforward application of the national pattern of flows on a regional level would be formidable. Depending on the number and magnitude of interregional linkages, which are certain to be very great for areas on the scale of the French program regions, many interindustry effects will pass to the rest of the world. Thus, links between local production and local consumption, as well as the effects of investment on employment, would require a great deal of special attention. Moreover, the prospects for utilizing operationally feasible interregional matrices are not bright. As Rodwin has aptly remarked, "the neglect of price effects, the difficulty of getting data for these models, the vastly increased computational problems which regional breakdowns entail coupled with the egregious simplifications of industry categories and the unrealistic linearity assumptions make one skeptical of the immediate, not to mention the long-term usefulness of this instrument."[35]

It should be pointed out that numerous attempts have been made in France to construct regional input-output tables similar to the one employed for national accounting purposes.[36] However, their usefulness for solving concrete regional problems remains, for the most part, to be seen. Even on a national level, "the precision of the input-output table in a medium-size economy like France, more and more open to foreign markets, actually seems questionable."[37] Moreover, the particular difficulties that have characterized French efforts at the regional level can only add to doubts concerning their feasibility as policy aids. Industrial statistics at the regional level have been generally insufficient. It is extremely difficult to identify the respective shares of the differing activities of multi-product firms. Declarations concerning salaries and business receipts are not available in uniform fashion, and they are sometimes reported according to plant location and at other times according to location of home office. Moreover, inter-regional monetary, financial, and merchandise movements are often impossible to evaluate, and the "final demand" category, including government, firm, and individual purchases, is difficult to specify because the planning system is only indicative.[38]

In general, then, while the notion of dominance has been given empirical verification for the structure of industry in the nation as a whole, it is not now operationally feasible to regionalize or otherwise give spatial content to the relevant national model. Nor is there any likely prospect that this end will be realized in the foreseeable future. However, the problem of analyzing the role of dominant sectors as localized development poles need not be limited to input-output techniques. As Paelinck has stated, it is not sufficient for the economist working on regional development problems to limit analysis to "the classical interdependencies (of either the Walras or Leontief type) of economic flux, whether in quantity or value terms. He must be able, in addition, to recognize the *technical origin* of this interdependence, which explains its ever increasing complexity."[39]

It will be recalled that the concepts of economic space and development poles have been defined both in terms of abstraction from spatial location and in terms of concrete geographical areas. It also should follow, then, that the dominance of a propulsive industry could be treated both in abstraction from spatial considerations and in terms of specific regions. This, in fact, has been the case.

Problems in the Development Pole Theory

Perroux's treatment of the growth process is consistent with his theory of economic space in that the industry remains his point of departure and the essential element in subsequent development. Philippe Aydalot has correctly maintained that while Perroux sometimes "seems to study the localization of the growth process, in fact, this localization seems secondary to him," since, "the primary phenomenon is 'the appearance and disappearance of industries,' 'the diffusion of the growth of an industry.' "[40]

The effects generated by a propulsive industry which qualify it as a development pole have been thoroughly explored by numerous writers. Some of these effects are internal to the industry itself; that is, its own growth generates increased investment, employment, and distribution of factor payments, including profits, which may be retained and reinvested. The internal growth of an industry also generates numerous external effects. Vertically and horizontally induced effects may of course be analyzed within the framework of input-output matrices. The effects of polarization may be further examined, at least in theory, by the application of appropriate matrices or vectors to the initial Leontief-type matrix. Here, several possibilities are available. For example, dynamic effects which alter the structure of industry as given by the original matrix may be introduced. Structural change involving lateral, or horizontal, production increases is termed a "Perroux effect" in the literature on development poles. There is also the so-called "Keynes effect," which involves the classic multiplier based on marginal propensities to consume applied to income increases. Yet another effect is that relating to the interplay of prices among related sectors and enterprises; this is generally called the "Scitovsky effect."[41] Nor does this list by any means exhaust the possible effects which a dominant industry may have. There is, in addition, a feedback phenomenon which generally is termed the "Aftalion effect." This involves increased investment resulting from the operation of the accelerator principle in connection with increases in final demand, which of course is related to the effects just mentioned. There is also "psychological polarization," which refers to the impacts on investment decisions of small and medium-size firms resulting from the creative activities of dominant propulsive sectors. Here, the degree of availability of technical information is important. The latter has a special designation, namely, the "publication effect."[42]

Although still other polarization classifications can be found in the literature, it is apparent that a propulsive industry (or firm) must have at least three basic characteristics. First, it must be relatively large in order to assure that it will generate sufficient direct and potentially indirect effects to have a significant impact on the economy; second, it must be a relatively fast-growing sector; and third, the quantity and intensity of its interrelations with other sectors should be important so that a large number of induced effects will, in fact, be transmitted.

The importance of bigness, first emphasized by Perroux, has been equally stressed in subsequent writings of other scholars. Pierre Bauchet, for example, writes that the growth of an underdeveloped region depends on the actions of large economic units. "Their mass alone is capable of starting the region on the path of economic growth."[43] Similarly, L. E. Davin maintains that "the principal poles are found in heavy, highly capitalized industry, and are the domain of large firms."[44] Thus, "the multiplicity of firms of small dimension, working in dispersed fashion without relying on a few large firms, is not of a nature to set in motion a truly dynamic regional economy."[45] Nevertheless, as will be discussed shortly, the notion of industrial bigness as an initiator of economic growth is not without its difficulties. That a propulsive firm or industry should be rapidly growing is unquestionable. However, when it comes to the third criterion, that of interrelations with other sectors, several problems may be raised.

Aydalot has argued that all things considered, the simplest definition that may be given of a propulsive industry is that it is a producer of external economies.[46] Here again, though, the question must be posed as to what kind of economic space is involved. Aydalot is quite correct in pointing out that *a priori,* the concept of polarization does not imply geographic concentration. Polarization "is the process by which the growth of an economic activity termed propulsive sets in motion that of other economic activities by the channel of external economies."[47] But this process takes place in abstract economic space. Thus, although a propulsive industry must certainly have a location in geographic space, the *process* of polarization is not amenable to unambiguous geographic location.

Moreover, if a propulsive industry is to initiate regional expansion, as the usual discussion would have it, it is essential to inquire into the criteria that govern the choice of location by a propulsive industry. In this regard,

> it is insufficient to bring in the effects of agglomeration once a propulsive industry is established. In other words, to say that Paris is a pole owing to the agglomerating power of its propulsive industries does not resolve the problem; it remains to explain why these propulsive industries are themselves agglomerated in Paris.
>
> One is necessarily led to the conclusion that the poles (spatial) possess characteristics which have a causal role in the implementation of propulsive industries.
>
> That is to say, and here is the essential point, that contrary to the conclusions of certain contemporary economists, the propulsive industry is not the primary phenomenon in the process of polarization.[48]

Thus, even if the propulsive industry does not induce other activities, it is itself induced and thereby constitutes only one link in the process of polarized growth; the propulsive industry as such "does not merit either the pedestal where it has been placed, or the prestige which has been given to it."[49] In conclusion, Aydalot finds that the propulsive industry does not represent the origin of the polarization; it is only an effect of it. Here, he concentrates on the importance of agglomeration effects, particularly those of a tertiary nature, in attracting industries, including those which, in turn, induce other activities.[50] One of the basic common denominators in the French-language literature is the notion that the process of economic growth has its origin and continuing stimulus in big industrial undertakings, a notion which derives from the theory of dominance. Some of the more naïvely enthusiastic interpretations of the theory would maintain that to generate economic growth in a region, it is merely necessary to implant a large firm, or several large firms, preferably in a relatively fast-growing industry. The fact that bigness alone is not sufficient in this regard is well illustrated by the case of the steel industry in Lorraine. The development of the steel industry in this region was not accompanied by a corresponding development in the region of industries consuming steel. As a result, Lorraine became highly dependent on exterior sources of supply for machinery and other equipment. Despite the existence of coal mines, energy sources, transportation facilities, and markets in close proximity to the steel complex, it would appear on the basis of input-output data that less than 10 per cent of steel production in the region was consumed by manufacturing industries in the region. Thus, there exists the paradox of relatively weakly developed industry existing side by side with conditions highly favorable to industrial location.[51] As Paelinck has emphasized, "the facts do not indicate that one can consider any isolated industrial implantation as a necessarily efficient development pole, by which effective polarization relations, technical or otherwise, are produced."[52]

If the stimulating effects on general economic growth of big industrial undertakings often have been overestimated, so has the importance of both bigness and industry. Boudeville considers that on a European scale, Denmark just fulfills the minimum requirements of an "independent" region. However, the prosperity of this region was not initiated and has not been sustained by a big propulsive industry, but rather by scattered (though closely cooperating) and relatively small agricultural units.

Moreover, even if a propulsive industry is considered to be as much an effect as a cause of the polarization process, it is clear that development pole theory fails to give a satisfactory explanation of the agglomerating process. The industries which are often most attracted by the external economies generated by large urban areas are not so much oligopolistic in structure, but rather have numerous small- and medium-size firms highly dependent on auxiliary business services and frequent, direct personal contacts with buyers and sellers.[53]

Another difficulty with the development pole theory of the French School is that criteria for regional policy have not been explicitly related to the goals often sought in practice. For example, Davin poses the following question: From the point of view of political economy, what is the nature of the principal polarizing activities (active or potential), and how can the flux among these poles be created or increased? In reply, he maintains that the industries or industrial sectors most favorable to regional growth (defined as a significant increase in the flux of products and of revenues) are those where (1) the value added per worker is the highest or most likely to increase; (2) the forseeable increase in production indicates an accelerated rate of expansion, and technical progress is the most rapid and the most probable; (3) the process of automation or semiautomation can be most easily applied; (4) the flux of products and of services with the development poles is the most intense; and (5) the constitution of large production units is achieved most easily, since these units are capable of releasing a maximum of induced reactions (through the existence of interenterprise or intersectoral technical linkages and the possibility of making general use of small, dependent suppliers) and of realizing a maximum of technical and commercial productivity.[54]

One problem raised by these criteria is that in themselves they do not really give insights into the objective, or objectives, of regional policy. Is the "increase in flux of products and of revenues" supposed to increase hourly earnings of workers, annual income per employed inhabitant, number of persons employed, or some other possible regional variables? The emphasis put on automation and high worker productivity would conflict with what is perhaps the most generally sought-after goal of regional policies, namely, increased employment opportunities. Even if one adds, for example, the goal of increased earning power per employed inhabitant, it is not clear that these criteria would guarantee success. In this regard, the outcome would depend largely on the extent to which induced effects actually are localized in the region in question. If regional policy is to aim for increased flux in economic activity in lagging regions, the flux may be dissipated as a result of linkages with other regions. A particular difficulty in this respect would be income flows to owners of capital who reside outside of the region. Lagging regions generally would not be the type to furnish the savings which would be invested in the big, capital-intensive undertakings described by Davin. In addition, there is the probability that increased commercial and industrial activity will be accompanied by higher per capita costs of public services. I have already described this phenomenon on the basis of highly standardized Belgian data.[55]

Finally, it cannot be emphasized too much that the theory of development poles is badly in need of a thorough semantic reworking; the concepts and language which characterize it need more precise definition and more consistent usage. Even the very notion of a development pole suffers in this regard. For example, Davin states: "The idea of a development pole is made more precise by that of a propulsive industry and of a key industry. The first engenders activities in other industries, either suppliers or clients for merchandise or services; the second determines the increase of maximum activity."[56] Paelinck, on the other hand, states:

> The development pole concept has often been misunderstood. It has been confused with the notions of key industry, basic industry, and industrial ensemble; from this follows the erroneous conception according to which the development pole would be an industrial monument raised to the glory of future regional industrialization, a guarantee of certain economic growth. Or again, to make this scarcely rigorous concept more precise some would have as a development pole any important implantation of firms, preferably industrial, which would exercise salutary effects on the geographic area where it is introduced.[57]

Then, too, there is the question of economic space. The same concepts are sometimes employed in the context of abstract, nongeographic space, at other times in the context of certain more or less well-defined geographic areas, and at yet other times in a fashion which indiscriminately mingles abstract and geographic space in the same context. Of course, a scholar should be free to define the terms of his own discourse, and there would be no objection to his doing so, provided that he then proceeds to employ them in a systematic and consistent manner. In the present instance, however, one finds all too often that once the writer has defined (no matter how vaguely) his essential concepts, he proceeds in the development of his thought to bring in references from other writers to nominally identical concepts which, unfortunately, have been defined or used differently by the other writers. Even this would not be objectionable if the various definitions or usages were critically contrasted or otherwise differentiated, but this is rarely the case.

A greater emphasis on conceptual clarity might also have the virtue of making the concepts of development pole theory more operational. It has been noted that in some respects, development pole theory may be viewed as an effort to grasp the complex technical origins and dynamic interrelations of the growth process to a degree not possible with classical input-output techniques. Yet practical expositions of the theory (or better, individual versions of it) are generally presented in an input-output framework, usually in terms of a regionalization of the basic Leontief-type model, or by applying modifying vectors or matrices to the basic model, or both. In other words, although this approach is more complete from a theoretical viewpoint than the simple classical model, it necessarily limits the analysis of the polarization process to essentially static effects. In any event, it has been through an input-output format that the development pole approach has made its most important original contributions to operationally meaningful theory; otherwise, this literature has been extremely eclectic, borrowing such well-known analytic devices as location coefficients, simple graph theory, and Edgar Dunn's distinction between proportionality and differential employment shifts. However, on the level of operationally feasible models, it is questionable that development pole theory has really contributed any fundamentally new method of analysis, since the theoretically useful modifications which it has made in classical input-output techniques suffer not only from the usual difficulties in this regard, but also from the frequent impossibility of actually quantifying the modifying variables which it employs.

On the positive side, it may be said that the difficulties involved in unifying the basic concepts of the French School within the context of operationally feasible models are a result of its effort to come to grips with the complexity of the growth process, a phenomenon which frequently tends to be oversimplified for the sake of "elegance." Perhaps the best approach to development pole theory as applied to regional problems is that given by Paelinck, who proposes that it be regarded as "a *conditional* theory of regional growth; it is valuable, above all, to the extent that it clearly indicates the conditions under which accelerated regional development can occur."[58] Of course, this conditional approach implies that the relevance of the theory to individual regional cases must be judged on the basis of the nature and prospects of the particular regions, or types of regions, in question; the value of the theory to regional policy problems is not independent of the actual context in which it is to be utilized.

NON-FRENCH CONTRIBUTIONS

Hirschman and Myrdal: Conflicting Tendencies in Spatial Development

Outside of France and Belgium, the development of growth center theory has not been associated with any "school" but has, rather, been characterized by diverse contributions of individual scholars. The first systematic treatment of growth centers in the American literature was that by Albert Hirschman, who examined the spatial concentration of economic activity within the framework of his theory of unbalanced growth. Hirschman argued that development strategies should concentrate on a relatively few sectors rather than on widely dispersed projects; the key sectors would be determined by measuring backward-linkage and forward-linkage effects in terms of input-output maxima.[59] He maintained that growth is communicated from the leading sectors of the economy to the followers, from one firm to another. The advantage of this approach "over 'balanced growth' where every activity expands perfectly in step with every other, is that it leaves considerable scope to *induced* investment decisions and therefore economizes our principal scarce resource, namely, genuine decision-making."[60]

Geographically unbalanced growth requires special consideration, for "while the regional setting reveals unbalanced growth at its most obvious, it perhaps does not show it at its best" because successive growth points may all "fall within the same privileged growth space."[61] The principal reason for the tendency for economic activity to become overconcentrated in one or a few growth poles is that the external economies associated with the poles are consistently overrated by investment decision-makers on the ground that "nothing succeeds like success." Thus, whereas a clustering of investment around the initial growth poles is beneficial at the beginning of development, it may be irrational at a later period. The actual effects of the growth points on their hinterlands depend on the balance between favorable effects that trickle down to the hinterlands from the progress of the growth points and the unfavorable, or polarization, effects on the hinterlands as a consequence of the attractiveness of the growth poles.

The most important trickling down effects are generated by purchases and investments placed in the hinterlands by the growth points, though the latter may also raise the productivity of labor and per capita consumption in the hinterlands by absorbing some of their disguised unemployment. On the other hand, polarization may take place in a number of ways. Competition from the growth points may depress relatively inefficient manufacturing and export activities in the hinterlands, and the growth points may produce a "brain drain" from the hinterlands, rather than create opportunities for their disguised unemployed.[62]

In the long run, Hirschman argued, public investment would cease to be pulled so heavily into the developed areas, largely because of considerations of equity and national unity. Moreover, after development has proceeded for some time in the growth points "the need for public investment in relation to private investment tends to decline and in any event an increased portion of public investment can be financed out of earnings of previous investments. This kind of change in the composition of investment is implicit in the term 'social *overhead* capital.'"[63] Thus, central government funds are released for use in other regions and, in the long run, regional differences will tend to disappear. Finally, Hirschman suggests that while some investment in utilities in the hinterlands may be indispensable, the provision of infrastructure is only a permissive inducement mechanism; the essential task is to provide the hinterlands with a continuously inducing economic activity in industry, agriculture, or services.[64]

Gunnar Myrdal's theory of circular causation, published at about the same time as Hirschman's analysis but developed independently, contains a number of conceptual tools that coincide with those of Hirschman. Myrdal maintained that a simple model of circular causation with cumulative effects is more consistent with actual social and economic processes than the static equilibrium analysis typical of economic theory. Myrdal found that whatever the reason for the initial expansion of a growth center, thereafter cumulatively expanding internal and external economies would fortify its growth at the expense of other areas. These economies include not only a skilled labor force and public overhead capital, but also a positive feeling for growth and a spirit of new enterprise.[65]

In developing his analysis, Myrdal employed the concepts of "backwash" and "spread" effects, which correspond closely to Hirschman's polarization and trickling down effects. The backwash effects involve the workings of population migration, trade, and capital movements. Like Hirschman, Myrdal noted the selective nature of migration from the hinterlands to the growth center, though he emphasized the fact that the young are the most prone to move. He also dwelt on the higher fertility rates of poor areas and their impact on the working-age group to total population ratio, which is likely to be relatively unfavorable in the hinterlands. Similarly, capital tends to flow to the growth centers because of increased demand. Consequently, incomes and demand increase again, resulting in yet another round of induced investment. The tendency to increased inequality is reinforced by the flow of savings from the hinterlands, where demand for investment capital remains relatively weak, toward the centers of expansion, where returns are high and secure. In addition, Myrdal recognized the critical significance of noneconomic factors to the cumulative process of maintaining poverty in the hinterlands. Their inability to support adequate health and education facilities, their generally conservative outlook—related to acceptance of the more primitive forms of tradition and religion—are all detrimental to the experimental and rational orientation of an economically progressive society.[66]

Among the spread effects, which may counter the backwash effects, are increased outlets for the hinterland's agricultural products and raw materials and a tendency for technical advance to diffuse from the growth centers. The spread effects will be stronger the higher the level of economic development of a country. Moreover, the attractiveness of the growth centers may be weakened by increasing external technological diseconomies and high labor costs. Finally, the governments of the wealthier countries are likely to initiate policies directed toward greater regional equality.[67]

Despite the similarities in approaches of Hirschman and Myrdal, there are considerable differences of emphasis. In particular, Hirschman is more optimistic about the long-run future of the less-developed countries; he seems to take for granted that strong forces eventually will create a turning point, once polarization effects have proceeded for some time. In any case, both approaches are primarily oriented toward problems of less-developed countries, and while the problems of lagging regions of industrialized countries may be similar to those of poor countries, they are certainly not so severe. For example, labor often is anxious to find employment and savings frequently are considerable, though they often flow to expanding regions rather than to local projects. And even in Appalachia, fertility rates are not very different from those in the United States as a whole.

Nevertheless, the persistence of interregional disparities in income and employment opportunities in industrial countries poses special problems neglected by Hirschman and Myrdal. For example, even if central government policy does favor the development of lagging areas, a high proportion of public investment is financed by state and local governments. There is evidence from U.S. and Belgian data that current investment per capita by state and local governments is greatest in places which have had the most public investment in the past, so that even if the central government deliberately favors lagging areas, total public investment may, on balance, still favor more advanced areas.[68] Moreover, the type of investments which central governments are prone to place in lagging areas are usually aimed at the support of directly productive activities and not at the development of human resources, even though there is considerable evidence that (1) the provision of infrastructure in the narrow sense (roads, power, industrial parks, etc.) is very often not sufficient to overcome the attractiveness of the external economies of existing growth centers and (2) the greatest relative need of lagging areas is for increased investment in human resources. The author has dealt with these issues at length elsewhere,[69] and they will be taken up again in this study.

Friedmann's Core-Periphery Model

Although Hirschman and Myrdal introduced the growth center concept to the development literature in English, the first attempt to formulate a systematic and comprehensive model was made by John Friedmann. His "core-periphery" analysis was initially set forth in a study of Venezuelan regional development policy,[70] but it has since been refined.[71]

Friedmann finds that development, that is, the unfolding of the creative potential in a society through a successive series of structural transformations, occurs through a discontinuous, but cumulative, process of innovation. Development originates in a relatively small number of "centers of change" located at the points of highest potential interaction within a communication field. Innovations diffuse from these centers to areas of lower potential interaction. "Core regions" are major centers of innovative change, while all other territory consists of "peripheral regions," which are dependent on the core regions and whose development is largely determined by institutions of the core regions. The process by which core regions consolidate their dominance over peripheral regions tends to be self-reinforcing as a consequence of six principal feedback effects of core region growth: (1) the dominance effect, or the weakening of the periphery by resource transfers to the core; (2) the information effect, or increased interaction and innovation in the core; (3) the psychological effect, or a higher rate of innovation due to greater visibility, higher expectations, and lower risks; (4) the modernization effect, or social and institutional change favoring innovation; (5) linkage effects, or the tendency of innovations to induce yet other innovations; and (6) production effects, which increase scale and agglomeration economies.

Core regions are located within a nested hierarchy of spatial systems, ranging from the province to the world. A spatial system exists when a core dominates some of the vital decisions of populations in other areas, and a spatial system may have more than one core region. Peripheral regions are dependent on core regions by virtue of supply and market relations, as well as administrative organization. For any spatial system, a loose hierarchy of core regions exists in relation to "the functional performance of each core for specified characteristics of system performance." Innovation is diffused to peripheral regions from the core, and core-region growth will tend to promote the development process of the relevant spatial system. Eventually, however, increasing social and political tensions between the core and the periphery will tend to inhibit the development of the core, unless these tensions can be alleviated by acceleration of spread effects or decrease of the periphery's dependence on the core. The conflict between the core and the periphery may result in the repression or neutralization of peripheral elites, the replacement of core-region elites by peripheral elites, or a more equal sharing of powers between core and periphery by means of political and economic decentralization and the development of new core regions in the periphery. In the last case, authority-dependency relations between cores and their peripheries may disappear with relatively minor exceptions in remote rural areas or in urban slums.

In general, then, Friedmann's theory "assigns a decisive influence to the institutional and organizational framework of society and, specifically, to the patterns of authority and dependency that result from the unusual capacity of certain areas to serve as cradles of innovation."[2] The theory is attractive in many respects. In particular, it includes all space and it treats variables in specific areas as parts of a larger system rather than as isolated phenomena. It also integrates cultural and political processes into the process of economic development. Finally, it is sufficiently general to cover a great number of cases. Unfortunately, the relevant cases include the newly developing countries or multinational regions characterized by core-periphery dependency relations, but not, as Friedmann clearly realizes, "the reasonably advanced and integrated spatial systems of the United States, West Germany, or Sweden."[3] Thus, while Freidmann's theory may provide some insights into interregional problems in the United States (readers of Harry Caudill's *Night Comes to the Cumberlands* may well recognize a case in point), it is not addressed to the larger contemporary policy issues related to spatial allocation of resources in the United States.

Lasuén: Growth Poles and Organizational Space

The most recent original contribution to growth center theory is that of José Lasuén, who has indicated a promising direction for future research on problems of regional development by linking growth pole theory to the study

of industrial organization. Lasuén takes as his starting point the works of
Perroux and the French School, but he emphasizes the ambiguity of many of
their concepts, and he deplores their restricted use of input-output techniques:

> The inter-industry technique ... has drained the growth pole
> concept of its original temporal and dynamic meaning and recharged
> it with a static and/or comparative static content. The heavy use of
> the input-output technique has shifted the school's attention away
> from Perroux's original translation of Schumpeterian development.
> They have failed to develop the point that the activity creating a
> growth pole was essentially a sectoral and a geographic disturbance
> not because of its larger than average size, nor because of its higher
> multiplier, but because it was an innovation.[74]

In response, Lasuén sets out to test, reformulate, and complete—within
the context of recent economic development—Perroux's work on growth pole
dynamics. For Lasuén, the critical factors in economic development are those
which determine the generation and diffusion of innovations and the spread of
adoptions. Perroux's thought, he maintains, was strongly influenced by the
vertical complexes of the Ruhr combine type, which, due to institutional,
cultural, and sociological factors, as well as to smaller national markets, were
dominant in Europe before World War II. Today, in contrast, the organizational
structure of the leading corporations has changed, and there is a new type of
management. The leading firm is now a loose organization that is less
concerned with one line of product than with marketing the most profitable
mix of products or services. It seeks to adapt to a changing flow of innovations
more than it aims at a breakthrough by means of a single innovation, which
may be copied or become obsolete in a short time. It markets a multitude of
products and services all over the world; it produces or assembles many of
these, but it also subcontracts numerous functions. Moreover, linkages have
been strengthened between large and small firms within an industry, as well as
among firms of all sizes in different industries. To illustrate the change in
corporation structure, Lasuén contrasts the rigidity of Krupp with the
"stupendous flexibility" of Litton. Under these conditions, Lasuén believes
that "the diffusion channels of specific information will become less and less
selective, the spread of adoptions more extensive over sectoral and geographic
space, and economic development faster and less polarized."[75]

Lasuén suggests that underdeveloped regions need to leapfrog not only
over the technological stages of past development, but also over the stages
of business reorganization. In general, he proposes a two-pronged strategy
to avoid problems of regional economic disparities. First, "what is required
is to create, as soon as possible, stronger interrelations between all plants
across all topological spaces (geographical, sectoral, etc.). That can be
achieved, as hinted, by consolidating all plants into large multi-plant/multi-
product/multi-city firms and/or by fostering inter-firms linkages."[76]
Second, there should be a very flexible policy to increase the relative
attractiveness of lagging regions. Capital, credit, training, service,
infrastructure, and other forms of assistance to public and private firms

should take account of the different priorities of firms at various stages of organization if they are to be really effective.

The present author has criticized Lasuén for, among other things, not giving sufficient attention to the importance of external economies of agglomeration as the origin of spatial polarization.[77] In a constructive reply, Lasuén points out that his policy suggestions were meant to apply broadly to the newly developing countries. "I am not unaware," he states, "of the economic and political problem Appalachia presents for the U.S.A., but I am also conscious that it is not by a long shot similar to the problems that the Italian Mezzogiorno or so many other 'souths' signify for their respective countries."[78] In general, he supports the development efforts being made for Appalachia on the ground that policies which did not make sense in underdeveloped Europe may make sense in the United States today. However, he cautions against any belief that "a geographical polarization of urban infrastructure attracting services or service-oriented manufacturing, instead of a geographical polarization of factors attracting manufacturing (like the French school recommended and I criticized), is going to do the trick."[79] He further remarks:

> From my perspective, it seems clear that the imagery of the Route 128 and El Camino Real complexes is not less dangerous than the imagery of the Ruhr complex. It leads to the defeatist attitude that in order to have the industries and services connected with Harvard and M.I.T. and with Stanford and Berkeley, the thing to do is to create smaller but similar research and education magnets. Or that in order to have small Manhattans, the thing to do is to create small First City Banks, Madison Avenue publicity firms and insurance companies.
>
> If that were the case, since the duplication of those magnets is simply not feasible, the hope of the world's future Appalachias would be rather gloomy.[80]

Nevertheless, Lasuén does advocate building up the urban infrastructure necessary to attract tertiary and quaternary activities to lagging areas of developed countries as one part of a larger development strategy. In addition, he would promote the inter- and intra-firm integration of these activities so that operations could be branched off from the original locations to the areas favored by public policy. Since "secondary and tertiary activities are in the real world intermixed at all levels of development" he proposes that consideration be given to whether the existing manufacturing network could not be used "to promote a similarly homogeneous spatial spread of tertiary and quaternary activities." He finally suggests that growth policies for developed countries consider promoting firms catering to the final market and encouraging them to branch out into other activities or to set up, through various contractual arrangements, other firms in market-related activities.[81]

Other Contributions

It is evident by now that growth center theory covers a great many concepts and issues. For this reason, detailed consideration has been given only to the more general approaches that have been formulated over the past fifteen years. However, there is now an abundant literature dealing with more specialized aspects of the theory.

For example, Vida Nichols has attempted to examine, using data from Georgia, the contention that economic growth will diffuse naturally from a medium-size growing city to the areas immediately surrounding it and eventually beyond to other parts of the region. Nichols concludes that although it is probably advisable to concentrate investment in towns with the strongest linkages, it might also be advisable to invest in lower-order centers, or even in agricultural areas, because increased incomes in these places will generate strong income multipliers in higher-order centers, whereas the converse is not true.[82]

Heiko Körner has attempted to make Perroux's theory of development poles more workable by analyzing broadly the inducement effect mechanisms transmitting economic growth from leading to lagging areas. He examines polarization in terms of economic, institutional, psychological, and geographic effects.[83]

Gordon Cameron recently has examined the analytical basis of spatial discrimination in terms of four arguments: (1) A planned build-up of infrastructure in optimal sites will avoid the external diseconomies of growth in large and congested cities and the high marginal costs of placing public overhead capital in minor centers of activity. (2) For any given level of subsidy, investment in spatially concentrated infrastructure is likely to maximize the inflow of exogenous capital. (3) The long-run spread effects of geographically unbalanced growth are likely to be substantial as the growth areas become the leading regional centers of innovation and technical efficiency. (4) A commitment to provide specific amounts and types of public investment in selected sites will facilitate the formulation of regional goals and priorities for where and how much to invest. He finds that all of these arguments have merits on *a priori* grounds. He also concludes that a policy designating a broad zone for special investment and seeking to improve the linkages among areas and centers within this zone is more fruitful than one favoring a very limited number of urban centers.[84]

In a forthcoming study by Brian Berry, it is argued that the role played by growth centers in regional development is a particular case of the general process of innovation diffusion. In particular, he maintains that the developmental role of growth centers involves the simultaneous filtering down the urban hierarchy of the innovations that cause growth and the spreading of the benefits accruing from the resulting growth both nationally, from core to hinterland regions, and within these regions, from their metropolitan centers outward to the intermetropolitan periphery.[85]

In another forthcoming paper, William Alonso and Elliott Medrich demonstrate that since the beginning of the century, a very large share of American metropolitan growth, and an even larger share of the net immigration into metropolitan areas, has been absorbed by those SMSA's which grew substantially faster than all SMSA's. This share has been increasing recently because of more active and selective intermetropolitan migration. They suggest that just as the SMSA transcended the city, now clusters of metropolitan areas are emerging as functional systems. On the other hand, spontaneous growth centers are lacking in lagging regions such as Appalachia and the Ozarks.[86]

Although the number of relevant contributions which can be considered here is necessarily limited, several surveys of the literature are available. In addition to works previously cited, particular attention may be called to *Regional Policy in EFTA,* an examination of the growth center idea in the context of the European Free Trade Association,[87] and David Darwent's review and evaluation.[88]

Before considering more critically the relevance of growth center theory to the United States, it is first necessary to examine the empirical evidence on the role of growth centers in promoting the development of lagging regions.

NOTES

1. See, for example, François Perroux, *L'économie du XXe siècle* (2nd ed.; Paris: Presses Universitaires de France, 1964), pp. 142-153, "Note sur la notion de pôle de croissance," originally published in *Economie appliquée,* Nos. 1-2 (January-June, 1955); Pierre Bauchet, "La comptabilité économique régionale et son usage," *Economie appliquée,* Vol. 14 (January, 1961), 69, 80; Jules Milhau, "La théorie de la croissance et l'expansion régionale," *Economie appliquée,* No. 3 (July-September, 1956), 361; and J. F. Gravier, *La question régionale* (Paris: Flammarion, 1970).

2. Benjamin Higgins, *Economic Development* (revised edition; New York: W. W. Norton, 1968), p. 477.

3. Eric E. Lampard, "The Evolving System of Cities in the United States," in Harvey S. Perloff and Lowdon Wingo, Jr., eds., *Issues in Urban Economics* (Baltimore: The Johns Hopkins Press, 1968), pp. 95-96.

4. E. A. G. Robinson, "Location Theory, Regional Economics and Backward Areas," in E. A. G. Robinson, ed., *Backward Areas in Advanced Countries* (New York: St. Martin's Press, 1969), p.5.

5. Lloyd Rodwin, *Nations and Cities* (Boston: Houghton Mifflin, 1970), p. 18.

6. Ralph W. Pfouts, "An Empirical Testing of the Economic Base Theory," *Journal of the American Institute of Planners,* Vol. 23, No. 2 (Spring, 1957), 64-69.

7. Hans Blumenfeld, "The Economic Base of the Metropolis," *Journal of the American Institute of Planners,* Vol. 21, No. 4 (Fall, 1955), 114-32.

8. Wilbur R. Thompson, "Internal and External Factors in the Development of Urban Economies," in Perloff and Wingo, eds., *op. cit.,* p. 53.

9. Edgar M. Hoover, "Some Old and New Issues in Regional Development," in E. A. G. Robinson, ed., *Backward Areas in Advanced Countries* (New York: St. Martin's Press, 1969), pp. 343-57.

10. Joseph J. Spengler, "Some Determinants of the Manpower Prospect, 1966-1985," in Irving H. Siegal, ed., *Manpower Tomorrow: Prospects and Priorities* (New York: Augustus M. Kelley, 1967), p. 91. See also J. Beaujeu-Garnier and G. Chabot, *Urban Geography* (New York: John Wiley & Sons, 1967), p. 162.

11. John Friedmann, *Regional Development Policy: A Case Study of Venezuela* (Cambridge, Mass.: The M.I.T. Press, 1966), p. 28.

12. Economic Development Administration, *Industrial Location as a Factor in Regional Economic Development* (Washington, D.C.: Government Printing Office, 1967), pp. 23-24.

13. Harvey S. Perloff, with Vera Dodds, *How a Region Grows* (New York: Committee for Economic Development, 1963), p. 24.

14. Perroux, *op. cit.*

15. Milhau, *op. cit.*, p. 361.

16. P. Pottier, "Axes de comunication et théorie de développement," *Revue économique*, Vol. 14 (January, 1963), 113-14.

17. *Ibid.*, pp. 70-113. Although Pottier's analysis is based on French experience, he points out that development axes are usually interregional or international in nature.

18. *Ibid.*, p. 128.

19. Perroux, *op. cit.*, p. 143.

20. Jean Paelinck, "La théorie du développement régional polarisé," *Cahiers de l'Institut de Science Economique Appliquée*, Series L, No. 15 (March, 1965), 10-11.

21. François Perroux, "Economic Space: Theory and Applications," *Quarterly Journal of Economics*, Vol. 64, No. 1 (February, 1950), 90.

22. *Ibid.*, p. 91.

23. *Ibid.*

24. *Ibid.*, pp. 94-97. See also Perroux, "Les espaces économiques," *Economie Appliquée*, No. 1 (January, 1950).

25. Jacques Boudeville, *Les espaces économiques* (Paris: Presses Universitaires de France, 1961), p. 8.

26. *Ibid.*, p. 10.

27. *Ibid.*, pp. 11-13.

28. Jacques Boudeville, "Un modèle des mouvements commerciaux interrégionaux de France," *Cahiers de l'Institut de Science Economique Appliquée*, Series L, No. 9 (October, 1961), 5-78. See also Boudeville, *Les espaces économiques, op. cit.*, pp. 14-15; and Jacques Boudeville, "La région plan," *Cahiers de l'Institut de Science Economique Appliquée*, Series L, No. 6 (January, 1960).

29. Boudeville, *Les espaces économiques, op. cit.*, p. 16.

30. Jacques Boudeville, "Les notions d'espace et d'intégration" (paper given at the International Conference on Town and Regional Planning, Basel, September 22-25, 1965), p. 2.

31. Perroux, *L'économie du XXe siècle, op. cit.*, p. 85.

32. *Ibid.*, p. 40.

33. *Ibid.*, pp. 142-53.

34. H. Aujac, "La hiérarchie des industries dans un tableau des échanges interindustriels, et ses conséquences dans la mise en oeuvre d'un plan national décentralisé," *Revue économique*, Vol. 11 (March, 1960), 169-238.

35. Rodwin, *op. cit.*, pp. 150-51.

36. See, for example, Pierre Bauchet, *Les tableaux économiques, analyse de la région lorraine* (Paris: Génin, 1955); Janine Capronnier-Spielhagen, *Comptes nationaux et régionaux de l'énergie* (Paris: Colin, 1962); R. Jouandet-Bernadat, *Les comptes du département de la Gironde* (Bordeaux: Imprimerie Bière, 1963); and R. Jouandet-Bernadat, *Comptabilité économique et espaces régionaux* (Paris: Gauthier-Villars, 1964).

37. Sylvan Wickham, "French Planning: Retrospect and Prospect," *Review of Economics and Statistics*, Vol. 45, No. 4 (November, 1963), 340.

38. André Trintignac, *Aménager l'hexagone* (Paris: Editions du Centurion, 1964), pp. 218-19.

39. Paelinck, *op. cit.*, p. 8.

40. Philippe Aydalot, "Note sur les économies externes et quelques notions connexes," *Revue économique*, Vol. 16 (November, 1965), 962.

41. For a fuller discussion of these phenomena, see, for example, Paelinck, *op. cit.*; Jacques Boudeville, "La région plan," *Cahiers de l'Institut de Science Economique Appliquée*, Series L, No. 6 (January, 1960); François Perroux, "La firme motrice dans une région, et la région motrice," *Cahiers de l'Institut de Science Economique Appliquée*, Series AD, No. 1 (March, 1961); and L. E. Davin, *Economie régionale et croissance* (Paris: Génin, 1964), pp. 54-72.

42. Paelinck, *op. cit.,* pp. 34-37.

43. Bauchet, *Les tableaux économiques, analyse de la région lorraine, op. cit.,* p. 10.

44. Davin, *op. cit.,* p. 56.

45. *Ibid.,* p. 64.

46. Aydalot, *op. cit.,* p. 963.

47. *Ibid.,* p. 964.

48. *Ibid.,* pp. 964-65.

49. *Ibid.,* p. 967.

50. *Ibid.*

51. Paelinck, *op. cit.,* pp. 10-13.

52. *Ibid.,* p. 13.

53. Raymond Vernon, *The Changing Economic Function of the Central City* (New York: Committee for Economic Development, 1959), pp. 28-37.

54. Davin, *op. cit.,* p. 57.

55. Niles M. Hansen, "The Structure and Determinants of Local Public Investment Expenditures," *Review of Economics and Statistics,* Vol. 47, No. 2 (May, 1965), 150-62.

56. Davin, *op. cit.,* p. 56.

57. Paelinck, *op. cit.,* pp. 10-11.

58. *Ibid.,* p. 47.

59. Albert O. Hirschman, *The Strategy of Economic Development* (New Haven: Yale University Press, 1958), pp. 100-17.

60. *Ibid.*, pp. 62-63.

61. *Ibid.*, p. 184.

62. *Ibid.*, pp. 187-90.

63. *Ibid.*, p. 194.

64. *Ibid.*, pp. 194-95.

65. Gunnar Myrdal, *Rich Lands and Poor* (New York: Harper & Brothers, 1957), pp. 23-27.

66. *Ibid.*, pp. 27-31.

67. *Ibid.*, pp. 31-33.

68. Niles M. Hansen, "Unbalanced Growth and Regional Development," *Western Economic Journal*, Vol. 4, No. 1 (Fall, 1965), 3-14; and Niles M. Hansen, "The Structure and Determinants of Local Public Investment Expenditures," *Review of Economics and Statistics*, Vol. 47, No. 2 (May, 1965), 150-62.

69. Niles M. Hansen, *French Regional Planning* (Bloomington: Indiana University Press, 1968), Chapters 1, 7-8; and Niles M. Hansen, *Rural Poverty and the Urban Crisis* (Bloomington: Indiana University Press, 1970).

70. John R. Friedmann, *Regional Development Policy: A Case Study of Venezeula* (Cambridge, Mass.: The M.I.T. Press, 1966).

71. Friedmann's paper "A General Theory of Polarized Development" has been in circulation since late 1967. In its definitive version, it will appear in Niles M. Hansen, ed., *Growth Centers and Regional Development*, to be published by The Free Press. The present summary is based on this paper.

72. Friedmann, "A General Theory of Polarized Development," *op. cit.*, pp. 29-30.

73. *Ibid.*, p. 31.

74. J. R. Lasuén, "On Growth Poles," *Urban Studies*, Vol. 6, No. 2 (June, 1969), 141.

75. *Ibid.*, p. 148.

76. *Ibid.*, p. 150.

77. Niles M. Hansen, "On Urban Hierarchy Stability and Spatial Polarization: A Note," *Urban Studies*, Vol. 7, No. 1 (February, 1970), 82-83.

78. J. R. Lasuén, "Urban Hierarchy Stability and Spatial Polarization: A Rejoinder," *Urban Studies,* Vol. 7, No. 1 (February, 1970), 86-87.

79. *Ibid.,* p. 87.

80. *Ibid.*

81. *Ibid.,* pp. 87-88.

82. Vida Nichols, "Growth Poles: An Evaluation of Their Propulsive Effect," *Environment and Planning,* Vol. 1, No. 2 (1969), 193-208.

83. Heiko Körner, "Industrielle Entwicklungspole als Instrumente der Regionalpolitik in Entwicklungsländern," *Kyklos,* Vol. 20, No. 3 (1967), 684-708.

84. Gordon C. Cameron, "Growth Areas, Growth Centres and Regional Conversion," *Scottish Journal of Political Economy,* Vol. 17, No. 1 (February, 1970), 19-38.

85. Brian J. L. Berry, "Hierarchical Diffusion: The Basis of Developmental Filtering and Spread in a System of Growth Centers," forthcoming in Niles M. Hansen, ed., *Growth Centers and Regional Development.*

86. William Alonso and Elliott Medrich, "Spontaneous Growth Centers in Twentieth Century American Urbanization," forthcoming in Hansen, ed., *Growth Centers and Regional Development.*

87. *Regional Policy in EFTA,* University of Glasgow Social and Economic Studies Occasional Paper No. 10 (Edinburgh: Oliver and Boyd, 1968).

88. David F. Darwent, "Growth Poles and Growth Centers in Regional Planning: A Review," *Environment and Planning,* Vol. 1, No. 1 (1969), 5-31. See also Byung N. Song, "A Theory of Regional Economic Growth: Growth Poles and Development Axes" (unpublished dissertation, University of Southern California, 1970).

CHAPTER

3

GROWTH CENTER EXPERIENCE
IN THE UNITED STATES
AND ABROAD

In recent years, numerous countries have attempted to implement growth center or growth area policies for the purposes of revitalizing depressed industrial areas dominated by stagnating or declining sectors and of stimulating economic development in regions which have always lagged behind their countries' more advanced regions. In many of these cases, governments have also been trying to divert migration flows away from large, congested cities. This chapter examines the nature and significance of these policies as they have been elaborated in other countries and in the United States.

FOREIGN EXPERIENCE

Growth Areas in Great Britain

Although some postwar legislation made favorable references to growth areas, the 1960 Local Employment Act abandoned this approach completely by restricting regional development measures to areas of high unemployment, regardless of their growth prospects. The Act represented an extreme position of taking jobs to workers, even though some places with good growth prospects outside of designated Development Districts were within commuting distance of high-unemployment areas. Moreover, many Districts, particularly in mining areas, were not suitable for industrialization. Critics of the Act argued that a broad view should be taken of a region's growth, rather than merely concentrating on the difficulties of problem areas, and that the benefits of regional policy measures should be extended to places in the region with the best growth prospects. This approach was first introduced at the official level in the White Papers on Central Scotland and North-East England in 1963.[1] The White Paper on Central Scotland took the following position:

> This programme represents a more positive approach to regional economic development than any Government in this country has yet attempted. It incorporates the conception of growth areas, chosen as potentially the best locations for industrial expansion. The development of these areas will be fostered by providing for them, in accordance with a coherent plan, all the "infrastructure" services, e.g., communications, water supplies, housing—that industry needs; and also by maintaining in them, as long as the economy of Central Scotland as a whole requires, the inducements available for industry in Development Districts.[2]

The political difficulties of a growth area policy were soon obvious. Within Central Scotland alone, eight such areas were designated, while in the North-East a large "growth zone" was selected covering most of the region. In addition, the economic criteria used to select growth areas were very vague. While some of the "growth points" selected had, in fact, demonstrated real growth potential, others were simply depressed areas whose designation would have little effect on private investment. In any event, when the Labor Party came to power, the growth area policies were largely abandoned.[3]

In 1966, new Development Areas were scheduled to replace the Development Districts. The new policy made regional policy benefits available on a wide regional basis instead of limiting them to small districts defined in terms of unemployment rates. Most of the natural growth points in the problem areas are included in the Development Areas, but there are significant exceptions. Gavin McCrone notes that Cardiff is not included in the Welsh Development Area and that Plymouth is not included in the South-West, though "both of these towns would appear to be the most natural growth points for the region that surrounds them and there is little indication that either of them are yet large enough to pose serious congestion problems. Their exclusion from their respective Development Areas, therefore, appears to be absurd." A similar argument might be made with respect to Edinburgh and its exclusion from the Scottish Development Area, though with half a million population it is more congested than either Cardiff or Plymouth. Furthermore, its economy is prospering without assistance, and there are numerous potential industrial sites just outside the city.[4]

In general, the growth area approach adopted in Great Britain has been primarily based on finding and promoting locations with the most suitable growth prospects, as well as considerations of efficient use of public investment. On the other hand, in relation to the continent, relatively little emphasis has been given to the importance of interindustry linkages and still less to external economies as the basis for concentrated investment. However, the problems which typify Great Britain are associated, for the most part, with depressed industrial areas rather than underdeveloped agricultural areas (the Scottish Highlands and the Irish Republic are exceptional in this regard). The concentrations of population and public overhead capital which already exist in older industrial areas make the need for a growth center policy less forceful than in underdeveloped areas. McCrone maintains that this is especially true with respect to the external economies argument. He states that planning authorities should seek out places in South Wales or Central Scotland where the return on public investment can be maximized but that Central Scotland and South Wales as a whole are the appropriate units for considering the external economies associated with a particular industrial structure.[5]

However, there is a danger here that geographic space may be too broadly defined because the notion of external economies is too narrowly defined. McCrone's emphasis on "the external economies which a particular industrial structure provides" overlooks the fact that employment growth today is likely to be in non-"industrial" sectors attracted by services and amenities which need to be more concentrated than interlinked industries. In any case, Lloyd Rodwin is correct in stating that the British goals "of encouraging growth centers and reducing unemployment in the lagging regions are so vague that they hardly provide an adequate basis for evaluating progress, or even for gauging how much of the changes in the character of urban development can be attributed to the measures undertaken.[6]

Italy's North-South Problem

Although Italy has depressed industrial areas, the country's principal problem is the presence of the largest underdeveloped area in industrial Europe. This area, the Mezzogiorno, comprises the seven southern administrative regions of the country and includes 41 per cent of the national territory and 38 per cent of its total population. When a regional policy for the South was introduced about twenty years ago, estimates placed its per capita income between less than 50 per cent and 60 per cent of that in the rest of the country. Behind these low-income figures were the characteristics often found in an underdeveloped area: predominance of agriculture, low productivity in all sectors, high birth rates, high unemployment, low education standards, and a high rate of outmigration.[7]

The reasons for the plight of the Mezzogiorno are numerous and complex. To begin with, the area has unfavorable natural conditions. The soil is poor, the climate is adverse, and water and minerals are scarce. The Mezzogiorno also was remote from the rich markets of Northern Europe at a time when transportation costs were a more critical factor than they are now. The North of Italy, on the other hand, received more stimulus from the countries that initiated the industrial revolution, and it cumulatively developed its industry through external economies, commercial and financial organizations, and wider opportunities for social and educational improvement. The political unification of Italy a century ago also appears to have worked to the detriment of the Mezzogiorno. At that time, it was generally believed that the free play of market forces would benefit both rich and poor regions, but the backwash effects turned out to be more powerful than the concomitant spread effects.[8]

A policy for developing the South was inaugurated in 1950 with the creation of the Cassa per il Mezzogiorno, a public body entrusted with the responsibility for administering government funds for that purpose. To give an indication of the magnitude of the operations of the Cassa, the annual average of its investments for the period 1963-65 was 1.8 per cent of the gross national product and 7.7 per cent of the gross southern product. This amounted to 7.7 per cent of the Italian gross investment and to 28.8 per cent of total investment in the South. Of course, to these investments must be added those of ordinary public agencies (which devoted 38.5 per cent of their investments to the South from 1950 to 1965) and public enterprises, which established the large iron and steel growth center complex at Taranto.[9]

Although the South is undoubtedly better off than it would have been in the absence of the Cassa, a comprehensive evaluation of effects to improve its economy concludes that "economic problems which for so long have plagued Southern Italy remain unsolved. There are still nearly one million unemployed (and maybe more, were all unemployment accounted for) and the vast majority continues to live in abject poverty."[10] An Italian authority also points out that the South's economic structure has been only slightly changed and estimates that per capita income at current prices rose from 59.5 per cent of the rest of Italy in 1951 to only 61.2 per cent in 1965 [11]

A principal reason why development policy for the South has not been more successful is that it has been primarily oriented toward improvements in agriculture, in infrastructure, and in incentives to private business. Since "what appears to be inadequate in the South is the economic, social and human environment required to allow everybody to exploit his own ability without having to move elsewhere," it is striking that "the Cassa activities began to show amounts earmarked for social and human investments for the first time only eight years after it started to operate."[12] Indeed, through 1965, not more than 5 per cent of the outlays of the Cassa were devoted to investment in human resources. This glaring disproportion is now coming to be recognized as a major factor in the lack of entrepreneurship in the South, which, in turn, is a major obstacle to the government's efforts to develop a growth center policy for the South.

Until recently, Italian authorities were preoccupied with reducing unemployment as widely as possible, but it is now clear that this approach resulted in an excessive dispersal of investments. The trend now is "to concentrate effort in areas possessing the essential requirements of a rational location of productivity,"[13] that is, to pursue a growth center strategy. But even this approach is difficult in an area such as the Mezzogiorno. Pasquale Saraceno finds that recent Italian experience shows that

> the location in an underdeveloped area of a large productive unit often remains an isolated incident, which does not give rise to those favourable repercussions on the rest of the economy which many expected from it. If, then, it is borne in mind that the number of *new* large production units that can be foreseen for the future in the Italian industrial system is very limited, it has to be concluded that important developments in the industrialization of the South must depend principally on a variety of medium and small undertakings. The question that arises today in Italy is whether this objective can be achieved under the conditions that exist at present.[14]

The recent decision of Fiat to build a major plant in the South is a case in point. Although Fiat will invest 250 million lire, only 19,000 jobs will be created. It is much harder to relocate small and medium-size firms, even though they are needed for the creation of an industrial framework. Indeed, many observers believe that even if large, capital-intensive operations are moved to the South, the immobility of smaller firms will constitute a permanent barrier to the South's industrial autonomy. If a breakthrough is made, it may well come in the electronics industry, since electrical component manufacturing requires relatively little capital but a great deal of unskilled and semiskilled labor.[15]

It would seem, therefore, that a growth center policy for the Mezzogiorno must rely on the personal initiative and ability of private entrepreneurs to set up the small and medium-size firms that are a necessary complement to the larger undertakings of major firms. Unfortunately, it is not easy to induce entrepreneurs from the North to move to the South to run newly formed firms of their own, and the South still does not have a sizable entrepreneurial class of its own. It would seem that the time is long overdue for the Italian government to acknowledge that any real solution to the problems of the Mezzogiorno must be based, in large part, on vastly greater investment in the region's human resources, coupled with a growth center policy that avoids the widely dispersed, and too often ineffective, investments of the past. Of course, after twenty years of development efforts, it may well be difficult politically to admit that the payoff from these measures will take place, for the most part, in the long run.

Regional Planning in France

During the past two decades, the French have developed the most comprehensive system of regional planning in Europe. The main policy objectives have been to balance the pull of the Paris region by stimulating economic growth in the provinces, to promote growth of urban centers in the Paris Basin, and to guide the expansion of the Paris region by a comprehensive Strategic Plan. Despite a certain lack of coherency and integration among various elements in their regional policy, the French are making relatively great strides in developing institutions and policies equal to their pressing regional problems.

The implementation of regional planning in France is carried out by agencies at both the national and regional levels. Coordination of planning activities at the national level is the responsibility of the Delegation for Spatial Planning and Regional Action or Délégation à l'Aménagement du Territoire et à l'Action Régionale (DATAR). This interministerial body insures that regional objectives are considered during the formulation of the national plan and that regional policy as embodied in the plan is effectively executed by government agencies. DATAR is not an administrative body in the usual sense, but in its tasks of coordination and impulsion, it works in close cooperation with the General Planning Commission. Through regionalization of the government budget, it watches over annual investment programs of various administrations, and through a special fund for regional action, it finances particularly urgent investment projects.

The long-term perspective within the medium-term (four- or five-year) plans are developed is formulated by the National Commission for Spatial Planning or Commission Nationale de l'Aménagement du Territoire (CNAT). CNAT, which is attached to the General Planning Commission, analyzes social, economic, and technical factors that will be most influential in shaping the future distribution of population and economic activity. Then it attempts to identify what influence public authorities can employ to achieve regional objectives. Finally, CNAT proposes the principal orientations for regional policy by fixing a number of long-term goals consistent with more geographically balanced growth. It was actively involved in preparing the regional aspects of the Fifth Plan (1966-70), defining the principal orientations within a perspective extending to 1985.

During the 1950's, there was growing recognition that the need for more local initiative could be met only by decentralization, combined with more democratic participation and greater horizontal coordination at the regional, departmental, and local levels. In 1959, a decree was promulgated that called for harmonization of administrative boundaries along regional lines, and in the following year, France was divided into twenty-one "program regions." The Paris region was placed under the authority of the General Delegation for the District of the Region of Paris. The remaining regions, grouping from two to eight departments, were each given a prefect to oversee and coordinate regionally significant economic programs. In 1964, administrative reform was furthered by a series of decrees that strengthened the authority of regional prefects and provided regional bases for economic policy coordination. At the same time, regional administrative conferences, composed of government administrators advised by outside experts, were created to consider the consequences of alternative public investment policies for each region.

The 1964 decrees also initiated Regional Economic Development Commissions, which bring together local public officials and representatives from all socio-occupational categories for consultation on regional problems and planning needs. A commission has from twenty to fifty members. A quarter of the members are chosen from local officials; a quarter are appointed by the Prime Minister on the basis of their expertise; and the remaining members are drawn from business, labor, agriculture, and other interest groups. Government consultation with the commissions, which are named for five years, is obligatory during the preparation of regional plans.

The national plan's regional objectives are specified in the regional sections, or *tranches*. Like the national plan, regional sections include a schedule of realizations, order of priorities, and indications of means of finance. They provide a framework for action over the length of the plan and are part of the government's budget, which specifies each year how regional objectives are to be realized.

In general, regionalization of the national plan and the administrative reforms of 1964[16] were intended to promote more effective implementation of the government's economic and social development programs, as well as to promote more concerted regional action among the central government, local authorities, and special interest groups. The degree to which decentralized decision-making can be harmonized with the national plan remains to be seen. This picture is further clouded by ambiguities in regional policy objectives developed at the national level. In particular, policy measures for the twenty-one regions have yet to be reconciled with the Fifth Plan's urban policy.

Although France's urban revolution is taking place later than in countries such as the United States, Great Britain, and Germany, it is moving rapidly. One French planner has pointed out that since, by the end of the century, 85 per cent of the total French population will live in cities, it is increasingly difficult to distinguish between the study of urban society and society as such.[17] In order to provide a balance to the pull of the Paris region—which nearly all Frenchmen acknowledge as overcrowded—and to provide a stimulus to economic activity in provincial areas, eight *métropoles d'équilibre* have been chosen for special development aid. They are Lyon-St. Etienne, Marseille-Aix, Bordeaux, Lille-Roubaix-Tourcoing, Toulouse, Strasbourg, Nantes-St. Nazaire, and Nancy-Metz. Concentration of projects around a relatively few spatial development poles permits firms to take maximum advantage of the technical and financial external economies generated by interaction of mutually interdependent activities. The locations were selected on the basis of studies of the quantity and kinds of services offered in France's principal cities, as well as of urban spheres of influence. The number of *métropoles* is relatively small because major projects such as large hospitals and airports can be justified economically only if they are assured a sufficient number of users. Nevertheless, the *métropoles* have been more broadly defined than single cities because polynuclear urban areas are beginning to form as automobile use increases.[18]

The Fifth Plan provides for decentralization of private and public tertiary activities by endowing the *métropoles* with renovated central cities and new business centers. The proportion of new housing accounted for by the *métropoles* is to be increased and a start made on subway systems for Lyon and Marseille if plans can be prepared in time. Government aid will also permit construction of a number of new towns in the vicinity of Lyon and Marseille. Fifty to 55 per cent of government research investment will be allocated to the *métropoles* (plus Grenoble and Rennes), as contrasted with 22 per cent during the Fourth Plan. Thy proportion for Paris will decline from 50 per cent to between 35 and 40 per cent. New urban agencies have been created to prepare "strategic plans" for the *métropoles* similar to the plan that presently guides the Paris region's growth.[19]

Six OREAM (Organismes d'Etudes d'Aménagement d'Aires Metropolitaines) have been established for the urban areas of Marseille, Lyon-St. Etienne, Metz-Nancy, the North, the Lower Seine, and the Lower Loire. The first task of the OREAM is to trace long-term development prospects and related urban planning needs, taking the year 2000 as a planning horizon. The results of these studies will be discussed by the relevant Regional Economic Development Commissions in the context of their reflections on long-term regional planning requirements. During the Sixth Plan, the OREAM will have as their principal mission the preparation of medium-term modernization and investment programs for each study area. However, there remain numerous political problems, especially those concerning cooperation between the central government, which created and directs the OREAM, and local authorities whose perspective is often limited by the next municipal and legislative election.[20]

At present, studies are being made to determine how much influence the *métropole* provinces have gained in relation to Paris. In particular, demographic and employment variables are being analyzed and compared to the goals of the Fifth Plan. In the Sixth Plan, less emphasis will be placed on defining an urban hierarchy, while more will be given to analyzing the interplay of functions and dependencies within the nation's urban structure (*armature urbaine*). In the continuing effort to limit growth of the Paris region, complementarities are sought among provincial cities so that social investment (housing, education, transportation, and so on) and investment in directly productive activities may be harmonized from a spatial perspective. In this regard, certain *métropoles* will be favored for investment in key sectors, for example, the chemical industry in Lyon, synthetic fibers in Lille, aeronautics in Toulouse, and steel in Fos, near Marseille. The Sixth Plan will also increase efforts to expand tertiary activites in the *métropoles*, and a Planning-Programming-Budgeting System will be introduced for projects of national concern. Programs for the development of the *métropoles* will be formulated between the middle of 1969 and October, 1970. From then until March, 1971, following parliamentary approval of the Sixth Plan, the regional sections for the *métropoles* will be specified in detail, including financing by project, origin of funds, and year.

In addition to the *métropoles,* another spatial orientation has been superimposed on the twenty-one program regions. The area within a 200-mile radius of Paris, including the city of Paris, the territory covered by the Strategic Plan (*Schéma directeur*) for the Paris region, and the remainder of the area, has been termed the Paris Basin.

The Strategic Plan envisions creation of new urban centers around Paris as the only cure for the lack of public overhead capital in the suburbs and congestion in the heart of the city. The future growth of the region's population will be channeled along certain "preferential axes," chosen to suit the region's physical, economic, and human geography.[21] The principal axis follows the Seine west to Rouen and Le Havre, in Normandy. Secondary axes will be developed east along the Seine and the Marne. It is hoped that this scheme will break up the radial-concentric pattern that has contributed to many of the region's difficulties. Along the new axes, self-sufficient towns are planned. Each of the eight projected new towns would supply a complete range of commercial, service, and entertainment activities. It is anticipated that by the end of the century, each town will be able to provide for the needs of from 300,000 to 500,000 persons and for the more specialized needs of from one million to 1.5 million persons.[22]

For planning purposes, the Paris Basin is comprised of fifteen departments surrounding the Paris region. In 1967, an interministerial planning group for the Paris Basin was established with its own secretariat and a research team of economists, geographers, urbanists, and specialists from related disciplines.

During 1969, general planning directives were formulated to furnish a framework for the relevant investment choices of the Sixth Plan.

In the past, the growth of Paris has checked the development of urban centers in the Paris Basin by attracting industrial and commercial activity to the capital. Thus, while the French population as a whole is about 66 per cent urban, the Paris Basin is only 50 per cent urban. Moreover, the Basin's cities do not represent a well-structured urban hierarchy. There are nine urban areas with over 100,000 inhabitants living 100 to 200 kilometers from Paris, and numerous cities with between 20,000 and 50,000 inhabitants, but only one with a population between 50,000 and 100,000. Decentralization policies have stimulated industrial growth in the Basin; in 1962, the departments immediately surrounding the Paris region accounted for 10 per cent of France's population but 40 per cent of all industrial decentralization operations. On the other hand, tertiary employment (services, commerce, and administration) is relatively low; the Paris region has been a brake on these specifically urban activities that form an essential basis for regional life.[23]

To check the growth of the Paris region, the development of regional centers in the Paris Basin has been proposed as an alternative to the *métropoles d'équilibre* on the one hand and the new towns envisaged in the Strategic Plan for the Paris region, on the other.[24] Between 1954 and 1962, the Basin had a net migration loss of 82,000 persons to the Paris region, though it showed a net gain of 15,700 in relation to the rest of France. Through a major effort to build up the tertiary activities of such Basin cities as Rouen, Le Havre, Caen, Le Mans, Tours, Orléans, Troyes, Reims, and Amiens and by continuing to support their industrial growth, it is argued that net outmigration from the Basin to Paris can be sharply reduced and that the Basin can serve as a zone of attraction for migrants from the rest of France.[25]

In evaluating French experience, it is important to first realize that the inclusion of the entire country in French policy promotes integrated planning for all types of regions, from underdeveloped to congested, and it facilitates comprehensive evaluation of particular projects in terms of alternative locations. French policy also includes an urban dimension which, though it needs further elaboration, provides alternatives to both rural poverty and the diseconomies and social costs of the congested metropolis.* It is to be hoped that the Sixth Plan, now in initial stages of preparation, will specify relative priorities for investments to be made among (1) the new towns specified in the Strategic Plan for the Paris region, (2) the eight provincial *métropoles d'équilibre*, and (3) the cities of the Paris Basin.

It would also be desirable for the Sixth Plan to specify the role of urban policy in relation to other major regional planning objectives, most notably the development of both the North Sea-Mediterranean axis and lagging regions of the country. The growth of the Common Market has led to considerable

---

*The fruits of French regional policy are beginning to become evident. Between 1962 and 1968, the population of the Paris region grew by 750,000 (that of the city proper declined by 200,000), only about 66 per cent of the increase that had been officially predicted. See *Le Monde*, Selection hebdomadaire (September 12-18, 1968), 9.

interest in the creation of an unbroken waterway from Marseille to Rotterdam. Although certain variations have been proposed, the basic axis would follow the Rhone north from Marseille, join the Saône at Lyon, and then proceed by a system of canals to the Moselle Valley, which would be the final link with the Rhine and the North Sea.

The relatively lagging area south of the Loire and west of the Rhone, which includes Languedoc, Midi-Pyrénées, Aquitaine, Auvergne, Limousin, Poitou-Charentes, and most of the Center, has only two cities (Bordeaux and Toulouse) that will benefit from development programs under the new urban policies. In particular, the two most underdeveloped regions, Auvergne and Limousin, are relatively far from any vital urban area. This situation implies considerable potential conflict between urban policies that attempt to build on existing agglomeration economies and program region participation in the formulation of the national plan. All of the urban approaches assume that there will continue to be outmigration from regions with relatively low growth potential. In contrast, planning within the program region context is place oriented; each region is concerned with its own development rather than with preparing a significant number of its residents for employment in areas with greater opportunities. What this suggests is that the program regions should be redefined (and reduced in number) so that each one includes at least one major urban growth center. This would enable lagging areas to be related to genuine growth centers within a planning framework that combines a national urban policy and decentralized participation in the planning process.

Policies in Other Foreign Countries

In 1957, the Greek government, in cooperation with the European Productivity Agency (EPA), initiated a systematic regional planning program. The program was based on the creation of "trial and demonstration areas" similar to that established earlier by EPA and the Organization for European Economic Cooperation in Sardinia at the request of the Italian government. After preliminary studies, the lagging province of Epirus was selected for the first development planning program. Three districts within Epirus were chosen as a trial and demonstration area, or pilot zone. In evaluating the "planning from below" approach to regional development in Greece—which added Peloponnesus and Crete to the Epirus experiment—Benjamin Higgins writes that as of mid-1964, the work in the three regions "delayed the finding of a solution to the problem of poverty in the lagging regions of Greece. In this respect one could even argue that the pilot project did considerable and lasting harm."[26]

The main problem in the Greek case is similar to that in Italy—growth center investments in infrastructure were placed in areas which should have received more investment in human resources. Higgins notes that in the pilot zone approach for Epirus there was "something of the *pôle de croissance* concept" but that "a focal point of growth must by definition be big enough and dynamic enough to generate spread effects to the entire region, in this case the whole of Epirus. The pilot zone project did not meet these criteria."[27] Indeed, Higgins finds that Greek policy should stress migration out of the poorer agricultural areas into the industrial centers and that Epirus should be one of the first regions selected for a reduction in total population.[28]

In Canada, too, regional development policy has been primarily aimed at helping poor areas. This has been true of the Area Development Administration, the Atlantic Provinces Development Board, and the Agricultural Rehabilitation and Development Agency, though the government does provide some assistance to persons willing to move to jobs. Even in the province of Québec, where French regional planning concepts are at least nominally espoused, the poorest and most stagnant part of the province, the eastern section, has been selected as a pilot region for development. However, in contrast to the Greek pilot zone, recommendations have been made to establish growth poles in the more dynamic cities of the pilot region and to reduce the population of the more stagnant areas.[29]

In Brazil, where a considerable effort has been made on behalf of the lagging Northeast, the Second Master Plan (1963-65) of the Superentendencia para Desinvolvimento do Nordeste contained no analysis of interregional trade, capital movements, or population movements. The Plan assumed that the problems of the Northeast must be solved in the region and failed to consider that investment outside the region may benefit the people of the region more than investment within it. The Third Plan (1966-68) paid more attention to the interrelations among areas of the region, the region and other regions of the country, and the region and the world economy. However, there is still no indication of changed investment priorities.[30]

Brazil also provides an example of the difficulties of trying to implant a major urban center in a rural hinterland. Higgins aptly states that

> one point is perhaps too little stressed in the literature: the simple fact that . . . the kind of people needed to launch and maintain a process of industrialization have urbane taste. The ludicrous spectacle of cabinet members in Brazil solemnly boarding their planes on Tuesday morning to fly to Brasilia for a cabinet meeting, and flying joyously back to Rio de Janeiro on Tuesday evening, is evidence enough of the difficulties involved in moving such people even from large cities to small ones. The painfully slow growth of Canberra since its establishment in 1920 provides further support for this argument.[31]

Finally, E. A. G. Robinson's survey of attempts to develop lagging areas in industrial countries concludes:

> One of the clearest lessons of the experience of attempts to regenerate backward areas in the past twenty years has been the failure of such attempts where they have been directed to small-scale projects, intended to help local communities. Not only the Italian, but also the Belgian, the Swedish and the Russian experience had been so clear in this respect that . . . the "peppering" of a backward

area with large numbers of small projects has come to be regarded as a recipe for failure. It is interesting but sad that British as well as American practice is notably backward in this respect.[32]

At this point, it is appropriate to consider whether and to what extent American practice has been "notably backward."

AMERICAN EXPERIENCE

Regional policy in the United States at this writing is based on two legislative acts, both passed in 1965: the Appalachian Regional Development Act (ARDA) and the Public Works and Economic Development Act. Both acts are intended to provide financial aid, as well as planning and technical assistance, to areas experiencing high unemployment and/or low income. Although no definitive growth center strategy has been worked out within the context of these acts, the agencies that have been created to implement the programs which they outline have utilized the growth center concept in their operations. This section briefly describes and evaluates the nature of their growth center policies.

The Appalachian Region

As defined by the ARDA, the Appalachian region extends from northeastern Mississippi to southern New York. It represents a rather unusual case among lagging regions of industrialized countries; these regions tend to be peripheral to their countries' economic heartlands, whereas Appalachia is located between two of the most highly industrialized and urbanized regions of the world—the Atlantic megalopolis and the industrial Midwest.

In 1966, the estimated population of the Appalachian region was 18.3 million. Between 1960 and 1966, the population of the United States grew by 9.8 per cent, whereas that of Appalachia increased by only 3 per cent. Net outmigration of 606,100 persons was largely responsible for the region's lower growth rate. The proportion of the Appalachian population living in metropolitan areas or in counties with a total urban population over 50,000 was 49.7 per cent in 1966, compared to a corresponding national value of 72.4 per cent.[33] In 1960, over 30 per cent of the families living in Appalachia had an annual income of less than $3,000, the frequently used approximate borderline between poverty and a minimally comfortable standard of living. Between 1959 and 1966, per capita personal income in Appalachia increased from $1,661 to $2,297; in the United States as a whole, the increase was from $2,161 to $2,963. Thus, the absolute income gap between the region and the nation increased from $500 to $666.[34]

Much has been made, and rightly so, in discussions of Appalachian development problems of the lack of urban centers in the region capable of providing the services, concentrated labor force, and other external economies needed to support growth. This lack is especially evident in Southern Appalachia. Many people feel that difficult adjustment problems related to migration would be less severe if the region's own cities could absorb more of the migrant population. Unfortunately, the performance of Southern Appalachia's SMSA's has not been bright.

From 1940 to 1950, the SMSA's of Southern Appalachia, as defined by Brown and Hillery, increased in population by 20 per cent, but from 1950 to 1960, the gain was only 7 per cent, while all SMSA's in the country were increasing in population by 26 per cent. During the 1950-60 decade, only 30 of the 212 SMSA's in the United States had population declines, or increases of less than 10 per cent. Four of the six Southern Appalachian SMSA's— Huntington-Ashland, Charleston, Asheville, and Knoxville—were among these. The growth rates of the other two—Chattanooga (13.3 per cent) and Roanoke (18.1 per cent)—were below the national median for SMSA's. Moreover, during the 1950-60 decade, the combined SMSA's of the region actually lost population related to migration, the net migration rate being -10.1 per cent. Only Roanoke did not lose population due to migration, and most of the other SMSA's had relatively high net outmigration rates. Thus, it is apparent that the region's SMSA's have been less attractive to migrants than have other SMSA's in the country.[35] Moreover, according to Bureau of the Census projections, this pattern is going to continue. The Bureau estimates that between 1965 and 1975, the six SMSA's in question will, taken together, grow only by 3.5 per cent. If Roanoke is excluded, the ten-year growth rate will be only 1.9 per cent.[36] Brown and Hillery have correctly pointed out:

> As metropolitan centers have become more important in national life, the incapacity of the Appalachian Region to develop and sustain many large metropolitan areas has resulted in a decline of its national significance. Furthermore, various parts of the area have tended to fall into the spheres of influence of the cities that have developed outside the Region. Consequently, it is less meaningful today to consider the Appalachians as a region in itself, since it is becoming increasingly segmented so far as its economic ties are concerned.[37]

Thus, a regional policy that is primarily concerned with people would give high priority to integrating the growth of urban areas outside of Appalachia with their Appalachian hinterlands and to providing comprehensive relocation assistance. In general, it is to be expected that migrants will be less and less influenced in choosing their destinations by the previous choices of their families and that they increasingly will become more sensitive to opportunities in the job market.[38] The Appalachian Regional Commission (ARC), the agency charged with implementing the provisions of the ARDA, has taken account of the commuting possibilities that are and can be made available to residents of the region who live relatively close to growing urban areas on the fringe of the region. Many of its human resource investments within the region also imply that the beneficiaries may have to relocate to find gainful employment for their skills and training. But, as yet, there has been no systematic effort to guide migration, particularly if it involves movement outside the region.

For the near future at least, the principal response to Appalachia's lack of urban centers capable of providing the services, trained labor, and other external economies needed to support sustained growth apparently will be to encourage the development of such centers within the region.

The ARDA specified that "the public investments made in the region under this Act shall be concentrated in areas where there is the greatest potential for future growth, and where the expected return on public dollars will be the greatest." At the outset of the Appalachian program, there was strong support in some quarters of the ARC to work with a relatively few major urban centers in response to this stipulation. However, states such as Kentucky—which represented to many the plight that the Act was to ameliorate—objected that they would be left out of a growth center approach that was built only on a few SMSA's. In consequence, the determination of growth centers was given to the various states.

Within each of the sixty development districts (the number has since grown slightly) into which the region was divided, the states attempted to identify areas where future economic growth would probably occur. In this process, distinctions were made among a growth center, a growth area, and the surrounding hinterland:

> By a "growth center" or "centers" is meant a complex consisting of one or more communities or places which, taken together, provide or are likely to provide, a range of cultural, social, employment, trade, and service functions for itself and its associated rural hinterland. Though a center may not be fully developed to provide all these functions, it should provide, or potentially provide, some elements of each, and presently provide a sufficient range and magnitude of these functions to be readily identifiable as the logical location for many specialized services to people in the surrounding hinterland. A *"growth area"* is an extension of the growth center itself. It is the adjoining area likely to experience residential and employment growth because of proximity to a center or location between centers. The hinterlands are surrounding rural areas which rely upon the growth center and growth area for services and employment. The hinterlands contribute resources and manpower to the overall district economy.[39]

Among the key factors to be considered in analyzing the relationship between centers and hinterlands were commuting patterns, wholesale trade services, education and cultural services, professional services, interfirm and interindustry trade, government services, natural resources and topography, and transportation networks.

It will be noted that the definitions of growth centers and growth areas are based on the performance of certain functions—there is no reference made to growth or to how the performance of the functions mentioned gives a center or area growth potential. This is a matter to which we will return shortly.

The ARC attempts to concentrate appropriate investments in designated growth areas, though human resource investment may be made in the hinterlands to enable the rural population to take advantage of the

opportunities expected to develop in the growth areas. Although the states
have followed diverse procedures in designating growth centers, the ARC has
classified them into three types: regional centers, primary centers, and
secondary centers.

> *Regional Centers* are important metropolitan centers providing
> specialized services and employment opportunities that extend well
> beyond the boundaries of the district in which they are located.
> Investments made in these centers are mainly "region-serving," i.e.,
> they help improve services and employment prospects for a large area
> of the Appalachian Region embracing several state planning districts.
> *Primary Centers* are communities or a complex of communities
> where preliminary analyses indicate a major portion of the future
> employment base of a district is likely to be located. Investments in
> these centers will develop their competitive advantages by providing
> the public facilities and services needed to make the area attractive to
> increased private investment and growth.
> *Secondary Centers* are communities from which it is necessary
> to provide services to a large surrounding rural hinterland if isolated
> populations are to be given the skills and training they need to
> compete for opportunities wherever they choose to live and work.[40]

The growth center policy of the Appalachian program is constrained in
principle by its district program. Instead of beginning by delimiting a select
number of growth centers, it has been necessary to define the centers so that
each of the districts has at least one. Thus, the states have designated some 125
areas which are deemed to have "significant potential for future growth." If
each district really has a genuine growth center, it would seem that there would
be no need for outmigration from Appalachia nor for commuting to outside
metropolitan areas. There would only need to be commuting—and perhaps
some limited relocation within each district—from the hinterlands to the
growth center.

Given the relatively low level of urbanization in Appalachia, given the
great comparative advantages of larger urban centers in terms of external
economies (proximity to suppliers, buyers, and services; a relatively skilled labor
force; amenities; infrastructure; etc.) attractive to most firms, and given the
enormous financial effort needed to bridge the gap between a "potentially
promising" location and one with enough external economies to be
competitive, it seems that greater selectivity should have been used in
designating growth centers. When one considers that public capital investment
in established metropolitan areas in the United States may range from 25 to 33
per cent of the total capital outlay,[41] it becomes apparent that
Appalachian program funds available for growth centers are not sufficient
to make all of the designated centers attractive relative to urban centers in
more advanced regions, at least not by a process of balanced growth of
public facilities within each center. The ARC is aware of this but believes
that the problem is less one of strategy than of inadequate funding. However,
even if "ample" funds were available, it still would seem inadvisable to spread

them over so many centers, especially when many of them do not really have promising growth potential.

In practice, Appalachian growth center investments have been relatively concentrated. During fiscal years 1965-69, the ARC placed about 40 per cent of its nonhighway investment in rural hinterlands. These expenditures were primarily for health and education. The other 60 per cent was placed in growth areas. However, about 75 per cent of the growth center investments were concentrated in thirty of the seventy-eight regional and primary centers.[42] In Northern Appalachia relatively great emphasis has been put on growth areas as service centers and on their potential for developing employment on principal transportation routes. In Central Appalachia, trade and service functions, proximity to the Appalachian Development Highway System, and plant site availability have been given particular attention. Recent population and employment growth have been emphasized in Southern Appalachia, while the Highlands have emphasized service functions, especially in relation to tourism and recreation. The areas listed in Table 3 have been principal recipients of growth center investments.

Although large absolute expenditures have been made in some of the region's bigger cities, the highest proportion of ARC obligations has gone to growth areas in the 10,000 to 250,000 range. These areas account for 75.3 per cent of all growth area obligations, compared to 15.6 per cent for areas with populations over 250,000 and 9.0 percent to areas with fewer than 10,000 inhabitants. It is the policy of the ARC to invest more in per capita terms in communities of 250,000 or less than in larger cities, because the impact of program funds is likely to be greater in these communities. Moreover, the most rapid growth in Appalachia is occurring in communities in the 10,000-50,000 population range, rather than in the larger cities or rural areas. Between 1960 and 1966, communities in the 10,000-50,000 range accounted for 40 per cent of Appalachia's population growth even though they had only 24 per cent of the region's population.[43]

In summary, then, the distribution of growth center investments has been more concentrated than might have been expected from a policy that would give each of sixty districts at least one growth center and some districts more. On the other hand, even though the designation of growth center has little economic basis in many cases, it may well have political and morale value. In any event, the decision to concentrate investment in human resources in the hinterlands and other investments in growth centers and growth areas was well taken. It should be noted, however, that the people in some of the nominal growth areas which are, in fact, hinterlands to more viable growth centers might benefit more from improvements in health and education facilities than from growth-type investments that are likely to be ineffective. Finally, the Appalachian Development Highway Program provides links to growing metropolitan areas outside of the region (for example, Atlanta, Cincinnati, Lexington, Nashville, Harrisburg, and the Piedmont Crescent cities in the Carolinas), but these links have primarily been viewed in terms of commuting opportunities for Appalachian people living near the fringe of the region or in terms of markets for Appalachian firms. In the future, a more systematic effort might be made to encourage and aid migration to growth centers out of, but still near to, Appalachia.

TABLE 3

Appalachian Regional Commission Growth
Center Investments, 1965-69

Northern Appalachia

Greater Pittsburgh, Pa.	$ 9,883,216
Cumberland, Md.	4,993,114
Wilkes-Barre-Scranton, Pa.	4,441,903
Altoona-Johnstown, Pa.	3,898,746
Binghamton, N.Y.	3,537,020
Sharon-New Castle, Pa.	3,498,638
New Philadelphia-Cambridge, O.	3,368,493
Hornell, N.Y.	2,717,173
Parkersburg-Marietta, O.	2,483,329
Williamsport, Pa.	2,432,975
Huntington-Ashland-Ironton, O./W. Va./Ky.	n.a.
Hagerstown-Martinsburg, W. Va./Md.	1,731,948
Elmira, N.Y.	1,773,357
Erie, Pa./N.Y.	1,650,000
Charleston, W. Va.	1,392,211

Southern Appalachia

Florence-Decatur-Huntsville, Ala.	$10,454,584
Gadsden-Anniston, Ala.	7,168,953
Greenville-Spartanburg, S.C.	4,914,596
Birmingham, Ala.	3,491,231
Tri-Cities, Tenn./Va.	2,997,983
Knoxville, Tenn.	2,344,287
Asheville, N.C.	2,133,906
Chattanooga, Tenn./Ala./Ga.	1,860,901
Carrollton, Ga.	1,869,889
Tuscaloosa, Ala.	1,771,742
Pontotoc-Tupelo, Miss.	1,479,529

Central Appalachia

Cookeville-Crossville, Tenn.	$ 3,083,841
Paintsville-Prestonburg-Pikeville, Ky.	2,859,256
London-Corbin-Middlesboro, Ky.	2,403,480

Appalachian Highlands

State College, Pa.	$ 1,465,523

Source: *The Role of Growth Centers and Growth Areas in Appalachian Development,* ARC Staff Paper, n.d.

The Economic Development Administration

The Public Works and Economic Development Act of 1965 authorized the Secretary of Commerce to designate, with the concurrence of the states involved, multistate regions that contain common problems of economic distress or lag that are beyond the capability of any one state to solve. Once a region has been designated, the relevant states are invited to participate in a regional commission, which is patterned in structure after that created for the Appalachian region. In 1966, five regional commissions were established. The regions concerned are the Ozarks, New England, the Four Corners, the Coastal Plains, and the Upper Great Lakes. Because of funding delays, the new commissions are only now getting off the ground, so it is not possible yet to evaluate their programs. However, some are developing growth center strategies.[44]

Implementation of the more general aims of the Public Works and Economic Development Act of 1965 is the responsibility of the Economic Development Administration (EDA). In addition to assisting the regional commissions, EDA provides development aid to "redevelopment areas," that is, counties, labor areas, Indian reservations, or certain larger municipalities. Redevelopment areas are designated on the basis of criteria that reflect chronic economic distress. These criteria include substantial and persistent unemployment, population loss, and low median family income. "Substantial and persistent unemployment" is defined by two criteria. First, 6 per cent or more of the work force must have been unemployed during the latest calendar year. Second, the annual average rate of unemployment must have been at least 6 per cent and (1) 50 per cent above the national average during three of the last four years or (2) 75 per cent above the national average during two of the last three years or (3) 100 per cent above the national average during one of the last two years.

Areas that lost 25 per cent or more of their population between 1950 and 1960 due to a lack of employment opportunities are eligible for designation as redevelopment areas, provided they did not have an annual median family income over $2,830 in 1960. An area where this figure was less than $2,264 may be designated as a redevelopment area without regard to rate of outmigration.

When loss of a major source of employment causes the unemployment rate of an area to exceed the national average by 50 per cent or more, or when such a loss is expected, redevelopment area designation is authorized. In addition, Indian reservations with a high degree of economic distress are eligible for designation as redevelopment areas. Finally, when a state does not have any area that qualifies on the basis of high unemployment, low family income, or population loss, the area in the state that most nearly meets these criteria may be designated as a redevelopment area.

Another kind of geographic entity eligible for EDA assistance is the multicounty economic development district. Individual redevelopment areas often lack efficient resources to provide a solid base for their development.

However, because of economic interdependencies among adjacent areas, successful development on a larger scale may be promoted by grouping together economically distressed areas and economically healthy areas. EDA has therefore encouraged groups of counties—usually five to fifteen in number—to pool their resources for effective economic planning and development. The district program offers incentives to promote the economic growth of the entire district, but it is aimed particularly at redevelopment areas. Thus, a district must contain at least two redevelopment areas. In addition to the benefits authorized for all redevelopment areas, those located within districts may receive up to 10 per cent more of the total cost in grant assistance for projects that are consistent with the district program. With the exception of an EDA-designated economic development center, counties in the district that are not redevelopment areas are not eligible for project funding from EDA. However, all participating counties are expected to benefit from coordinated, district-wide development planning.

Counties that wish to form a district must submit a formal proposal for qualification to EDA through the governor of the state involved. In considering whether, and to what extent, a proposed district will effectively foster economic development, EDA considers a number of factors, including the percentage of district population living in redevelopment areas, district per capita income, the percentage of families with annual incomes of less than $3,000, trading area patterns, the character of the proposed development center and its ties to the redevelopment areas, and unemployment and labor-force participation rates. Once a district becomes qualified, its major organizational task is to formulate a district Overall Economic Development Program, which must be approved by EDA before a district can be formally designated. EDA requires that the district organization be broadly representative of the major economic groups of the area, including business, labor, agriculture, minority groups, and representatives of the unemployed and underemployed.

Each economic development district must contain an economic development center (growth center). The center must be a city or an area with sufficient population, resources, public facilities, industry, and commercial services to insure that its development can become relatively self-sustaining.

The growth of the development center is then expected to carry over into the redevelopment areas within the district. Cities or contiguous groups of incorporated places outside the redevelopment area may be designated as economic development centers if they have a population of 250,000 or less. Once designated, development centers are eligible for EDA assistance on the same basis as redevelopment areas. It may also be noted that EDA distinguishes between economic development centers and redevelopment centers; the latter lie within redevelopment areas, whereas the former do not.

The development center is expected to provide an economically efficient marketing and service center for surrounding counties, both by providing job opportunities for depressed area residents who could commute to jobs and by encouraging those rural area residents who do migrate to move to the center. EDA's program would relieve migration pressure on the big cities while, at the same time, lifting rural areas by the boot straps. This approach implies that job opportunities can be easily induced because growth factors are already present, even though the community may be located in a low-income area. It is hoped that migration flows can be channeled to the growth centers through a combination of forces including jobs, schools, transportation systems, social amenities, and improved equal-opportunity programs. The program can also be linked with parallel programs for resettlement assistance and manpower training and development to assist the rural migrant to adjust to an urban employment environment.

Total authorizations over the life of the Public Works and Economic Development Act of 1965 amounted to $3,250 million. As of June 30, 1969, EDA had approved 1,542 public works projects amounting to $773.8 million. There were 253 approved business development projects, involving $175.3 million in loans and $21.4 million in working capital. A total of $40.537 million was provided for technical assistance and $14.8 million for planning grants. All programs together received $1,053 million. California received the most money ($86.4 million); followed by Kentucky ($73.8 million), the clear leader in per capita terms; Tennessee ($50.8 million); Georgia ($49.2 million); and West Virginia ($48.8 million).[45]

It is now necessary to consider the realities of EDA's development policy compared with the strategy just outlined. First, while a development center strategy implies the concentration of projects in a relatively few locations,[46] EDA simply does not have the funds to create the many external economies that will be needed if rapid, self-sustained growth is to be induced or reinforced in development centers. It will be recalled that the Appalachian Regional Commission has placed a relatively large amount of its growth center funds in a relatively few centers. This is also the case for EDA. In 1968, EDA obligated public works and business development loans to only 21 development centers and in 1969 to only 24 development centers. However, the total outlay per center was still only $904,400 in 1968 and $870,700 in 1969.[47] While these amounts are not negligible, they are hardly likely to induce a major shift in growth rates.

Second, even if EDA had considerably more funds to devote to growth centers, the nature of the centers that are actually being chosen leaves great doubt as to their ability to provide a significant number of increased job opportunities for migrants from rural areas.

It will be recalled from Chapter 1 that, as Brian Berry states,

> examination of the gradients of influence of smaller centers indicates clearly that there seems little sense in trying to use small urban places as growth centers—their regional influence is too limited. Indeed, very few cities of less than 50,000 population appear to have any impact on their regional welfare syndrome, although admittedly the few that do are located in the more peripheral areas.[48]

It should be pointed out, of course, that EDA growth centers are often likely to be in peripheral areas. In any case, the growth centers that have been designated by EDA are generally much smaller than Berry's 50,000 population level. The data in Table 4 show that as of April 15, 1970, there were 87 EDA-designated economic development districts with 171 development centers

(126 economic development centers and 45 redevelopment centers). Only 30 of the development centers had a population greater than 50,000 and only 13 had a population greater than 100,000. Forty-two of the centers had fewer than 10,000 persons.[49] Moreover, between 1960 and 1970, 61 per cent of the development centers that had been designated as of April 15, 1970, had population growth below the national average; 38 per cent of the development centers (and more than 50 per cent of the redevelopment centers) experienced population *declines*.

TABLE 4

Economic Development Administration Development Centers in Eighty-Seven Districts[a], 1960, by Population Size Class

| | Number of Centers | | |
Population	Total	Economic Development Centers	Redevelopment Centers
Less than 10,000	42	24	18
10,000-24,999	59	43	16
25,000-49,999	40	32	8
50,000-99,999	17	15	2
100,000-249,999	13	12	1
TOTAL	171	126	45
Total Population	5,892,091	4,966,977	925,114
Average Population	34,457	39,420	20,558
Median Population	18,612	22,000	14,682

[a]Districts designated as of April 15, 1970.

Source: Computed from data supplied by the Economic Development Administration.

The approach taken by EDA poses several problems. First, it leaves out of consideration areas that are neither congested urban agglomerations nor towns and small cities that are part of or in proximity to lagging areas. This no man's land—in terms of policy considerations—has growth centers which may absorb more migrants more efficiently than the EDA growth centers, especially if they too benefitted from federal aid aimed at helping migrants from lagging areas to find employment. Of course, it might be argued that rapidly growing centers obviously have no need for federal subsidies. This would be true if one were concerned only with the rapidly growing center and its own population. However, the relationship of concern here is that of centers of rapid growth to the people of lagging areas. If a federal subsidy can accelerate growth in a center which is already rapidly growing and if this subsidy is made conditional on providing employment opportunities for residents of lagging areas, then it may well be more efficient for EDA to tie into the growing environment than to attempt to create growth in a relatively stagnant area by putting in water or sewer lines.

One way in which EDA might relate lagging areas to viable growth centers is to structure multicounty districts around economic centers as defined by the Regional Economics Division of the Office of Business Economics (OBE), U.S. Department of Commerce (see Map 1). Within the continental United States, 171 centers have been delineated, along with their functional economic areas. These OBE economic areas provide an exclusive and exhaustive regionalization of the country. For the most part, the centers are SMSA's, but where several SMSA's are parts of larger integrated economic complexes, they are combined. In rural areas, centers of 25,000 to 50,000 have been used, provided they are wholesale trade centers. Counties have been allocated to centers primarily on the basis of commuting flows (journey to work patterns and time and distance of travel to the centers) and, in the more peripheral areas, on the basis of other links such as television viewing and wholesale trading patterns. Very small economic areas are combined if they comprise larger television or wholesale markets in order to satisfy a minimum population size criterion of 200,000. In general, the areas are defined to approach closure with respect to residentiary industries, and therefore self-sufficiency in the tertiary sector, while specializing in export activities to other areas.

The counties in many EDA districts are located in different OBE regions. Thus, to the extent that the OBE centers are really the focal nodes for their areas, the districts are being pulled apart by existing trade and commuting patterns (see Map 1). Moreover, as of January, 1969, only 17 out of 171 OBE centers were also EDA development centers. This is, no doubt, because OBE areas were defined only in 1967 and because redevelopment areas choose "growth centers" from within or in close proximity to themselves.

Another difficulty with EDA's programs is that it is not clear that the public works projects with which the agency is primarily involved, largely as a consequence of restrictive legislation, will lead to a rational migration policy, even though EDA claims that "by linking lagging areas with adjacent communities, the Growth Center provides new opportunities for jobs and services close to home. Under the concept, many of the unemployed and underemployed rural populace will choose to commute or move to nearby

LEGEND: Map 1, Office of Business Economics Economic Areas and Economic Development Administration Districts

EDA districts are shaded and hatched.

OBE areas, outlined and numbered as follows, are named for the largest SMSA or, where there is no SMSA, for the largest city.

1 Bangor, Maine
2 Portland, Maine
3 Burlington, Vt.
4 Boston, Mass.
5 Hartford, Conn.
6 Albany-Schenectady-Troy, N.Y.
7 Syracuse, N.Y.
8 Rochester, N.Y.
9 Buffalo, N.Y.
10 Erie, Pa.
11 Williamsport, Pa.
12 Binghamton, N.Y.-Pa.
13 Wilkes Barre-Hazelton, Pa.
14 New York, N.Y.
15 Philadelphia, Pa.-N.J.
16 Harrisburg, Pa.
17 Baltimore, Md.
18 Washington, D.C.-Md.-Va.
19 Staunton, Va.
20 Roanoke, Va.
21 Richmond, Va.
22 Norfolk-Portsmouth, Va.
23 Raleigh, N.C.
24 Wilmington, N.C.
25 Greensboro-Winston Salem-High Point, N.C.
26 Charlotte, N.C.
27 Asheville, N.C.
28 Greenville, S.C.
29 Columbia, S.C.
30 Florence, S.C.
31 Charleston, S.C.
32 Augusta, Ga.
33 Savannah, Ga.
34 Jacksonville, Fla.
35 Orlando, Fla.
36 Miami, Fla.
37 Tampa-St. Petersburg, Fla.
38 Tallahassee, Fla.
39 Pensacola, Fla.
40 Montgomery, Ala.
41 Albany, Ga.
42 Macon, Ga.
43 Columbus, Ga.-Ala.

44 Atlanta, Ga.
45 Birmingham, Ala.
46 Memphis, Tenn.-Ark.
47 Huntsville, Ala.
48 Chattanooga, Tenn.-Ga.
49 Nashville, Tenn.
50 Knoxville, Tenn.
51 Bristol, Va.-Tenn.
52 Huntington-Ashland, W. Va.-Ky.-Ohio
53 Lexington, Ky.
54 Louisville, Ky.-Ind.
55 Evansville, Ind.
56 Terre Haute, Ind.
57 Springfield, Ill.
58 Champaign-Urbana, Ill.
59 Lafayette-West Lafayette, Ind.
60 Indianapolis, Ind.
61 Muncie, Ind.
62 Cincinnati, Ohio-Ky.-Ind.
63 Dayton, Ohio
64 Columbus, Ohio
65 Clarksburg, W. Va.
66 Pittsburgh, Pa.
67 Youngstown-Warren, Ohio
68 Cleveland, Ohio
69 Lima, Ohio
70 Toledo, Ohio
71 Detroit, Mich.
72 Saginaw, Mich.
73 Grand Rapids, Mich.
74 Lansing, Mich.
75 Fort Wayne, Ind.
76 South Bend, Ind.
77 Chicago, Ill.
78 Peoria, Ill.
79 Davenport-Rock Island-Moline, Iowa-Ill.
80 Cedar Rapids, Iowa
81 Dubuque, Iowa
82 Rockford, Ill.
83 Madison, Wis.
84 Milwaukee, Wis.
85 Green Bay, Wis.
86 Wausau, Wis.

87 Duluth-Superior, Minn.-Wis.
88 Eau Claire, Wis.
89 La Crosse, Wis.
90 Rochester, Minn.
91 Minneapolis-St. Paul, Minn.
92 Grand Forks, N.D.
93 Minot, N.D.
94 Great Falls, Mont.
95 Billings, Mont.
96 Bismarck, N.D.
97 Fargo-Moorhead, N.D.-Minn.
98 Aberdeen, S.D.
99 Sioux Falls, S.D.
100 Rapid City, S.D.
101 Scotts Bluff, Nebr.
102 Grand Island, Nebr.
103 Sioux City, Iowa-Nebr.
104 Fort Dodge, Iowa
105 Waterloo, Iowa
106 Des Moines, Iowa
107 Omaha, Nebr.-Iowa
108 Lincoln, Nebr.
109 Salina, Kans.
110 Wichita, Kans.
111 Kansas City, Mo.-Kans.
112 Columbia, Mo.
113 Quincy, Ill.
114 St. Louis, Mo.-Ill.
115 Paducah, Ky.
116 Springfield, Mo.
117 Little Rock-North Little Rock, Ark.
118 Fort Smith, Ark.-Okla.
119 Tulsa, Okla.
120 Oklahoma City, Okla.
121 Wichita Falls, Tex.
122 Amarillo, Tex.
123 Lubbock, Tex.
124 Odessa, Tex.
125 Abilene, Tex.
126 San Angelo, Tex.
127 Dallas, Tex.
128 Waco, Tex.
129 Austin, Tex.

130 Tyler, Tex.
131 Texarkana, Tex.-Ark.
132 Shreveport, La.
133 Monroe, La.
134 Greenville, Miss.
135 Jackson, Miss.
136 Meridian, Miss.
137 Mobile, Ala.
138 New Orleans, La.
139 Lake Charles, La.
140 Beaumont-Port Arthur-Orange, Tex.
141 Houston, Tex.
142 San Antonio, Tex.
143 Corpus Christi, Tex.
144 Brownsville-Harlingen-San Benito, Tex.
145 El Paso, Tex.
146 Albuquerque, N.M.
147 Pueblo, Col.
148 Denver, Col.
149 Grand Junction, Col.
150 Cheyenne, Wyo.
151 Salt Lake City, Utah
152 Idaho Falls, Idaho
153 Butte, Mont.
154 Spokane, Wash.
155 Seattle-Everett, Wash.
156 Yakima, Wash.
157 Portland, Ore.-Wash.
158 Eugene, Ore.
159 Boise City, Idaho
160 Reno, Nev.
161 Las Vegas, Nev.
162 Phoenix, Ariz.
163 Tuscon, Ariz.
164 San Diego, Calif.
165 Los Angeles-Long Beach, Calif.
166 Fresno, Calif.
167 Stockton, Calif.
168 Sacramento, Calif.
169 Redding, Calif.
170 Eureka, Calif.
171 San Francisco-Oakland, Calif.
172 Anchorage, Alaska
173 Honolulu, Hawaii

MAP 1

OFFICE OF BUSINESS ECONOMICS ECONOMIC AREAS AND
ECONOMIC DEVELOPMENT ADMINISTRATION DISTRICTS

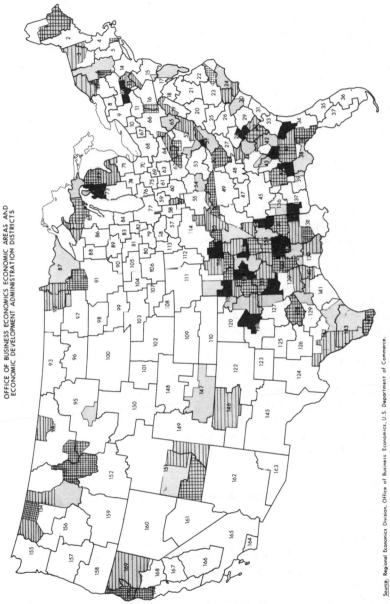

Source: Regional Economics Division, Office of Business Economics, U. S. Department of Commerce.

61

Growth Centers rather than to move to distant big cities."[50] However, if the unemployment and welfare difficulties of rural migrants in large metropolitan areas are largely related to lack of job skills and education, then it would seem that migration of these people to smaller centers would still pose similar problems.

Finally, it should be noted that there has been some disharmony between EDA and ARC programs in that area. EDA and the ARC have agreed to accept common multicounty districts in Appalachia, but there has been a tendency for local officials to bypass the state plans of the governors in favor of dealing directly with Washington for EDA assistance. In addition, early in its existence EDA considered a "worst-first" strategy, which sought to give first priority in financial assistance to places with the most severe problems. This approach obviously would be inconsistent with a meaningful growth center strategy. It would also be inconsistent with the ARC's objective of concentrating public works projects in areas with significant growth potential. Whereas 58 per cent of ARC nonhighway investment went to growth areas through 1968, only 42 per cent of EDA investment went to these areas.[51]

On the other hand, a number of informed persons not directly connected with either EDA or the ARC have indicated to the writer that EDA's economic development districts may have been more effective than the ARC's equivalent multicounty organizations. EDA has set forth in some detail a model of what it wants with respect to a district organization, whereas the ARC has felt that it is more appropriate to let each state formulate its own district program. The fact that EDA-organized districts have become going concerns in many areas before the formulation of state Appalachian plans has often tended to make local leaders and officials more responsive to EDA than to ARC programs.

From the foregoing analysis, it may be concluded that the public works and business-oriented programs of EDA should be concentrated in viable growth centers and that top priority in the worst areas should be given to investments in human resources to enable their people to take advantage of opportunities in growth centers. There is little likelihood that EDA's investments can attract significant private investment to the worst areas. It might also be advisable to modify EDA's authorizing legislation so that its activities may be brought more into line with those of the ARC.

SUMMARY AND CONCLUSIONS

Growth center strategies have been instituted in numerous industrial countries during the past two decades. For the most part, they have been designed to promote the development of lagging regions by concentrating investment so as to reap scale and agglomeration economies. In addition, growth centers also have been conceived as points of attraction for migrants who otherwise would go to large, congested urban areas.

To date, these strategies have not been notably successful, primarily because they have suffered from a tendency toward proliferation of a large number of relatively small centers. Even where a few large centers have been selected, as in the case of France's eight *métropoles d'équilibre*, inadequate funding has been a problem.

Although there is growing realization that a viable growth center strategy demands greater selectivity in choice of centers, it still is uncertain that the spread effects from induced growth centers can really lift income and employment opportunity levels in lagging or declining regions to levels comparable to those in more advanced regions. Indeed, it is possible that the public works bias, which inevitably accompanies growth center policies, has done a disservice by shifting attention away from the critical health, education, and social problems which plague underdeveloped regions. Preoccupation with spread effects also has hindered efforts to explore the opportunities which growth centers in intermediate areas (that is, viable growth centers which are neither merely relatively bright spots in lagging areas nor large, congested cities) offer to migrants from lagging regions. These issues will now be examined in more detail in the context of the United States.

NOTES

1. Gavin McCrone, *Regional Policy in Britain* (London: George Allen and Unwin, 1969), pp. 208-10.

2. Quoted in *ibid.*, p. 210.

3. *Ibid.*, pp. 210-12.

4. *Ibid.*, pp. 212-13.

5. *Ibid.*, pp. 220-21.

6. Lloyd Rodwin, *Nations and Cities* (Boston: Houghton Mifflin, 1970), pp. 275-76.

7. Francesco Vito, "Problems of the Underdeveloped Regions of Italy," in E. A. G. Robinson, ed., *Backward Areas in Developed Countries* (New York: St. Martin's Press, 1969), pp. 210-12.

8. *Ibid.*, pp. 211-13.

9. *Ibid.*, p. 221.

10. Gustav Schachter, *The Italian South* (New York: Random House, 1965), p. 193.

11. Vito, *op. cit.*, p. 216.

12. *Ibid.*, p. 219.

13. *Ibid.*, p. 220.

14. Pasquale Saraceno, "Development Policy in an Overpopulated Area: Italy's Experience," in Robinson, ed., *op. cit.*, p. 235.

15. Philippe Simonnot, "Italy—Waiting for the Second 'Miracle,'" *Le Monde*, Weekly Selection (June 10, 1970), p. 2.

16. For more detailed information on developments in these regards through 1966, see Niles M. Hansen, *French Regional Planning* (Bloomington: Indiana University Press, 1968).

17. Jacques Antoine, "La préparation du VIᵉ Plan dans sa dimension régionale," in *Aménagement du territoire et développement regional*, Vol. 2, 61.

18. See Hansen, *op. cit.*, pp. 228-49. See also, *Urbanisme*, No. 89 (1965), a special number devoted to the *métropoles d'équilibre.*

19. *Cinquième Plan de développement économique et social (1966-1970)*, Vol. 1 (Paris: Imprimerie des Journaux Officiels, 1965), pp. 132-33.

20. Antoine, *op. cit.*, pp. 58-62 and 74.

21. See David N. Kinsey, "The French Z.U.P. Technique of Urban Development," *Journal of the American Institute of Planners*, Vol. 35, No. 6 (November, 1969), Figure 1, 370.

22. *Schéma directeur d'aménagement et d'urbanisme de la Région de Paris* (Paris: Societé Parisienne d'Imprimerie, 1965). For recent developments concerning the Strategic Plan, see Pierre Trey, "Le Schéma directeur est-il remis en cause?" *Le Monde*, Sélection hebdomadaire (November 21-27, 1968), 12.

23. "Vers l'aménagement du Bassin Parisien," *Expansion régionale*, No. 44 (1967), 15-27; and *La politique de l'aménagement du territoire en 1968* (Paris: Délégation à l'Aménagement du Territoire et à l'Action Régionale, 1967), p. 31. See also, *Urbanisme*, Nos. 96 and 97 (1966), a special issue devoted to the Paris Basin.

24. *Décentralisation des activités "tertiaires"* (Paris: Délégation à l'Aménagement du Territoire et à l'Action Régionale, 1968), p. 25.

25. "Vers l'aménagement du Bassin Parisien," *op. cit.*, pp. 17-18.

26. Benjamin Higgins, *Economic Development* (revised edition; New York: W. W. Norton and Co., 1968), p. 786.

27. *Ibid.*, p. 784.

28. *Ibid.*, p. 785.

29. *Ibid.*, p. 789.

30. *Ibid.*, pp. 738-39.

31. *Ibid.*, p. 466.

32. E. A. G. Robinson, "Introduction," in Robinson, ed., *op. cit.*, p. xv.

33. Eli P. March, "Indicators of Appalachian Progress: Population and Income," *Appalachia*, Vol. 2, No. 7 (March, 1969), 24.

34. Data supplied by the Appalachian Regional Commission.

35. James S. Brown and George A. Hillery, Jr., "The Great Migration, 1940-1960," in Thomas R. Ford, ed., *The Southern Appalachian Region* (Lexington: University of Kentucky Press, 1962), pp. 59-61.

36. U S. Bureau of the Census, "Projections of the Population of Metropolitan Areas, 1975," *Current Population Reports*, Series P-25, No. 415 (Washington, D.C.: Government Printing Office, 1969), pp. 16-18.

37. Brown and Hillery, *op. cit.*, p. 71.

38. *Ibid.*, p. 76; and Niles M. Hansen and Richard YuKhin, "Locational Preferences and Opportunity Costs in a Lagging Region: A Study of High School Seniors in Eastern Kentucky," *Journal of Human Resources* (Summer, 1970).

39. *State and Regional Development Plans in Appalachia, 1968* (Washington, D.C.: Appalachian Regional Commission, 1968), p. 12.

40. *Ibid.*, pp. 19-20.

41. John W. Dyckman, "The Public and Private Rationale for a National Urban Policy," in S. B. Warner, Jr., ed., *Planning for a Nation of Cities* (Cambridge, Mass.: M.I.T. Press, 1966), p. 28.

42. Testimony of John B. Waters, Jr., Federal Cochairman, Appalachian Regional Commission, before the Special Subcommittee on Economic Development Programs, Committee on Public Works, House of Representatives, October 2, 1969.

43. "The Role of Growth Centers and Growth Areas in Appalachian Development," Appalachian Regional Commission Staff paper, n.d.

44. See, in particular, Brian J. L. Berry, *et al.*, "Potential Growth Centers and Growth Center Potentials in the Upper Great Lakes Region," a report to the Upper Great Lakes Regional Commission, October 15, 1968.

45. Economic Development Administration, *Jobs for America: Economic Development Administration Annual Report, Fiscal 1969* (Washington, D.C.: Government Printing Office, 1969), p. 150.

46. Gerald L. Duskin and Ronald L. Moomaw, "Economic Development Centers: A Review," Economic Development Administration, Office of Economic Research, staff paper (August, 1967), p. 7.

47. Data supplied by Economic Development Administration.

48. Brian J. L. Berry, "Spatial Organization and Levels of Welfare: Degree of Metropolitan Labor Market Participation as a Variable in Economic Development," paper presented to the Economic Development Administration Research Conference, Washington, D.C., October 9-13, 1967.

49. Mary A. Toborg, "Assistance to Development Districts and Growth Centers," Economic Development Administration staff paper, October, 1969, pp. 16-18.

50. Economic Development Administration, *1968 Progress Report of the Economic Development Administration, U.S. Department of Commerce* (Washington, D.C.: Government Printing Office, 1968), p. 8.

51. "Evaluation of the 1965 Economic Development Legislation," Appalachian Regional Commission staff paper, n.d., pp. 31-33.

4

CRITERIA FOR
GROWTH CENTER
POLICY REVISION

In previous chapters, it has been argued that growth pole theory in its present state does not provide specific criteria for identifying the location of relevant urban centers, for determining how big they should be, or for deciding what kinds of investments should be placed in them. This is true of the French School, as well as later formulations, and it is especially true for problems of lagging areas in industrialized countries. Nevertheless, growth center strategies have been adopted by numerous countries but without apparent success even in terms of the various goals pursued by these countries. In any event, growth center analysis implicitly or explicitly involves deliberate policies; otherwise one is left with only a mere description of spatial distribution and growth of population and economic activity.

This chapter develops the general outline of a growth center policy for the United States. However, before examining the central issues in our approach, it may be useful to specify certain notions that it either ignores or rejects. These include the doctrine that economic growth should be "balanced" geographically, the approach which takes growth centers to be either exclusively or primarily generators of spread effects to hinterlands, reliance on central place theory in growth center determination, and the identification or association of new towns with growth centers.

NONRELEVANT FACTORS

The Notion of Balanced Growth

A common theme in growth center strategies is the notion of "balanced" growth or a "balanced" distribution of economic opportunity. However, what this means is rarely specified in more concrete terms. Does it mean that equality of per capita public overhead capital, income, or economic activity (however defined) should be the goal? Should the growth of less-developed regions be promoted solely by moving resources to them or creating new resources within their boundaries? Precisely what public and private activities should be located in various types of cities and regions? What effects will the location of various types of activities in a given region have on other regions as a result of induced activities (on both the supply and the demand sides) of an interregional nature? What conflicts might arise between maximizing regional and national welfare, and how should they be resolved? It would seem apparent that until we are able to answer questions such as these, the appeal to balance is not operationally feasible. Of course, the fact that answers to some of these questions involve explicit or implicit value judgments which the economist must take as given does not preclude attempts to find out the nature of public preference patterns.

Growth Centers as Generators of Spread Effects

In addition to the notion of spatial balance, American growth center policy is posited on the alleged ability of centers to help spread economic growth into their hinterlands. In the last chapter, this emphasis in current federal policy was pointed out, but the notion is also prevalent in the most august realms of the scholarly community. The following passage from a recent article on growth poles is instructive:

> The following definition, which I shall adopt for the purposes of this paper, is one which was once agreed upon at a seminar in the regional science department, University of Pennsylvania. "A growth pole is an urban centre of economic activity which can achieve self-sustaining growth to the point that growth is diffused outward into the pole region and eventually beyond into the less developed region of the nation."[1]

Reliance on Central Place Theory

Another preoccupation in scholarly approaches to growth center policy in the United States is central place theory and the analysis of urban hierarchies.[2] The relationship between this type of study and studies which view growth centers as primarily generators of spread effects is close, because communication of growth involves transmission of stimulating effects through an urban hierarchy. Thus, although it was noted in Chapter 2 that growth pole theory originated in France in part as a reaction to central place theory, it is instructive to give somewhat more detailed attention to the incorporation of central place theory into some versions of growth pole theory.

The boundary of a polarized region is often defined as the line beyond which flows and connections are predominantly in some other direction, toward some other pole. A polarized region can exist at any scale, and smaller polarized regions will tend to "nest" within larger ones. The idea of a polarized region is, therefore, compatible with the central place structure of a hierarchy of cities of ascending size and function, with the growth centers normally being the larger city or cities in the region, at whatever scale is being considered.

The "range of a good" and "threshold population" are the key concepts in central place theory. The range of a good denotes the zone around the central place from which persons travel to the center to purchase the good or service offered at the place. In theory, the upper limit of this range is the maximum possible sales radius. Beyond this limit, the price of the good is too high because the distance results in too high a price or because of the closer proximity of consumers to alternative centers. The lower limit of the range is the radius that encloses the minimum number of consumers necessary to provide a sales volume adequate for the good to be supplied profitably from the central place. This lower limit is the threshold population. The lowest level of center performs certain functions or provides certain goods that are limited in number and kind by the limited population within usual range of the center. The center of the next highest order performs all the functions of the lower-order center plus a group of additional functions. The next higher order of center will offer all the goods offered by the first two levels but will be differentiated from the order just beneath it by a group of goods with greater ranges than those possessed by any of the goods of the next smallest center. In this manner, a hierarchy of centers is determined. It should be pointed out that population by itself is not a good measure of centrality. A large, specialized-function town may have only a small tributary area and little influence on its surrounding hinterland. Thus, centrality is generally discussed in terms of centralized services, including administration, culture, health, social services, organization of economic and social life, finance, trade, service industries, the labor market, and traffic.

One problem with the study of urban hierarchies is whether differentiated classes actually exist as discrete entities. The number of classes in any given study may be a result of arbitrary decision, whether conscious or unconscious. Moreover, if discrete classes actually exist, they may vary among countries or even among regions within a single country. An even greater problem is identifying precisely how growth is transmitted through a given hierarchy. Central place theory is essentially static, whereas what is required is an explanation of the dynamics of growth in its spatial dimensions. Research into the spatial diffusion of innovations through the urban hierarchy has attempted to remedy this difficulty. It has indicated that innovations will spread where there is a developed communications network but that there may be a considerable time lag in the process of diffusion from the innovating center to its hinterland and to major centers in peripheral areas. However, Harry Richardson accurately maintains that

this theory is an inductive theory, developed from particular cases that are not representative of the many different types of innovation.

In particular, case studies have been based on new types of consumer goods rather than on industrial innovations and new production techniques. Yet when we are considering the impact of the spatial transmission of technical progress on growth in fringe areas, it is these latter innovation categories that we have in mind.[3]

For innovations to be adopted in peripheral regions, more is required than a well-developed communications system and outward-looking major cities. The peripheral region must have people and organizations capable of evaluating the potential of innovations and of taking risks. However, the agglomeration economies of the innovating center will probably keep growth industries and their personnel closely tied to the center. Branch plants of national firms may be sources of receptivity to innovations, but they are not likely to flourish in industries with sizable economies of scale. Also, "if economic conditions favour a fast growth in factor inputs at core areas, these same conditions are likely to result in these core areas being the main innovation centres in the economy and to militate against a rapid, wide diffusion of technical progress to outlying regions."[4]

New Town Developments

Finally, a distinction must be made between growth centers and new towns, since the two notions are sometimes associated or made identical. New town proposals call for completely new urban centers, whereas growth center strategies are based on existing places. New town advocates usually espouse self-contained labor markets, whereas the growth center approach taken in this study stresses the role of job creation for migrants from other—though not necessarily distant—areas. New towns also are generally proposed as means of channeling population growth away from large cities; although growth centers may also perform this function, their primary function is to provide economic opportunities for persons from areas with limited opportunities.[5] Existing examples of new towns—most notably Columbia and Reston, near Washington, D.C.—may prove to be successful experiments in town planning, but they are primarily vehicles for relocating people within a metropolitan area. Their costs are such that they have little relevance to people in the income categories of migrants from lagging regions.

In sum, then, the approach of this study assumes not only that economic growth is spatially unbalanced as a matter of fact, but also that growth center policy should be based on unbalanced growth, favoring urban places which are intermediate to congested areas, on the one hand, and lagging areas, on the other. It also concentrates on growth centers as poles of attraction for commuters and migrants and gives less emphasis than most approaches to growth centers as generators of spread effects. Relatively little use is made of central place theory or new towns.

The following sections deal, in turn, with the need for human resource investment in lagging regions, problems of congested regions, and the nature of intermediate growth centers.

INVESTMENT IN HUMAN RESOURCES

One of the major developments in economics during the 1960's was the immense attention devoted to the significance of investment in human resources or, as some would have it, human capital. Indeed, it now seems almost incredible that at the outset of the decade so little work had been done in this field. It now is apparent that among the factors which contribute to economic growth, the quality of the human input ranks very high. Conversely, one of the principal factors retarding the development of lagging regions is a relative deficiency in human resource development. The lack is particularly evident in areas which have not experienced economic development, as contrasted with declining industrial areas in need of conversion of economic activities and readaptation of the labor force. These points were mentioned in Chapter 3, and they have been developed at considerable length by the author elsewhere.[6]

The disadvantages which lagging areas encounter on account of deficiencies in the health, education, and training of the labor force are familiar. However, lack of investment in human resources also has adverse effects on the political and business leadership of these areas. Although especially vigorous political and business leadership is needed if improvements are to be made in social and economic problems, as Melvin Levin has pointed out, "each of the essential elements in the leadership-technical-expert pattern tend to be relatively weak in distressed areas."[7] The political leadership "is often inbred, weak and factionalized to the point of near paralysis. A dearth of alternative opportunities combined with decades of selective outmigration have removed young, dedicated, well-educated, and well-motivated men and women whose views extend beyond limited local horizons." Entreprenuership in lagging areas "has been diluted over the years by the dissolution or relocation of stronger local firms that, whatever their faults in 'milking' their business and community, nevertheless retained strong local ties and supplied civic direction at critical junctures." To the extent that new firms are attracted, their managers tend to be persons with brief tenure in branch plants of national firms or else marginal operators dependent on the favor of local politicians. In either case, the newcomers have little political impact, and they frequently endeavor to retain their ties with other areas of the country. Finally, technicians employed in lagging areas "are often underpaid, substandard professionals more akin in quality and outlook to local civil servants than to professional staff found in metropolitan communities. The occasional capable elected official finds himself seriously handicapped by the absence of technicians qualified to seek out federal and private outside capital and to design and implement effective programs."[8]

In many cases, inadequate investment in human resources has occurred not only because of inadequate local funds, but also because available funds have been squandered on attempts to attract industry. Instead of building better schools and using public amenities to attract firms, there has been a pronounced tendency to extend financial inducements directly to firms and to let the schools wait. What Ralph Widner has termed "the era of chasing smokestacks" began with an effusion of brochures representing more or less sophisticated versions of boosterism. However, as communities and states began to outbid one another, some 14,000 industrial development organizations came into being to compete for 500 to 750 new plant locations per year. In the scramble to attract industry, many communities even went so far as to grant tax moratoria to new firms, thereby losing the principal gain that industrial development was supposed to bring. Thus, instead of upgrading community services, a burden of services to the new plant had to be assumed without any financial benefit from the company. Moreover, the types of firms that were attracted tended to be labor-intensive (often employing mostly women), slow-growing industries paying low wages. In some cases, they would also pull out when another community offered a more favorable subsidy.[9]

Realization of the dangers in trying to subsidize footloose and often marginal firms still has not overcome reluctance to upgrade human resources in many places. Because of the selective nature of outmigration, many communities know that better health facilities and schools will only lead to an accelerated exodus of young people. There is something to be said for the people in relatively poor regions not wanting to see the payoff from their investment in mobile human beings go to relatively prosperous areas. Under these conditions, poor regions are justified in asking the nation as a whole to support investment in their people, although public works and business-oriented programs so favored in regional development legislation are difficult to justify because of better alternatives in regions with greater external economies.

A recent study points up the relative underinvestment in human resources in lagging areas.[10] U.S. Office of Economic Opportunity (OEO) data on federal investments by county and by SMSA in 1967 and 1968 are divided into economic overhead capital (EOC)—primarily public works in the narrow sense—and social overhead capital (SOC)—investment in human resources.[11]* Observations were taken for (1) the fifteen largest SMSA's, (2) a random sample of thirty-five SMSA's with relatively high employment growth, (3) a random sample of thirty-five SMSA's with relatively low employment growth. These eighty-five SMSA's comprised 257 counties with a total population of 90 million, about 45 per cent of the national total. Then non-SMSA counties were divided into those qualified for EDA assistance and those not qualified. Each of these groups were then divided into relatively high-growth and relatively low-growth classes. Thus, in addition to three sets of SMSA's, four sets of fifty counties each were used: (4) high-growth, non-EDA, (5) low-growth, non-EDA, (6) high-growth, EDA, and (7) low-growth, EDA. (In the cases of both the SMSA's and the non-SMSA counties, "relatively high-growth" and "relatively low-growth" refer to the sample observations and not to all SMSA's or counties in the nation.)

---

*In Miller's study, 62 per cent of the SOC outlays were accounted for by the Department of Health, Education, and Welfare (HEW), 11 per cent by the Department of the Interior, and 8 per cent by the Office of Economic Opportunity. Of the EOC outlays, 61 per cent were accounted for by the Department of Transportation, 14 per cent by the Department of Agriculture, and 12 per cent by the Department of Commerce.

The data in Table 5, which shows unweighted average per capita federal EOC and SOC outlays, indicate that counties designated for EDA assistance receive less per capita SOC investment than any other group except low-growth SMSA's. In contrast, they receive much higher per capita EOC investment than any other group, a reflection of the public works bias toward lagging areas. In terms of SOC as a proportion of total federal investment, the EDA counties are much lower than any other group, with the low-growth EDA group having by far the lowest value of all, 39.2 per cent.

TABLE 5

**Unweighted Average Per Capita Federal SOC and EOC Investment,
Fiscal Years 1967 and 1968, by Type of Area**

	SOC		EOC	
Type of Area	Amount (dollars)	SOC as a Percentage of OC	Amount (dollars)	EOC as a Percentage of OC
All States	175	57.0	132	43.0
85 SMSA's	157	63.8	89	36.2
15 Largest	206	70.5	85	29.5
High-Growth	137	60.6	88	39.4
Low-Growth	128	58.7	90	41.3
200 Counties	172	54.1	146	45.9
High-Growth, Non-EDA	242	67.0	119	33.0
Low-Growth, Non-EDA	178	70.0	114	39.1
High-Growth, EDA	135	48.8	142	51.2
Low-Growth, EDA	134	39.2	208	60.8

Source: Computed from data supplied by the Office of Economic Opportunity.

The per capita SOC and EOC values in Table 6 are weighted by population. The per capita SOC value for high-growth, EDA counties is below that for SMSA's and for all counties; the comparable value for low-growth, EDA counties is somewhat above that for all counties but below that for all SMSA's and each category of SMSA's. However, the SOC-EOC structure of total investment shows that the proportion of SOC is lowest in the EDA counties, and especially in the low-growth, EDA counties.

TABLE 6

Weighted Average Per Capita Federal SOC and EOC Investment, Fiscal Years 1967 and 1968, by Type of Area

	SOC		EOC	
Type of Area	Amount (dollars)	SOC as a Percentage of OC	Amount (dollars)	EOC as a Percentage of OC
All States	159	64.1	88	35.9
85 SMSA's	166	62.8	94	37.2
15 Largest	181	70.2	77	29.8
High-Growth	141	56.8	106	43.2
Low-Growth	156	61.4	98	38.6
200 Counties	127	55.6	101	44.4
High-Growth, Non-EDA	102	62.2	61	37.8
Low-Growth, Non-EDA	152	63.9	85	36.1
High-Growth, EDA	116	53.5	100	46.5
Low-Growth, EDA	138	46.9	154	53.1

Source: Computed from data supplied by the Office of Economic Opportunity.

During a visit with a federal official in Washington in the spring of 1970, the author was shown a tabulation by type of area, based on the OEO federal investment data but more comprehensive in geographic coverage than the data in Tables 5 and 6. The official explicitly pointed out that the author's contention that lagging areas are not receiving adequate SOC investment was clearly borne out by the data. However, their use was denied the author by another official on the ground that "they have policy implications."

That the most fundamental problem of lagging areas is underinvestment in human resources is perhaps indicated best by the return migration which occurs when a new plant does locate there. Two clear cases of this phenomenon are seen in Central Appalachia.

In 1956, Kaiser Aluminum and Chemical Corporation built an aluminum reduction and rolling mill at Ravenswood, West Virginia, fifty miles north of Charleston. When the plant was first built, the company attempted to maximize hiring of workers from the local area. It soon became evident, however, that directly applicable skills and even adequate basic schooling were lacking in the local manpower pool. The kind of worker needed by Kaiser was likely to be employed, to be a migrant from the area who desired to return, or to be on temporary layoff from some other plant in the Ohio Valley. The direct effects of the plant from the standpoint of lesser-qualified persons seeking employment were disappointing. Moreover, the induced employment attributable to the plant's operations could be traced from Ohio (power) to Louisiana (bauxite), but very little could be found in Ravenswood. Only three firms located there to furnish services to the plant. Perhaps 300 jobs were created locally as a result of the town's growth, but they were primarily low-skill jobs in retail trade. New professional jobs were almost all filled by persons from outside the community. Lack of capital and of local entrepreneurship prevented local people from establishing new businesses. In all, about 4,000 new jobs were created in Ravenswood as a consequence of Kaiser's location there. Of this number, only about 300 to 500 local persons worked in the plant and another 300, in establishments which came into existence because of Kaiser's growth. In his analysis of the impact of Kaiser on Ravenswood, Irwin Gray concludes that "more local people could be at work, at the expense of immigrants, if they had had the necessary minimum education or training. . . . That more were not hired brings up some pointed questions about education and skills in general."[12]

Another case is provided by the location of a plant by American Standard, the nation's ninetieth largest industrial corporation, near Paintsville, Kentucky. American Standard is the first major firm to locate a manufacturing plant in Eastern Kentucky, but it was clear from the outset that the company counted on migrants who had left for northern cities to return to work in their home region. Among the transplanted Eastern Kentuckians who hoped to find employment with American Standard was Trevert Blackburn, who went to work for Whirlpool Corporaton in Ohio and had been gone from Eastern Kentucky for seventeen years. When the Paintsville newspaper ran an item requesting to know if former Eastern Kentuckians would return if work were available, Blackburn circulated it among sixty natives of the region who had been in Ohio for fifteen to twenty years. Blackburn found that "they all said they would come back if there were work. The people of Ohio don't seem to want much to do with us. They like our work, but that's about it." American Standard, according to the *Louisville Courier-Journal,* "is gambling that it, too, will like their work, and that the 'homing instinct' demonstrated by Blackburn and his friends will provide a loyal and stable work force. Their performance will be critical to Eastern Kentucky's industrial future. 'If this doesn't work, no other major industry will go to Eastern Kentucky,' said Roger I. McKenzie, who will manage the new American Standard facility."[1 3]

The history of the Kenwood site, where American Standard has located, is itself instructive concerning the difficulties of attracting industry to an area where industry expects to find barefoot children, broken-down shacks, and a population with poor health and education and dependent on "the welfare" as the prime source of income.

In the early 1960's, the Area Redevelopment Administration, the predecessor of EDA, awarded a $50,000 contract to MacDonald Associates to determine the feasibility of establishing a wood products complex that would utilize the abundant, but inferior, wood resources of Eastern Kentucky. The report prepared by this company recommended establishing a plant which would utilize the whole tree, instead of cutting lumber and discarding up to 60 per cent of the tree as waste. Sales, marketing, and financial plans also were proposed. Meanwhile, a site for such a plant was purchased between the Big Sandy River and U.S. Highway 23 by the Kentucky Power Company and held for the nonprofit Big Sandy Industrial Foundation, whose purpose was to attract industry to the area. After failing to attract plants from existing firms, the Foundation decided to create Kenwook Products Incorporated to implement the proposals of the MacDonald report. Kenwood received a $60,000 grant from the Kentucky Highway Department to build an access road to the site, and EDA provided a $425,000 grant for grading, paving, and other improvements to the site. EDA also gave Paintsville a $278,000 grant and a $70,000 loan to link the Kenwood site to Paintsville water. A bridge over the Big Sandy was constructed for $489,000, the cost being shared by the state and the Appalachian Regional Commission. In addition to approximately $1.3 million in public works, Kenwood Products applied for a low-interest, EDA loan of $3.4 million and asked that EDA guarantee 90 per cent of a private loan of $1 million for working capital. However, EDA required that a minimum of 15 per cent of the aggregate cost of the project be financed from nonfederal sources. To raise the money, Kenwood made a public offering of 700,000 shares at $2.50 a share; it sold only 101,000 shares. Kenwood then tried to obtain private loans from Ohio and South Carolina companies and offered a controlling interest to several national lumber companies. When these efforts failed, Kenwood folded. Community leaders then began to look for other firms to locate on the Kenwood site, and after a number of unsuccessful negotiations with such companies as Hobart Manufacturing and Armco Steel, they finally reached an agreement with American Standard.

As of April, 1970, American Standard had received 4,742 applications for employment, with new applications arriving at the rate of about 30 per day. The company expected a total of 7,000 applications by the end of the summer.

Although there were initial reports that the plant would employ from 450 to 600 persons, by the summer of 1970 it was only employing 242 persons. Despite the fact that Paintsville is the site of the Mayo State Vocation-Technical School, many of the jobs at American Standard have gone to returned migrants; the plant manager states: "We've had many move back from Ohio and Michigan. They've learned their skills in the North, and they now can use them here. I've got 500 applications in the file, most of which would be highly acceptable, highly employable, in a big-city labor market. We're able to be very selective."[14]

In general, then, it is apparent that without substantially more investment in human resources, too many of the people of lagging regions will be unprepared not only for employment opportunities in other regions but even in their own communities, should the prospect be opened.

Even though the prospect is not bright, advocates of rural development still claim that every effort should be made to give everyone a job where they now live because migration to big cities results in greater social costs than those that would be involved in implementing their proposals. This raises two questions. First, are big cities really too big? And second, are rural areas and small towns, on the one hand, and big cities, on the other, the only alternatives? On the first question, it is quite likely that the rural development proponents are correct. However, on the second question they are wrong, because they ignore job opportunities in intermediate-size cities. (Some acknowledge that there may have to be some migration from areas no longer viable to towns, but they are usually quite conservative on the size of the town, as EDA growth center policy illustrates.) These propositions will be considered in detail in the following sections.

THE ROLE OF BIG CITIES

Whether or not our big cities are too big cannot be proven. The author has considered both sides of this issue elsewhere[15] and has suggested that they probably are too big in terms of alternatives available to individuals and firms in intermediate-size cities. More recent evidence indicates that larger cities continue to experience diseconomies of scale in providing public services,[16] but this argument can never be decisive until it is possible to measure adequately the quality of the services rendered by cities—a prospect which does not seem near at hand. Nevertheless, it is abundantly clear from the media that there is a growing disenchantment with life in our big cities. Thus, Alexander Ganz notes:

In recent years it has become fashionable to write off the future of our large cities. Observers point to the shift of population and jobs to the suburbs, the riots of the mid-1960's, the postwar and projected polarization of blacks in the cities and whites in the suburbs, the traffic congestion and pollution, the obsolescence of public facilities and private structures, the poverty of low income families, the fiscal squeeze affecting large city governments and the deterioration of the environment.[17]

Since Ganz obviously suffers no myopia about these difficulties, it is instructive to consider at some length his defense of the big city. The economies of big cities, he argues, are showing new strength and a larger potential. Since at least 1963, they have not been net losers of jobs. The earlier loss of manufacturing jobs has been more than offset by increased employment in government, business, and personal services. The total number of jobs in eleven large cities for which comparable data were available rose by 5.3 per cent between 1963 and 1967, a rate of growth that exceeded that of the growth of their populations. This phenomenon was experienced by slower-growing cities such as Boston, Philadelphia, and St. Louis, as well as rapidly growing cities such as Denver, New Orleans, and Washington, D.C. Between 1950 and 1967, the eleven cities lost nearly 600,000 manufacturing and trade jobs, but they gained more than a million jobs in government employment at all levels, finance, communications, advertising, publishing, legal services, the arts, theater, fashions, recreation, medical services, business services, private educational institutions, nonprofit institutions, and travel and tourist activities. Productivity has been increasing in all of the cities and even manufacturing has been expanding in some cities at a faster rate than in the suburbs. In general, the industry mix in most large cities now shows as high a proportion of fast-growing activities as the mix of their suburbs.[18]

Ganz also finds that alleviation of central city traffic congestion is in prospect. Although automobile use and trips are expected to increase substantially in SMSA's, trips to and from the central city may rise only fractionally. Ganz therefore suggests that transportation improvements already under way or planned, including mass transit and highways, may be expected to accommodate the slower growth of travel in large cities. Moreover, he also finds that a notable revitalization of the large cities is under way in response to their new economic functions and to rising personal income and public expenditures.[19]

A new beginning of advance and development is occurring as a result of new initiatives in urban ghetto communities. In addition to a great number and variety of efforts for and by black communities, the prediction of rapid growth of the Negro population in the central cities has not been borne out. The rate of Negro population increase in central cities has fallen from 400,000 per year during the 1960-66 period to 111,000 per year in the 1966-68 period. At the present rate, the Negro population in central cities, now numbering 12 million, may not exceed 14 million by 1985, in contrast to the 20 million anticipated by the Kerner Commission. Perhaps even more significant is the increasing suburbanization of Negroes. From 1960 to 1966, the Negro population in the suburbs grew by 33,000 annually, but from 1966 to 1968, the rate jumped to 220,000 per year, sufficient to create a suburban Negro population of about 7 million by 1985. Moreover, Negro median family income rose from 54 per cent of that for whites in 1965 to 60 per cent in 1968.[20]

"Our studies," Ganz writes, "show that despite all of the limitations of life in the ghetto, non-white labor force migrating to the large cities are experiencing notable gains in wages and earnings. The absorption and upgrading of this disadvantaged population is a national problem and a national task which the cities are performing."[21]

The conclusions drawn from this survey are quite explicit: "The large role of the large cities as producers of goods and services suggests that national growth and welfare would be enhanced by policies and programs favoring their upgrading and transformation."[22] And again:

> Federal policy should be explicitly designed to favor the large cities and their ghettos through expenditure, grant, loan guarantee and regulatory programs, in accordance with a measure of their need and their potential contribution to national growth and welfare. Federal policy has recently begun to move in this direction on a number of fronts, but an explicit policy determination would help assure that Federal policy would no longer work at cross purposes.[23]

It is noteworthy that the arguments advanced by Ganz and other advocates of the big city seldom take account of the unquantifiable social costs of urban congestion, nor do they adjust incomes to reflect cost of living. If data limitations preclude our making the relevant subtractions from private pecuniary gain to firms and individuals, it is still unwise simply to ignore these problems. If big cities have so many net advantages over other areas, it is curious that a Gallup Poll survey released in 1968 found that 56 per cent of the respondents would prefer living in rural areas or small towns, if jobs were available. In comparison with a poll taken two years earlier, the proportion of persons expressing a preference for city or suburban living dropped by seven percentage points.[24] The condition of job availability is, of course, critical, but as Wilbur Thompson has pointed out, "if blue-collar, middle-income workers should happen to prefer small towns or medium-size cities as places to live and to fish, such a preference is irrelevant as a locational factor. What could be most relevant is that the wives of corporate managers prefer the theater. Under unionism [*i.e.*, equal wages in all places], managers become increasingly free to locate where *they* would like to live."[25]

Thompson and others who emphasize the importance of urban amenities assume that management will always tend to locate in big cities. Up until recently, this has been true, but now there is mounting evidence that the managers who determine where the workers will live are increasingly inclined to shun the big city. *Business Week* recently reported that

> New York's well-publicized life-style, composed of poor transporation, dirty streets, costly housing, rising crime, strikes, bad air, and bad telephone service, is also getting to business. . . . The proverbial Big Apple for many a corporate career has turned out to have a worm in it. Executives are choosing not to take

that big promotion that will involve moving to headquarters in Manhattan.[26]

The article goes on to point out that whether they admit it or not, all of the major corporations in New York are having trouble getting people to move there and that New York offers a preview of what will take place in other big cities if they continue to expand.

Similarly, the *Wall Street Journal* reports that business executives are increasingly reluctant to take jobs in big cities because of their expensiveness and discomfort. Executives located in New York, Chicago, and Cleveland are the most inclined to leave for jobs elsewhere, even at lower pay. While there always have been people who cannot endure large cities, "suddenly, to the growing dismay of corporations, executive talent hunters and management consultants, the metrophobes are legion."[27]

It may be that the difficulties of the big cities are not so much inherent in their size as in their structure, particularly where it is a question of a bifurcation between blacks in the central city and the whites in the suburbs. Indeed, this position is widely held among the supporters of the big cities. In this event, there are two fundamental solutions to the problems of the cities: break down the barriers imposed on the black population by discrimination and pump more money into the cities to make them more habitable.

But these are not convincing. In the first place, nations all over the world are finding that their big cities are too big, and an ever-increasing number of urban policies are aimed at checking their growth. While it is obvious that we have structural problems in our cities, this should not be an excuse for evading the difficulties of sheer size and density. Moreover, to the extent that we have structural problems, they would be easier to deal with if a migration policy would encourage migrants to locate in places other than the big cities. Finally, the argument that the big cities can be saved by means of huge doses of federal investment is not, in itself, appealing; it is the same argument used by the proponents of rural areas and the small towns to save many of them from a natural death, and no doubt Eastern Kentucky, South Texas, and the Indian reservations *could* be made into very attractive places for people and industry if *enough* money were pumped in. The real question must be posed in terms of spatial opportunity cost: Are there better alternatives in other places? The big cities and the small towns and rural areas obviously need, and will receive, a great deal of public investment, but it does not seem wise to single them out for special favor, especially when a growth center strategy based on intermediate-size cities offers more opportunities in terms of existing external economies than do small towns and rural areas and fewer diseconomies than do the big cities.

THE ROLE OF INTERMEDIATE-SIZE CITIES

Without speaking of disadvantages, do the big cities have real economic advantages over intermediate-size cities? The issue here is not one of optimum size, but rather of the minimum size required to provide the range of services needed by people and firms and the impact of size on growth potentials.

In a study discussed earlier, Brian Berry found that above a population of 250,000, "the necessary conditions for self-sustaining growth seem satisfied," and he suggests that the greatest payoff in terms of increasing employment and reducing unemployment would be to use "the public treasury to enable centers close to this point to achieve self-sustaining growth," rather than to put resources into places much smaller than this maximum.[28]

Wilbur Thompson proposes that there is an urban size ratchet and that when the population growth of an urban area reaches a critical size of around 250,000, it appears that "structural characteristics, such as industrial diversification, political power, huge fixed investments, a rich local market, and a steady supply of industrial leadership may almost ensure its continued growth and fully ensure against absolute decline—may, in fact, effect irreversible aggregate growth."[29]

Since the 250,000 population figure appears so frequently in discussions of efficient city sizes, it is instructive to examine what happens to SMSA's as they approach this threshold.

Population data at ten-year intervals between 1900 and 1960, as well as estimates for 1965, were used for each of the 231 SMSA's as defined in 1967. Of these 231 SMSA's, the 25 which had not yet reached a population of 100,000 in 1965 were omitted, along with the 32 which had well exceeded the 250,000 population when the first observations were made in 1900. This left 174 for consideration. Of these, 74 had yet to attain a population of 200,000. This means that of 231 SMSA's, 100 fit into the category of interest, in that they had arrived at a population of 250,000 during the sixty-five-year span.

Population was plotted against time for each SMSA. Plots were also made of first differences, percentage changes, and growth on a semilogarithmic scale. As the cities approached the 200,000 level, 88 of the 100 experienced a growth spurt, that is, a large leap in absolute population. The growth spurts tended to range in magnitude from 50,000 to 200,000 over the relevant ten-year period, with the average being 70,000. This increase of 5,000 to 7,000 per year was substantially larger than any comparable previous growth. The average population at which the spurt began was 173,000 and the average population at the end was 248,000. Some SMSA's continued growing at an ever-increasing rate in subsequent periods, while in other cases growth tapered off. Many of the SMSA's reached 250,000 population during their spurt, but those that did not arrived at it early in the next ten-year period.

When graphs of the percentage changes were considered, no real conclusions could be drawn. In general, the spurt period occurred during one of the larger percentage changes in growth, but it was by no means always the largest. Percentage change in population during the spurt ranged from highs of 200 per cent to lows of 20 per cent. The average change during the spurt period was between 40 and 50 per cent. The semilogarithmic analysis indicated that city growth was somewhat linear in its natural log form. The spurts also were apparent on a semilog scale. Only twelve cities showed a population decline after the initial spurt period had occurred. In cities which had not experienced a growth spurt, some twenty-six showed population declines. The twelve cities which did experience population declines (see Table 7) could all be classified as being dependent on a single industry or sector for their existence. They did not generally have the "structural characteristics" which Thompson feels are necessary for self-sustained growth. Many had a single base industry or sector (*i.e.*, coal, iron ore, or a naval base) upon which fluctuations in population and economic well-being were directly dependent.

The cities which did not undergo a growth spurt showed no similar characteristics in either their structure or in their growth patterns. The growth patterns ranged from unusually consistent and stable to fairly eratic.

In general, then, the evidence supports the proponents of a growth spurt threshold but suggests that the threshold tends to be in the 150,000 to 200,000 range, somewhat lower than the usual estimate. However, there is no evidence of automatic self-sustained growth following the spurt.

Australian data indicate that most of the advantages of a city of 500,000 probably also are found in a city of 200,000 but that if a city gets much beyond the 500,000 level, external diseconomies are likely to begin to outweigh the concomitant economies. On the basis of Australian experience, G. M. Neutze suggests that many firms will maximize their profits in centers with populations between 200,000 and one million.[30]

In an earlier study, Colin Clark examined structural differences in American, Canadian, and Australian cities of different sizes. He concluded that a city of about 200,000 provides practically all important services and that it is "full grown" with respect to manufacturing at a population level of around 500,000.[31]

Such data as we have with respect to the provision of public services indicate that both small towns and big cities fare worse than intermediate-size cities. For example, Werner Hirsch estimates that the greatest economies of scale occur in the 50,000 to 100,000 population range, whereas the Royal Commission on Local Government in Greater London found the range to be from 100,000 to 250,000.[32] Gordon Cameron finds a "U-shaped" infrastructure cost curve with the minimum cost lying between somewhat less than 30,000 and somewhat more than 250,000.[33] Critics of such studies usually point out the difficulty of holding the quality of services constant when estimating costs. However, the fact that these studies almost invariably find the range of maximum efficiency to be considerably less than the size of our big cities suggests that until evidence is produced to the contrary, the burden of proof lies with the defenders of the big city.

Finally, it is pertinent to note the conclusion drawn by participants at a conference—sponsored by the International Economic Association—in response to the question, "How large must a successful growth point be?" E. A. G. Robinson reports that

> the general sense of our discussions was that the minimum size of growth points that experience had shown to be successful was nearer to a population of 100,000 than to one of 10,000 and that even 100,000 was more likely to be an underestimate than an overestimate. It must be large enough to provide efficiently the main services of education, medical facilities, banking, shopping

TABLE 7

Intermediate-Size SMSA's That Experienced Population Spurts and Subsequent Declines, 1900-65

SMSA	Decade of Spurt	Population (thousands) at Beginning and at End	Decade(s) of Decline	Population (thousands) at Beginning and at End
Akron, Ohio	1910-20	138-322	1930-40	387-386
Allentown-Bethlehem, Pennsylvania	1900-10	231-290	1910-20	290-247
Charleston, West Virginia[a]	1940-50	185-240	1960-65	253-245
Duluth-Superior. Minnesota-Wisconsin	1900-10	119-211	1920-30	256-251
			1940-50	254-253
			1960-65	277-267
Jersey City, New Jersey	Pre-1900	--	1930-40	691-652
			1940-50	652-647
			1950-60	647-611
Johnstown, Pennsylvania	1900-10	154-234	1940-50	298-291
			1950-60	291-281
			1960-65	281-270
Norfolk-Portsmouth, Virginia	1910-20	169-246	1920-30	246-233
Pittsburgh, Pennsylvania	Pre-1900	—	1960-65	2,405-2,372
Scranton, Pennsylvania	1900-10	194-260	1930-40	310-301
			1940-50	301-257
			1950-60	257-235
			1960-65	235-226
Spokane, Washington[a]	1900-10	165-222	1960-65	278-267
Tulsa, Oklahoma	1920-30	81-208		
	1930-40	208-299	1940-50	299-291
Wilkes Barre-Hazleton, Pennsylvania	Pre-1900	—	1930-40	445-442
			1940-50	442-392
			1950-60	392-347
			1960-65	347-346

[a]Decline forecast for 1960-65 period.

Source: Jean Shackelford, "On Thresholds, Take-Offs and Spurts: A Place for SMSA's in Growth Center Strategy," Discussion Paper Number 27, Center for Developmental Change, University of Kentucky, Lexington, 1970.

facilities. . . . Above all, it must be large enough both to provide an efficient infrastructure of public utility services, and to permit the early and progressive growth of external economies for its local industries.[3 4]

In other words, though it is agreed that small towns rarely make viable growth centers, the intermediate-size city often does have the necessary conditions.

In general, the foregoing material indicates that encouraging (or at least not discouraging) migration from lagging areas may be coupled with a growth center policy based on external economies in cities in the 200,000 to 750,000 population range. Of course, these are rough indicators, not magic numbers, and the limits could be made more flexible to accommodate cities in, say, the 50,000 to one million range. There is evidence for believing that self-sustained growth is easier to maintain in a city of 200,000 than in smaller places. On the other hand, external diseconomies may make expansion of alternative locations desirable from an opportunity-cost viewpoint after a city passes the 750,000 mark. It has been proposed that the solution to finding an optimum city size consists in finding the "point at which the economies of scale (or agglomeration) are equalled or exceeded by the diseconomies."[3 5] Although measurement of these variables is not a realistic prospect for the foreseeable future, the formulation of the problem in this manner is not quite correct. Even if expansion of a big city yielded a positive net social product (economies greater than diseconomies) it would be preferable to have the expansion take place in an intermediate-size city if the net social product were even greater there. The case for the intermediate-size city is based on considerable evidence that it has most of the external economies of a big city but that it has not yet become a generator of significant external diseconomies.*

IMPLEMENTING A GROWTH CENTER STRATEGY

What measures should be taken to implement a growth center strategy along the lines that have been discussed? Since development policy will focus on areas which are already economically healthy and growing, rather than on areas which have relatively poor growth prospects, there should be more emphasis on measures that will appeal to growing industries and less emphasis on subsidies whose principal appeal is to small firms in slow-growing, low-wage

---

*Even with respect to amenities, one must be careful not to overestimate the advantages of the big city. New York may offer 300 plays, concerts, and recitals in a given week, while a city of 600,000 may offer only 25. Though the overall quality may be better in New York, the average person still has time only to take in a fraction of the offerings in the intermediate-size city. Though there is a wider range of choice in New York, it would be difficult to argue that the cultural advantages of living there are twelve times greater than in the intermediate-size city. Modern home entertainment equipment also has served to lessen the importance of living in a big city.

industries. More effort might be devoted to equipping relatively sophisticated industrial sites and less to building water and sewer lines (which may be sorely needed in rural areas but which should not be a primary concern of an agency whose purpose is to stimulate or accelerate growth).

Placement of Aid

The kinds of tools should be more varied and flexible than those presently applied in small towns and rural areas. The latter need so many improvements in order to make them relatively attractive to firms, especially the bigger and more rapidly growing ones, that whatever a development agency can do within the constraints of its limited resources is not likely to change greatly the total "package" of factors that a firm considers when making a location decision. This is especially true to the extent that a "worst-first" policy is either explicitly or implicitly followed. On the other hand, the growth centers that have been proposed here have a large variety of external economies. This means, in the first place, that a given type of aid extended by an economic development agency would not be so visible as it would be in a lagging area. However, if used wisely, a given type of aid could produce more employment opportunities in the growth center because it could be combined with these external economies. The development agency should seek out the bottlenecks that are hindering or preventing a firm from locating or expanding in the growth center and attempt to provide the assistance needed to overcome the resistance. The situation may call for a certain type of investment in amenities or in more directly productive infrastructure or for a labor training subsidy or for some combination of aid devices. Efforts also should be made to enlist the cooperation of prominent business leaders as is now being done for job creation programs in the ghettos. A properly dramatized program of public investment and plant location in growth centers could be a strong force in attracting new economic activity and migrants from lagging areas. Investigations should be made of the degree to which and conditions under which the private sector could be brought into active cooperation in developing growth centers. Large, national firms should be involved, as well as local business and civic leaders. In any case, it is essential that the aid be made conditional on the extension of job opportunities to persons from lagging regions (and, in part, to the unemployed and underemployed residents of the center).

The emphasis that is given here to the development of intermediate-size cities as the principal focus for a national regional policy is based not only on the job growth potential of these cities, but also on the fact that problems related to their growth are still amenable to solution. The massive renewal needs of our large metropolitan areas can still be avoided by careful planning in growth centers. "A city of 'optimal size,'" writes Benjamin Higgins, "must be big enough to be urbane in its range of activities and small enough to provide effective proximity to these activities for its residents, with the available techniques of city planning and transportation."[36] Unless the government knows what places are going to grow, it can provide public facilities only after the demand has appeared. If there is planned growth of a relatively few centers, then they can be provided with an integrated and coherent system of public facilities in advance of the demand. Of course, it is not necessary that a growth center be limited to one city. A system of cities or towns linked by adequate transportation and communications might serve as well or better. Such a system could take the form of a cluster of urban centers or a development axis.

Human Resource Development Versus Migration

The selective nature of outmigration from lagging areas means that they tend to lose their most vital people—the best workers, the young, the better educated. Thus, outmigration may cause cumulative difficulties in a lagging region, and the benefits from an increase in local employment opportunities may help return migrants more than the local residents. Of course, the positive multiplier effects of any new activity will indirectly benefit the community as a whole, especially if leakages to other areas are minimal. Whatever may be the consequences of outmigration from lagging areas, it is still clear that policies that merely try to check migration—even by attempting to subsidize the industrialization of rural areas—do little service to either the nation or the individuals concerned, at least from an opportunity-cost viewpoint. Return migration, in particular, shows that the real problem of lagging regions is underinvestment in their human resources, rather than migration as such, which is a symptom rather than a cause.

Hopefully, a national regional policy would aid areas with problems occasioned by outmigration to attain new equilibria with a minimum of friction. The nation may also deem it desirable to aid persons in these areas whose prospects either for local employment or for retraining and migration are not bright; older workers in particular would fall into this category. However, it must be recognized that we are talking here about welfare and not about economic development policy. In any case, public policy for lagging regions should still emphasize manpower and human resource development programs, including comprehensive job information and relocation assistance.

If growth center policy is to be coordinated with human resource development in lagging regions, we need much more knowledge concerning the trade-offs between "regional development" and worker relocation. As has been argued, many problems of regional development might be dealt with more effectively if they were treated as problems of human resource development and manpower mobility. There is a pronounced need to integrate the research of place-oriented regional economists and the research of labor economists and others concerned with manpower programs in the broadest sense. For example, regional research could benefit from a number of social science disciplines with respect to our knowledge of attitudes and preferences. When we speak of making spatial resources allocation more rational, it is implied that we are in some sense attempting to increase the aggregate level of welfare. But this, in turn, implies that we know something of the preferences we presumably are trying to satisfy.

Although it is not possible to give empirical content to all of the issues raised here with respect to implementing a growth center strategy, many of the opportunities (and difficulties) which it offers are critically examined in the following chapters in the context of regional problems in the United States.

NOTES

1. Vida Nichols, "Growth Poles: An Evaluation of Their Propulsive Effect," *Environment and Planning,* Vol. 1, No. 2 (1969), 193.

2. See, for example, *Growth Centers and Their Potentials in the Upper Great Lakes Region* (Washington, D.C.: Upper Great Lakes Regional Commission, 1969), a report prepared for the commission by Brian J. L. Berry and associates; and *The Role of Growth Centers in Regional Economic Development* (Ames: Iowa State University Department of Economics, 1966), a report prepared for the Office of Regional Economic Development, U.S. Department of Commerce.

3. Harry W. Richardson, *Regional Economics* (New York: Praeger, 1969), p. 316.

4. *Ibid.*

5. See William Alonso, "What Are New Towns For?," *Urban Studies,* Vol. 7, No. 1 (February, 1970), 37-56.

6. See Niles M. Hansen, *French Regional Planning* (Bloomington: Indiana University Press, 1968), Chapters 1, 7, and 11; and Niles M. Hansen, *Rural Poverty and the Urban Crisis* (Bloomington: Indiana University Press, 1970).

7. Melvin R. Levin, *Community and Regional Planning* (New York: Praeger, 1969), p. 203.

8. *Ibid.,* pp. 203-204.

9. Ralph R. Widner, "Economic Development and Social Change," paper presented at the Government Relations and Planning Policy Conference, American Institute of Planners, Washington, D.C., January 25, 1969. See also Gerald W. Sazama, "State Industrial Development Loans: A General Analysis," *Land Economics,* Vol. 46, No. 2 (May, 1970), 171-80.

10. Duncan R. Miller, "Public Investment and Regional Economic Development" (Lexington: University of Kentucky, 1970; doctoral dissertation).

11. The economic overhead capital (EOC) and social overhead capital (SOC) breakdowns were based on procedures in Niles M. Hansen, "The Structure and Determinants of Local Public Investment Expenditures," *Review of Economics and Statistics,* Vol. 47, No. 2 (May, 1965), 150-62; and Niles M. Hansen, "Municipal Investment Requirements in a Growing Agglomeration," *Land Economics,* Vol. 41, No. 1 (February, 1965), 49-56.

12. Irwin Gray, "Employment Effect of a New Industry in a Rural Area," *Monthly Labor Review,* Vol. 92, No. 6 (June, 1969), 29.

13. Rod Wenz, "Paintsville Plant: A Point for East Kentucky's Future," *Louisville Courier-Journal* (July 6, 1969), p. G1.

14. David V. Hawpe, "Plant at Paintsville is Luring Workers Back to Mountains," *Louisville Courier-Journal* (June 28, 1970), p. 1.

15. Hansen, *Rural Poverty and the Urban Crisis, op. cit.,* pp. 240-48. See also, Niles M. Hansen, *Urban and Rural America: Policies for Future Growth* (Washington, D.C.: Advisory Commission on Intergovernmental Relations, 1968), pp. 54-57.

16. L. R. Gabler, "Economies and Diseconomies of Scale in Urban Public Sectors," *Land Economics,* Vol. 45, No. 4 (November, 1969), 425-34.

17. Alexander Ganz, "Our Large Cities: New Directions and New Approaches," a summary of findings (Cambridge: M.I.T. Laboratory for Environmental Studies, December 3, 1969), p. 1.

18. *Ibid.,* pp. 8-13.

19. *Ibid.,* p. 13.

20. *Ibid.,* pp. 16-19.

21. *Ibid.,* p. 25.

22. *Ibid.,* p. 15.

23. *Ibid.,* p. 25.

24. Cited in an address by Secretary of Agriculture Orville Freeman to the Conference on Rural-Oriented Industry, Washington, D.C., May 13, 1968.

25. Wilbur R. Thompson, "The Economic Base of Urban Problems," in Neil W. Chamberlain, ed., *Contemporary Economic Issues* (Homewood, Ill.: Richard D. Irwin, 1969), p. 11.

26. "For Executives, Fun City Can Be a Hardship," *Business Week* (February 7, 1970), 64.

27. *Wall Street Journal* (March 24, 1969), 1.

28. Brian J. L. Berry, "Spatial Organization and Levels of Welfare: Degree of Metropolitan Labor Market Participation as a Variable in Economic Development," paper presented at the Economic Development Administration Research Conference, Washington, D.C., October 9-13, 1967, p. 18.

29. Wilbur R. Thompson, *A Preface to Urban Economics* (Baltimore: The Johns Hopkins Press, 1965), p. 24.

30. G. M. Neutze, *Economic Policy and the Size of Cities* (New York: Augustus M. Kelley, 1967), pp. 163 and 109-18.

31. Colin Clark, "The Economic Functions of a City in Relation to its Size," *Econometrica*, Vol. 13, No. 2 (April, 1945), 97-113.

32. Werner Z. Hirsch, "The Supply of Urban Public Services," in Harvey S. Perloff and Lowdon Wingo, Jr., eds., *Issues in Urban Economics* (Baltimore: The Johns Hopkins Press, 1968), pp. 509-11.

33. Gordon Cameron, "Growth Areas, Growth Centres and Regional Conversion," *Scottish Journal of Political Economy,* Vol. 17, No. 1 (February, 1970), 24-25.

34. E. A. G. Robinson, "Introduction," in E. A. G. Robinson, ed., *Backward Areas in Advanced Countries* (New York: St. Martin's Press, 1969), p. xvi.

35. D. J. Reynolds, *Economics, Town Planning and Traffic* (London: Institute of Economic Affairs, 1966), p. 21.

36. Benjamin Higgins, *Economic Development* (revised edition; New York: W. W. Norton, 1968), p. 468.

5

This chapter examines the potential relevance of two intermediate size growth centers in Kentucky—Lexington and Louisville—to the problems of poverty-stricken Eastern Kentucky (see Map 2). The average annual rate of growth in population in Kentucky between 1960 and 1966 was 0.7 per cent. The comparable rate in Louisville was 1.2 per cent, and in Lexington, 3.5 per cent, one of the highest in the nation.[1]

The poverty of Eastern Kentucky has been well documented.[2] Estimates prepared by the Appalachian Regional Commission indicate that per capita personal income in the Appalachian portion of Kentucky in 1966 was $1,378 (and only $1,066 in rural areas), as compared to the corresponding national value of $2,963 and the total Appalachian value of $2,297. The increase in per capita income in Appalachian Kentucky between 1959 and 1966 was $454; the corresponding national value was $802. The unemployment rate in Appalachian Kentucky in 1967 was 9.1 per cent, much higher than the national rate of 3.8 per cent and considerably higher than that in the Appalachian portion of any of the twelve other states with counties in the region.[3] In 1967, nineteen Eastern Kentucky counties had average annual unemployment rates in excess of 10 per cent; Owsley county had an average annual rate of 28 per cent and five other counties had rates higher than 20 per cent.[4] In view of these conditions, it is not surprising that Appalachian Kentucky had an estimated net migration deficit of 76,500 persons between 1960 and 1966.[5]

LEXINGTON AS A GROWTH CENTER
FOR THE PEOPLE OF EASTERN KENTUCKY

To determine the degree to which, and the conditions under which, problems of low income and high unemployment in lagging areas can be related

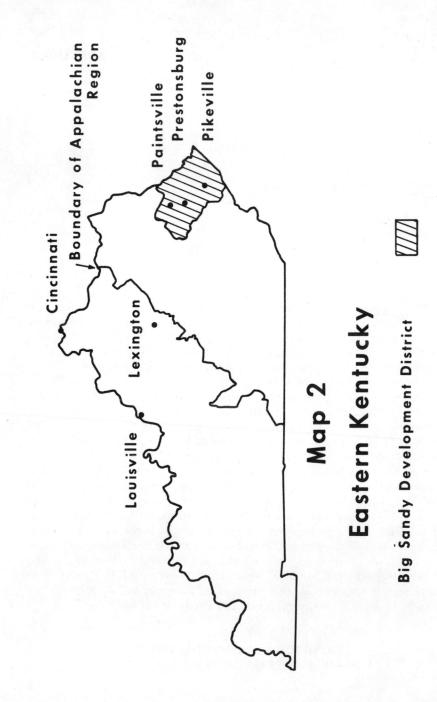

Map 2

Eastern Kentucky

Big Sandy Development District

Boundary of Appalachian Region

Cincinnati

Lexington

Louisville

Paintsville

Prestonsburg

Pikeville

to economic opportunities in an intermediate-size growth center, the author in the spring of 1969 interviewed leading industrial decision-makers in the Lexington, Kentucky, area, as well as Employment Service officials of the Kentucky Department of Economic Security who had direct knowledge of employment conditions and migration potentials in Eastern Kentucky.

Lexington is the county seat of Fayette County. Clark County, immediately to the east, is considered by the Appalachian Regional Commission to be part of Appalachia. Immediately to the east of Clark County is Powell County, where begins some of the worst poverty conditions in the United States. In contrast to the situation in Eastern Kentucky, Lexington has experienced rapid growth in recent years. Between 1960 and 1965, the Lexington SMSA increased from 132,000 to 159,000 persons. Estimates by the Bureau of the Census indicate that between 1965 and 1975, Lexington will be the fourteenth fastest growing SMSA in the nation; the increase for the decade 1960-70 was 31.1 per cent.[6] Accompanying this rapid growth has been a very low unemployment rate, 1.2 per cent in 1969.[7]

In an attempt to establish whether, and under what conditions, Lexington firms would hire people from Eastern Kentucky as part of a systematic effort to link labor surpluses in Eastern Kentucky to job opportunities in the Lexington area, the author first interviewed the executive vice president of the Lexington Chamber of Commerce, who supplied a list of names of relevant corporate executives, as well as considerable information on attempts being made to attract industry to Lexington. The executives interviewed represented the following national corporations: International Business Machines, Square D, Westinghouse Air Brake, American Can, and Texas Instruments. Two presidents of locally based enterprises were also interviewed, as well as the president of the Blue Grass Personnel Association.

The Chamber of Commerce reported that about two firms per week made inquiries concerning locating plants in Lexington, though it had been nearly a year and a half since any major new location had taken place. One of the principal reasons for firms' shying away from Lexington, according to the Chamber of Commerce, was fear of labor shortage in the area. This would seem reasonable in view of the low "official" unemployment rate. In marked contrast, however, the firms already in the area did not perceive any general labor shortage. Skilled labor appeared to be in short supply but this was the case throughout the country—even in parts of Central Appalachia. Most large firms in the Lexington area primarily employ relatively unskilled labor, and the local supply seemed to be quite adequate in view of the firms' actual and projected needs. One firm that was planning to expand expected to meet its labor needs from commuters from the rural hinterland if not from closer sources. The vice president of one of the major employers, who demonstrated considerable first-hand knowledge of the determinants of plant location, as well as of EDA and its activities, stated that firms frequently find adequate labor in areas which have low unemployment rates. He suggested that much more research is needed on the "true" number of workers that a firm has potentially available (through commuters from other counties and the locally underemployed) in any given place. He had very little faith in the operational usefulness of published unemployment figures.

The attitudes of Lexington employers toward workers from Eastern Kentucky was somewhat mixed, but in general, there was little or no reluctance to hire workers from that area, especially if they could present some skill. On the other hand, there was no interest in involvement in any federal program that might be devised to create job opportunities for Eastern Kentuckians in Lexington. This was the case with respect to any kind of direct or indirect loan or subsidy, including the development of plant sites. Indeed, there seemed to be little enthusiasm even for such programs as Manpower Development and Training Act (MDTA) training, which apparently had not been responsive to the needs of most local employers. In general, the local firms preferred to train their own workers, and some even preferred to have an untrained (but trainable) worker to one who had been trained under a government program. It should also be noted that some firms would be hostile to any program to expand industry in Lexington because they fear that wage rates would be bid up—even though this would not necessarily be the case if the labor supply were increased by importing workers. One major firm which has taken a real interest in helping to provide employment for persons in the hard-core poverty category has concentrated on helping local Negroes and sees little point in bringing in people from Appalachia so long as poverty and unemployment exist in Lexington.

In general, the only federal programs of direct relevance to the problems under discussion that met with approval from the interviewees were those that would develop human resources in Eastern Kentucky and those that would provide better interarea labor market information. It was felt that given these, the employment problems of Eastern Kentucky would correct themselves. It is particularly instructive that no firms had any interest in locating any activity in Eastern Kentucky. It was universally agreed that the projects engaged in by EDA and other federal agencies trying to attract economic activity to Eastern Kentucky would not be successful, beyond perhaps attracting a few marginal firms. The author was especially impressed by the degree to which amenities were cited as a major, perhaps the major, factor in determining plant location—at least where national corporations that are relatively "footloose" are concerned. And on this score, Eastern Kentucky has little to offer.

LEXINGTON AND LOUISVILLE FIRMS
VIS-À-VIS EASTERN KENTUCKY

A more comprehensive picture of the opportunities that firms in Lexington, as well as in Louisville, represent for Eastern Kentucky is contained in responses to a survey made by Richard YuKhin in 1969.[8] YuKhin's questionnaire was sent to private firms in Lexington and Louisville that had more than 50 employees. One hundred replies were received, representing 45 per cent of the companies to which the questionnaire was sent. The response rate was the same for both medium-size and large firms (a large firm is defined to be one employing more than 250 persons).

The companies were asked: If your firm expands during the next five years, will you seriously consider locating a new plant (or branch office) in Eastern Kentucky? No respondent expressed "extremely high" interest and only two expressed "high" interest. Ten stated they had a "moderate" interest, but seventy-five had "low" or "no interest." About 90 per cent of medium-size firms and about 80 per cent of the large firms had little or no interest.

Of particular interest is the response pattern to the following question: If various financial inducements are offered (e.g., industry grants, low interest loans and loan guarantees, renting of buildings to new firms) would you seriously consider locating a new plant (or branch office) in Eastern Kentucky? The proportion of medium-size firms indicating no interest jumped from 57 per cent in the case of the previous question to 64 per cent in this case; the corresponding increase for large firms was from 41 to 61 per cent. The already low proportion of expressions of "extremely high," "high", and "moderate" interest remained the same. The same general result obtained when firms were asked if they would consider locating in Eastern Kentucky if given liberal tax advantages or if given preferential treatment in the placing of government contracts. In other words, the initial reluctance of firms to locate in Eastern Kentucky was made even stronger by the presence of any kind of federal inducement mechanisms. This finding is in harmony with the author's interviews in the Lexington area.

YuKhin's survey results show that while firms generally do not want to locate in Eastern Kentucky, they are much more willing to cooperate in programs to bring Eastern Kentuckians to Lexington and Louisville. Eighty per cent of all the respondents and about 90 per cent of the large firms stated that they would cooperate with agencies to help create job opportunities for Eastern Kentuckians by recruiting workers trained by MDTA and other federal training programs. Of all firms, 87 per cent would cooperate in helping Eastern Kentuckians by providing job information to, and utilizing the services of, an agency concerned with interarea labor market information and placement programs. Again, however, there is pronounced evidence that firms are not so ready to become too directly involved with federal programs. Of all respondents, 45 per cent were *not* willing to hire workers who had received "satisfactory" on-the-job training, even if a substantial part of training expenses were reimbursed by the federal government. There was little difference between medium-size and large firms in this regard, but there was a notable difference between the responses of firms with headquarters in Kentucky and those with headquarters out of the state. Seventy per cent of the former group, but only 35 per cent of the latter, were willing to give Eastern Kentuckians on-the-job training with substantial cost reimbursement from the federal government.

In general, the survey results underscore the pronounced reluctance of firms—medium-size or large, Kentucky-based or with headquarters elsewhere— to locate in Eastern Kentucky. Federal inducements seem only to reinforce this attitude. On the other hand, there is considerable willingness to cooperate in giving Eastern Kentuckians employment in Lexington and Louisville.

LABOR MOBILITY AND LOCATIONAL PREFERENCES
IN EASTERN KENTUCKY

To gain increased understanding of attitudes toward labor mobility in Eastern Kentucky, the author interviewed persons likely to be familiar with the migration patterns and preferences of persons in the region, and persons in

Lexington who have dealt with Eastern Kentuckians working there. The latter interviewees were primarily personnel directors. For the most part, however, the author relied on interviews with Employment Service officials in Eastern Kentucky, Lexington, and Frankfort. The director of the Lexington office was particularly helpful because of his direct personal involvement in efforts to place Eastern Kentuckians in jobs in Lexington as part of a recent Kentucky Labor Mobility Demonstration Project carried out by the Kentucky Department of Economic Security in accordance with the MDTA.

Most Eastern Kentuckians who find employment outside the state through the U.S. Employment Service are now going to Indiana and Illinois. The Employment Service demand from Michigan has dried up because of efforts in Detroit to give jobs to ghetto residents. However, large numbers of migrants probably still go to Michigan without using the Employment Service. The greatest number of migrants probably goes to Ohio, but these are not generally known to the Employment Service. The migration streams tend to follow the paths traced by previous migrants. Most Eastern Kentuckians have some relative or friend in the North who may act as a source of job information and with whom the migrant can stay or otherwise count on for help when he goes North. (More will be said in this regard later in this chapter.) Despite a great deal of talk about "hillbilly ghettos," most Eastern Kentuckians apparently receive better wages in the North than they could in Lexington, and if and when they are laid off, they tend to return to Kentucky until they are called back to work. Moreover, there was little demand for workers from Eastern Kentucky in Lexington as far as requests reaching Employment Service offices in Eastern Kentucky were concerned (the exception was requests for skilled workers who were not generally to be found in Eastern Kentucky).

Those directly familiar with the economic problems of Eastern Kentucky generally agreed that there is little chance of attracting significant economic activity to the region, with the possible exception of firms seeking cheap labor. It is also agreed that federal programs, such as those of EDA, which are designed to stimulate private investment in the area, will probably not succeed in making the area more attractive to industry in relation to other areas. Similarly, welfare programs are viewed in a negative light. While they may be needed for the aged and for disadvantaged children, they have created a culture of dependency among many able-bodied persons in the age groups normally in the labor force. It is not difficult to "get on welfare" and to stay there, even though an individual could find gainful employment in other areas if not at home. The Kentucky Labor Mobility Project clearly showed that persons with a history of being on a welfare program were not good selections for relocation to new areas. There is widespread feeling among those familiar with the people of Eastern Kentucky that they would be better off in Lexington than in a northern city, primarily because of the former's proximity to their native area. However, some persons feel that those who permanently leave Eastern Kentucky might be better off in the North because wages are higher there.

Unfortunately, we know very little about the preferences of the people in question. To increase our understanding in this regard, a survey was made of 625 graduating seniors from seven high schools in one of Appalachia's poorest areas, the Big Sandy Region of Eastern Kentucky.* Graduating seniors were chosen because, at this stage of life, they must consider various job and residence alternatives. Their preferences were analyzed in terms of alternative opportunities in (1) their home area, (2) northern metropolitan areas, and (3) Lexington or Louisville.

The data in Table 8 show the locational preferences of all respondents under differing wage rate assumptions. Eight different relative wage structures were given for three locations: the student's own community; Lexington or Louisville; and a northern city.

If the wage rate is higher in the Eastern Kentucky community than in other locations (Case V) then more than 80 per cent of the respondents would stay in their home town. Most of the remaining respondents would move to Lexington or Louisville, even though they would receive $1.00 less per hour. In Case I, where wages are equal in all locations, almost 66 per cent would stay at home, but over 25 per cent would go to Lexington or Louisville, and 10.0 per cent would go North.

What is particularly striking is that in any case where the wage in Lexington or Louisville exceeds that in the home community, more respondents would prefer these cities to the home community. Moreover, the preference for these cities increases consistently with the magnitude of the wage differential between the home community and the urban centers. For example, when the difference is only $0.25 (Case II), those who would move to Lexington or Louisville outnumber those who would stay in Eastern Kentucky by 36 per cent to 25 per cent. When the wage differential is increased to $0.50 (Case III), the ratio becomes 40 per cent to 18 per cent. When the differential is increased to $0.75 (Case IV), it becomes 36 per cent to 10 per cent; at a differential of $1.00 (Case VII), it becomes 35 per cent to 9 per cent; and at $2.00 (Case VIII), 27 per cent to 6 per cent.

No less striking is the disposition of the students to avoid going to a northern city. In the two cases where the wage in Lexington or Louisville exceeds that in the northern city (Cases V and VI), very few respondents would go North. In Cases II and III, where the northern wage rate is highest, about as many respondents would prefer to go to Lexington or Louisville as to go North. Even in Case VII, 35 per cent would move to Lexington or Louisville, even though they could make $1.00 more in the North, and in Case VIII, 27 per cent would move to the Kentucky urban centers, even though they could make $2.00 more in the North.

Table 9 breaks down locational preferences by male and female groups. Where the wage spread is relatively wide, the groups have similar patterns. When the wage rate is equal in all locations (Case I), there is a much stronger

---

*The Big Sandy Region includes five counties at the extreme eastern end of Kentucky: Floyd, Johnson, Magoffin, Martin, and Pike. In 1966, the unemployment rate in the area was 14.7 per cent. Per capita income in 1963 was less than $1,025, compared with $1,799 for Kentucky and $2,488 for the nation as a whole. See "Community Cooperation for Development: Kentucky's Big Sandy," *Appalachia* (June-July, 1969), pp. 8-10.

TABLE 8

Locational Preferences of Eastern Kentucky High School Seniors Under Differing Wage Structure Assumptions, All Students

Place	Wage	Relative Frequency of Preferences	Place	Wage	Relative Frequency of Preferences
Case I			*Case V*		
Eastern Kentucky	$1.50	64.2	Eastern Kentucky	$3.50	81.3
Lexington-Louisville	1.50	25.8	Lexington-Louisville	2.50	13.4
Northern City	1.50	10.0	Northern City	1.50	5.3
Case II			*Case VI*		
Eastern Kentucky	1.50	25.1	Eastern Kentucky	1.50	10.0
Lexington-Louisville	1.75	35.8	Lexington-Louisville	3.50	81.1
Northern City	2.00	39.1	Northern City	2.50	8.9
Case III			*Case VII*		
Eastern Kentucky	1.50	18.0	Eastern Kentucky	1.50	8.7
Lexington-Louisville	2.00	39.6	Lexington-Louisville	2.50	34.9
Northern City	2.50	42.4	Northern City	3.50	56.4
Case IV			*Case VIII*		
Eastern Kentucky	1.50	9.7	Eastern Kentucky	1.50	6.5
Lexington-Louisville	2.25	36.5	Lexington-Louisville	3.50	27.1
Northern City	3.00	53.8	Northern City	5.50	66.5

TABLE 9

Locational Preferences of Eastern Kentucky High School Seniors Under Differing Wage Structure Assumptions, by Male and Female Groups

Place	Wage	Relative Frequency of Preferences Male	Female
Case I			
Eastern Kentucky	$1.50	73.6	56.2
Lexington-Louisville	1.50	18.8	31.8
Northern City	1.50	7.6	12.0
Case II			
Eastern Kentucky	1.50	31.2	19.7
Lexington-Louisville	1.75	32.4	38.7
Northern City	2.00	36.4	41.6
Case III			
Eastern Kentucky	1.50	21.6	15.0
Lexington-Louisville	2.00	36.9	41.8
Northern City	2.50	41.5	43.2
Case IV			
Eastern Kentucky	1.50	8.4	11.0
Lexington-Louisville	2.25	37.3	35.7
Northern City	3.00	54.3	53.3
Case V			
Eastern Kentucky	$3.50	86.5	76.6
Lexington-Louisville	2.50	10.4	16.1
Northern City	1.50	3.1	7.3
Case VI			
Eastern Kentucky	1.50	9.1	10.8
Lexington-Louisville	3.50	84.2	78.3
Northern City	2.50	6.6	10.8
Case VII			
Eastern Kentucky	1.50	7.3	10.0
Lexington-Louisville	2.50	34.2	35.6
Northern City	3.50	58.5	54.5
Case VIII			
Eastern Kentucky	1.50	4.0	8.8
Lexington-Louisville	3.50	26.7	27.4
Northern City	5.50	69.2	63.8

tendency for females to leave Eastern Kentucky, with a great majority of the migrants preferring Lexington or Louisville to a northern city. As the wage spread becomes wider to the detriment of Eastern Kentucky, both males and females increasingly prefer to leave Eastern Kentucky. That both groups clearly prefer Lexington or Louisville to a northern city is seen by comparing Cases VI and VII, where the wage rates in Lexington and Louisville are reversed from that in the North, with Eastern Kentucky held constant.

The data in Table 10, which breaks down preferences by college-bound (CB) and non-college-bound (NCB) students, show that CB students are less attached to Eastern Kentucky than NCB students. They also indicate that CB students leaving Eastern Kentucky have a relatively greater preference for Lexington or Louisville than do NCB students, who are more inclined to move to industrial centers in the North. For example, even when wage rates are equal in all locations (Case I), approximately 33 per cent of the CB students would still prefer Lexington or Louisville; in the case where the Lexington-Louisville wage is highest (Case VI), 87 per cent of the CB students prefer these cities.

In the regression equations shown in Table 11, the proportion of students preferring to remain in a given location is related to the opportunity cost of remaining. An opportunity-cost unit is here defined by:

$$\frac{\text{wage in given location - wage in best alternative location}}{25}$$

Thus, the opportunity cost of remaining in Eastern Kentucky in Case I is 0; in Case II, -2; in Case III, -4; in Case IV, -6; and so forth. Similarly, the opportunity cost of remaining in a northern city in Case V is -8; in Case VI, -4; in Case VII, +4; and in Case VIII, +8.

For all students and for each subgroup of students, the degree of responsiveness to opportunity cost is high; in only three equations is R^2 less than .50. For each subgroup, the degree of responsiveness, or goodness of fit, is highest when the opportunity cost of living in a northern city is considered. Degree of responsiveness is lowest when considered from the perspective of Lexington or Louisville.

Although the students are generally responsive to wage differences, they are also influenced in their choice of location by where their friends and relatives have gone. About 50 per cent of the students, male (47 per cent) as well as female (50 per cent), are influenced by this factor. It is particularly noteworthy that 62 per cent of the NCB students are influenced by friends and relatives who have migrated, whereas this is the case for only 37 per cent of the CB students. The difference is probably a reflection of the more immediate need of NCB students for help in migration; the CB students can defer specific decisions in this regard, and college experiences will also give them more information on which to act.*

---

*Most of the CB students would not be severing regional ties by going to college. Slightly over 66 per cent of the CB students indicated that they intended to go to college in Eastern Kentucky. (This figure includes those intending to go to Eastern Kentucky University, which lies just outside the region proper.)

TABLE 10

Locational Preferences of Eastern Kentucky High School Seniors Under Differing Wage Structure Assumptions, by College-Bound (CB) and Non-College-Bound (NCB) Groups

Place	Wage	Relative Frequency of Preferences CB	NCB	Place	Wage	Relative Frequency of Preferences CB	NCB
Case I				*Case V*			
Eastern Kentucky	$1.50	61.7	67.2	Eastern Kentucky	$3.50	79.8	83.1
Lexington-Louisville	1.50	31.9	18.6	Lexington-Louisville	2.50	15.8	10.5
Northern City	1.50	6.4	14.2	Northern City	1.50	4.4	6.4
Case II				*Case VI*			
Eastern Kentucky	1.50	19.7	31.4	Eastern Kentucky	1.50	6.6	14.3
Lexington-Louisville	1.75	40.8	29.8	Lexington-Louisville	3.50	87.1	72.6
Northern City	2.00	39.4	38.8	Northern City	2.50	6.3	12.1
Case III				*Case VII*			
Eastern Kentucky	1.50	14.9	21.6	Eastern Kentucky	1.50	6.6	11.3
Lexington-Louisville	2.00	45.4	32.9	Lexington-Louisville	2.50	38.1	30.9
Northern City	2.50	39.7	45.5	Northern City	3.50	55.3	57.8
Case IV				*Case VIII*			
Eastern Kentucky	1.50	7.0	12.9	Eastern Kentucky	1.50	3.6	10.0
Lexington-Louisville	2.25	40.6	31.6	Lexington-Louisville	3.50	31.4	21.7
Northern City	3.00	52.4	55.5	Northern City	5.50	65.0	68.3

103

TABLE 11

**Regressions Relating Opportunity Cost (X) to Per Cent
of Students Preferring a Given Location (Y)**

	Regression Equation[a]	R^2	Beta Coefficient	t
All Students				
Eastern Kentucky	Y = 47.5 + 3.89X	.687	.82	3.63
	(1.07)			
Lexington-Louisville	Y = 46.1 + 4.15X	.534	.73	2.62
	(1.58)			
Northern City	Y = 31.8 + 4.46X	.830	.91	5.41
	(0.82)			
CB Students				
Eastern Kentucky	Y = 45.0 + 3.95X	.675	.82	3.53
	(1.12)			
Lexington-Louisville	Y = 51.4 + 4.39X	.557	.75	2.76
	(1.68)			
Northern City	Y = 30.0 + 4.78X	.799	.89	4.88
	(0.92)			
NCB Students				
Eastern Kentucky	Y = 50.9 + 3.90X	.705	.84	3.78
	(1.03)			
Lexington-Louisville	Y = 40.1 + 3.82X	.505	.71	2.47
	(1.55)			
Northern City	Y = 33.9 + 4.45X	.848	.92	8.79
	(0.77)			
Male Students				
Eastern Kentucky	Y = 53.1 + 4.56X	.722	.85	3.95
	(1.10)			
Lexington-Louisville	Y = 44.4 + 4.18X	.443	.67	2.18
	(1.91)			
Northern City	Y = 31.0 + 4.78X	.818	.90	5.20
	(0.91)			
CB Male Students				
Eastern Kentucky	Y = 50.7 + 4.46X	.704	.84	3.78
	(1.18)			
Lexington-Louisville	Y = 50.0 + 3.93X	.392	.63	1.97
	(2.00)			
Northern City	Y = 27.4 + 4.27X	.814	.90	5.13
	(0.83)			
NCB Male Students				
Eastern Kentucky	Y = 55.7 + 4.59X	.737	.86	.410
	(1.12)			
Lexington-Louisville	Y = 37.3 + 4.65X	.512	.72	2.51
	(1.85)			
Northern City	Y = 36.3 + 5.44X	.821	.91	5.24
	(1.04)			
Female Students				
Eastern Kentucky	Y = 43.2 + 3.42X	.642	.80	3.29
	(1.04)			
Lexington-Louisville	Y = 43.3 + 4.04X	.616	.79	3.10
	(1.30)			
Northern City	Y = 32.7 + 4.13X	.822	.91	5.26
	(0.79)			
CB Female Students				
Eastern Kentucky	Y = 39.2 + 3.46X	.627	.79	3.17
	(1.09)			
Lexington-Louisville	Y = 52.6 + 4.89X	.707	.84	3.81
	(1.29)			
Northern City	Y = 33.3 + 4.62X	.772	.88	4.51
	(1.02)			
NCB Female Students				
Eastern Kentucky	Y = 47.7 + 3.39X	.664	.81	3.44
	(0.98)			
Lexington-Louisville	Y = 41.7 + 3.13X	.452	.67	2.23
	(1.40)			
Northern City	Y = 32.3 + 3.58X	.876	.94	6.50
	(0.54)			

[a]Numbers in parentheses are standard errors.

These considerations may also explain why the regression equation with the best fit in Table 11 is that for NCB males.

In addition to analyzing preference patterns under various hypothetical conditions, it is instructive to know where the respondents actually expect to live. Responses in this regard were as follows:

Proportion Expecting to Live in:

	Lexington or Louisville	Eastern Kentucky	Outside Kentucky
Total	30%	30%	40%
Males	26%	29%	45%
Females	34%	31%	36%
CB	35%	32%	33%
NCB	25%	27%	48%

Expectations are specified for five years in the future to allow for graduation from college by the CB students. Seventy per cent of all students expect to reside outside of Eastern Kentucky, with 40 per cent expecting to live outside of Kentucky and 30 per cent expecting to live in Lexington or Louisville. Contrary to the usually accepted belief that poor regions lose a relatively large proportion of their better-educated people, 32 per cent of the CB students expect to reside in Eastern Kentucky, as contrasted with only 27 per cent of the NCB students. Male and NCB students are particularly inclined to leave the state, whereas female and CB students were more inclined to stay within the state and to live in Lexington or Louisville.

These findings have important implications for regional policy. First, they demonstrate that even in one of the most lagging of Appalachian areas, there is considerable willingness and readiness to move to areas which offer better economic opportunities.

Second, it is erroneous to believe that outmigrants from lagging rural regions prefer to go to big metropolitan areas, in this case in the North. There is a clear tendency to prefer intermediate areas between the lagging rural area and the northern metropolitan areas. Unfortunately, there is limited evidence that actual migration patterns do not conform to either preferences or expectations. Migration estimates based on a 1 per cent sample of employees covered by the Social Security System show that between 1960 and 1965, 500 persons left the Big Sandy Region for Lexington or Louisville, whereas the number of persons migrating to northern SMSA's was 2,400, of which 1,000 went to Ohio SMSA's and 300 to Detroit.[9] These figures refer, of course, to all covered employees and not to high school seniors. However, there is abundant evidence that migrants from Eastern Kentucky have tended for several decades to move primarily to Ohio cities.[10] The home, or "stem," family supports the family branches in northern urban-industrial areas, while the branch family also supports relatives who migrate from home by helping them find a job and place to live in the new community.[11] Brown and Hillery have noted that while this process has caused migration flows to follow the path of the first migrants, in the future "fewer migrants will be guided to destination areas primarily because family members are already located there, and migration will become more sensitive to the job market."[12] The results presented here indicate that although family considerations are still important in influencing migration paths, especially for those who do not go to college, there is, in fact, considerable sensitivity to relative wages in location preferences and expectations.

Finally, the results support policies which would divert rural outmigrants from big cities toward intermediate-size areas and which would give potential migrants skills and training to match job opportunities in intermediate-size areas, as well as comprehensive relocation assistance. In the present case, this would mean matching education and training programs in Eastern Kentucky with the job requirements of industries in Lexington or Louisville, where labor markets are tight. The question is not one of "moving out" people—in our market system, it is no more possible to compel mountain people to leave than it is possible to compel industry to move to the mountains—but it is a question of giving people viable alternatives and, therefore, the possibility of genuine choice.

SUMMARY AND CONCLUSIONS

Since 1965, a major effort has been made to help the people of Eastern Kentucky by means of regional development programs. The region has received a relatively high proportion of Appalachian Regional Commission funds,[13] and it has probably received considerably more money per capita from the Economic Development Administration than any comparable area in the country.[14] To date, these efforts have borne relatively little fruit. Yet, on balance, federal programs for Eastern Kentucky continue to emphasize development of the region's infrastructure rather than its people.

For example, some insight into the SOC-EOC structure (see pp. 73-75) of federal investment in Eastern Kentucky may be gained by comparing the outlays of OEO, HEW, and the Department of Labor to those of the Department of Commerce (which includes EDA), the Department of Transportation, and the Small Business Administration. The first three agencies clearly are oriented toward SOC programs, and the last three, toward EOC programs. In 1967, Eastern Kentucky received 46 per cent of the state EOC total but only 28 per cent of the SOC total.[15] In the first half of fiscal 1968, Eastern Kentucky received 50 per cent of the state EOC total but only 31 per cent of the SOC total. In 1967, the proportion of the SOC-EOC total going to SOC in the United States was 85 per cent; in Kentucky, 82 per cent; and in Eastern Kentucky, only 73 per cent. The situation was quite similar for the first half of fiscal 1968.

In addition to expanding human resource development programs in Eastern Kentucky, there is a clear need to link these programs to economic opportunities in growth centers outside the region. The evidence indicates that a substantial number of firms in Lexington and Louisville would cooperate in giving jobs to Eastern Kentuckians at relatively small expense to the government (indeed, the degree of cooperation from private firms seems to be inversely related to the amount of federal investment). Outmigration of Eastern Kentuckians to northern cities continues to be heavy, but there is clear evidence that a combination of improved human resource development and comprehensive relocation assistance could divert a large number of migrants to Lexington and Louisville. Such a program would be more efficient than present efforts to force-feed economic growth in Eastern Kentucky, and even more important, it would be consistent with the locational preferences of a substantial number of the people in Eastern Kentucky, especially if jobs continue to be lacking in their home communities.

NOTES

1. U.S. Bureau of Census, "Estimates of the Population of Counties and Metropolitan Areas, July 1, 1966: A Summary Report," *Current Population Reports, Series P-25, No. 427 (Washington, D.C.. Government Printing Office,* 1969), pp. 30 and 68.

2. See Mary Jean Bowman and W. Warren Haynes, *Resources and People in East Kentucky* (Baltimore: The Johns Hopkins Press, 1963).

3. Data supplied by the Appalachian Regional Commission.

4. Data supplied by the Kentucky Department of Economic Security.

5. Eli P. March, "Indicators of Appalachian Progress: Population and Income," *Appalachia,* Vol. 2, No. 6 (March, 1969), 24.

6. U.S. Bureau of the Census, "Projections of the Population of Metropolitan Areas: 1975," *Current Population Reports,* Series P-25, No. 415 (Washington, D.C.: Government Printing Office, 1969), p. 17; "1970 Census of Population Preliminary Report PC(P2)-107" (Lexington: U.S. Bureau of the Census, 1970).

7. Data supplied by the Kentucky Department of Economic Security.

8. The survey is part of Richard YuKhin's doctoral dissertation, now in the process of completion at the University of Kentucky, Lexington.

9. Data supplied with the cooperation of David Hirschberg, Office of Business Economics, U.S. Department of Commerce.

10. James S. Brown and George A. Hillery, Jr., "The Great Migration, 1940-1960," in Thomas R. Ford, ed., *The Southern Appalachian Region* (Lexington: University of Kentucky Press, 1962), pp. 54-78.

11. James S. Brown, Harry K. Schwarzweller, and Joseph Mangalam, "Kentucky Mountain Migration and the Stem-Family: An American Variation on a Theme by LePlay," *Rural Sociology,* Vol. 28, No. 1 (March, 1963), pp. 48-69.

12. Brown and Hillery, *op. cit.,* p. 76.

13. "Appalachian Regional Commission Annual Report, 1968" (Washington, D.C.: Appalachian Regional Commission, 1969), pp. 117-53.

14. Economic Development Administration, *Jobs for America, Economic Development Administration Annual Report, Fiscal 1969* (Washington: Government Printing Office, 1970), p. 150.

15. Data in this section based on estimates supplied by the Office of Economic Opportunity. See Niles M. Hansen, *Rural Poverty and the Urban Crisis* (Bloomington: Indiana University Press, 1970), pp. 92-95.

6

THE
PIEDMONT
CRESCENT

Wilbur Thompson has written:

While the remote small one-industry town would seem to be highly vulnerable, even obsolete, in a country which has achieved an advanced stage of economic development, an interesting and perhaps highly significant exception may exist. A number of small and medium size urban areas, connected by good highways and/or other transportation facilities may form a loose network of interrelated labor markets. . . . This federated local economy may achieve the minimum size necessary to activate the urban size ratchet effect, . . . preserving the *collective* existence of these smaller urban places.[1]

THE NORTH CAROLINA PIEDMONT

"Some evidence of this pattern," he notes, "can be seen in North Carolina, a state filled with small and medium size urban areas, where a research and development triangle is being created in the Chapel Hill-Durham-Raleigh triangle, fifteen to thirty miles on a side, and enclosing about a quarter of a million people."[2]

The triangle of which Thompson writes is part of an even larger polynucleated urban region, the Piedmont Crescent, which includes, in North Carolina, five SMSA's (Raleigh, Durham, Greensboro-High Point, Winston-Salem, and Charlotte) and a number of smaller towns (*e.g.*, Burlington, Thomasville, Lexington, Salisbury, Gastonia) (see Map 3). The Bureau of the Census estimates that between 1960 and 1965, the population of the United States grew by 8.1 per cent, while that in SMSA's grew by 9.1 per cent. During

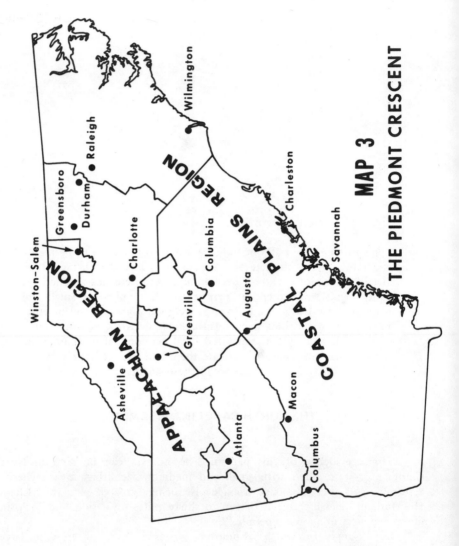

MAP 3

THE PIEDMONT CRESCENT

APPALACHIAN REGION

PLAINS REGION

COASTAL

Winston-Salem

Greensboro

Durham

Raleigh

Charlotte

Asheville

Greenville

Columbia

Augusta

Macon

Atlanta

Columbus

Wilmington

Charleston

Savannah

the same period, the SMSA's of the North Carolina Piedmont had the following estimated percentage growth rates: Raleigh, 15.7; Charlotte, 14.7; Durham, 9.8; Winston-Salem, 9.5; and Greensboro-High Point, 8.1.[3] In other words, four of the SMSA's grew more rapidly than the national average for SMSA's, and the fifth grew at the same rate as the nation's total population. Further evidence of the importance of Piedmont SMSA's is provided by a factor analysis of the Southeast's socio-economic development, where Piedmont cities show a strong affinity to the economic growth center factor. Variables loading highly on the factor, which has only positive loadings, are construction, business services, and financial and professional employment, all indicative of a rapidly growing economy.[4]

While there is no evidence that the Piedmont Crescent will become an enormous urban area in the foreseeable future, there is evidence of a high degree of interaction among Crescent cities. Commodity flow studies give a fairly strong indication of interaction at the preretail level, reflecting characteristics often associated with metropolitan areas. The economic integration of the area is also indicated by the patterns of branch banking and labor mobility, as well as growth along the Interstate Highway System.[5] The most thorough analysis of the Crescent tentatively concludes that "while the distances involved in the belt-like physical spread of urban development effectively preclude the Crescent from becoming one metropolis, nevertheless, there is every indication that, barring conscious efforts otherwise, this area is destined to become continuously urbanized."[6]

Studies of the adaptation of migrants to Crescent cities show that "the characteristics of life in these cities have not prevented them from achieving a reasonably contented existence. This, in view of the prevailing notions in some circles about 'the City' and its alleged malevolent effects on the human spirit, is an important finding."[7] A major reason for the successful adaption of migrants to the Crescent is that most are from the Southeast and find that they do not have to make many serious readjustments in their ordinary routines of living. Many newcomers also are able to maintain frequent contacts with friends and relatives who live relatively nearby. Increasingly high levels of educational attainment are another factor in easing adaptation for migrants both from the Southeast and from elsewhere.[8]

Nearly forty years ago, Rupert Vance wrote:

The diffused pattern of urbanization now taking shape in the Piedmont has much to commend it to the regionalist. . . . While the South develops the small city, the medium city, and a few large cities, it need not produce the metropolis. Thus it may avoid traffic congestion, the creation of slum areas, the loss of time going to and from work, and the corrupt and inefficient municipal housekeeping almost inevitably attached to over-developed population centers. If such a program is possible, the South may finally attain many of the advantages of contemporary industrialization without suffering its accompanying deficiencies and maladjustments.[9]

An eminent student of the region concludes that despite problems occasioned by the growth that has taken place in the intervening years, "this opportunity for a happier solution to the Piedmont's problems of growth than has been achieved in other sections of the country still exists today."[10]

MIGRATION AND HUMAN
RESOURCE DEVELOPMENT

The Appalachian counties of western North Carolina, which do not include the Piedmont, have been at least implicitly encouraged by the regional commission approach to solve their problems within the context of their own area. Similarly, the counties of eastern North Carolina have been grouped together to form a part of the area for which the Coastal Plains Regional Commission is responsible. This Commission, which also includes eastern South Carolina and eastern Georgia, was created by the Public Works and Economic Development Act of 1965 and is patterned in structure after the Appalachian Regional Commission. Thus, its activities are likewise to be carried out within the perspective of its own domain. However, C. E. Bishop suggests that relocation assistance that attempts to guide migration to the Piedmont Crescent would have a greater payoff than efforts to attract economic activity to the lagging areas on either side or to increase education at all levels. In North Carolina, he writes, "we are trying to alter the migration pattern. Instead of having our people concentrate in New York, Washington, or Philadelphia, we are attempting to encourage a shift into the Piedmont from the Coastal Plains."[11]

The North Carolina Mobility Project was carried out under a provision of the 1963 amendments to the Manpower Development and Training Act authorizing creation of small pilot relocation projects for unemployed workers. The goal of the North Carolina project was to demonstrate that unemployed persons in economically depressed rural areas of the state could be employed satisfactorily in the Piedmont. Over 90 per cent of the relocatees were nonwhites from thirty eastern counties, the rest being from twelve Appalachian counties. The unemployment rate in these forty-two counties rose from 5.5 per cent in 1960 to 5.9 per cent in 1967; meanwhile, in the demand-area counties, the rate declined from 3.6 per cent to 2.9 per cent.

An analysis comparing relocatees and a control group of nonrelocatees[12] indicated that the project increased total migration, though its effect on net outmigration was less clear. It was estimated that only 33.6 per cent of relocated workers would be retained in the demand area for at least one year; however, this was still greater than the control group outmigration rate of 16 per cent. It was clear that the project was influential in rechanneling the migration stream. All relocatees were within North Carolina, whereas 62 per cent of the control group movers went to other states. The latter value is in accord with an estimate that 75 per cent of the nonwhites who left the supply area counties during the 1955 to 1960 period migrated to points out of North Carolina. Relocatees had significantly higher earnings than the control group, a consequence of both higher earnings per unit time employed and more regular employment. However, the increase in employment and earnings was dependent on the relocatees' staying in the demand area; relocatees who returned home fared worse in employment and earnings than the control group. On balance, despite difficulties, the project did "clearly demonstrate that assisted relocation can play an important role in reducing poverty among the rural poor."[13]

Most of the workers relocated by the North Carolina Mobility Project were employed in textiles and furniture. The data in Table 12 show that in 1960, the textile sector accounted for over 50 per cent of all manufacturing employment in the North Carolina Piedmont. The employment projections shown in Table 12 indicate declines for the tobacco, textile, and lumber sectors in the North Carolina Piedmont; the combined employment in these sectors accounted for slightly over 60 per cent of all manufacturing employment in 1960.

It is apparent that in the past, relatively slow-growing industries have been attracted to the Crescent by its abundance of cheap labor. If the area is to attract a larger share of capital-intensive, high-wage, fast-growing sectors it will be necessary to upgrade the education and skills of the labor force.

By nearly every means of measuring the quantity and quality of education, the South falls short of the national average; Georgia, North Carolina and South Carolina fall short of the regional average; and the Piedmont Crescent falls short of the average for these three states of which it is a part. For instance, nationwide in 1960, the median level of formal schooling among residents 25 years and older was 10.6 years. For the South it was 9.3 years; for Georgia, 9.0 years; North Carolina, 8.9 years; and South Carolina, 8.7 years. In the Piedmont, the median was 8.5 years—more than two years below the national figure.[14]

In addition, the illiteracy rate in the Piedmont Crescent, again including the relevant portions of South Carolina and Georgia, was two and a half times the national rate. The dropout rate for young persons between fourteen and seventeen years of age is almost twice the national rate, and the three states as a whole rank at the very bottom with respect to percentage of young men passing the Selective Service mental test. In any discussion of education in these states, two fundamental problems always appear: the need for much more money and the need to equalize educational opportunities.[15] Real progress is being made, but a still greater effort is required if economic opportunity is to be improved by upgrading the Piedmont's industry mix. "One of the really significant challenges posed by the development of the Crescent," C. E. Bishop and F. A. Mangum conclude, "is whether the surrounding areas will train and send into the Crescent people who have the qualifications to upgrade the area's industry, or whether large numbers of people who have little or no marketable skills will migrate into the urban complexes of the Piedmont as they have to many of the cities in the northern part of the United States. The Piedmont Crescent will grow, but how it will grow depends to a large degree on the programs we develop to make the area a desirable place to live."[16]

TABLE 12

Projected Manufacturing Employment for North Carolina and the Piedmont Crescent in North Carolina

Industry	North Carolina			North Carolina Piedmont		
	1960	1975	Per Cent Change	1960	1975	Per Cent Change
Food	29,610	44,770	51.2	16,463	22,877	39.0
Tobacco	34,960	33,010	(-) 5.6	16,641	13,864	(-) 16.7
Textile	236,540	217,620	(-) 8.0	202,951	193,247	(-) 4.8
Apparel	36,800	69,210	88.1	24,030	41,526	72.8
Lumber	31,200	27,490	(-) 11.9	15,132	14,845	(-) 1.9
Furniture	42,490	67,620	59.1	37,051	61,196	65.2
Paper and Publishing	14,520	21,190	45.9	11,195	18,372	64.1
Printing	9,970	15,030	50.7	6,889	11,062	60.6
Chemicals	14,460	21,850	51.1	9,182	14,836	61.6
Petroleum	310	540	74.2	126	302	140.0
Rubber	2,260	4,990	120.8	1,950	4,402	107.3
Leather	1,040	1,730	66.3	615	1,323	24.0
Stone, Clay, Glass	9,860	19,590	98.7	6,567	12,400	88.8
Primary Metals	2,380	2,710	13.9	1,923	2,260	17.5
Fabricated Metals	8,010	19,140	138.9	6,544	14,010	114.1
Nonelectric Machinery	11,850	21,040	77.5	9,444	17,042	80.5
Electric Machinery	24,310	53,490	120.0	16,604	43,113	160.0
Transportation Equipment	3,610	7,700	113.3	1,523	4,335	184.6
Instruments	670	1,880	180.6	543	1,523	180.5
Miscellaneous Manufacturing	2,080	2,570	23.6	1,419	1,444	1.8
Ordnance			—			—
Total, All Industries	516,930	653,170	26.4	386,792	493,619	27.6
Total, Growth Industries	245,430	402,540	64.0	152,068	271,663	78.6

Source: James G. Maddox, ed., *Growth Prospects of the Piedmont Crescent* (Raleigh: North Carolina State University Agricultural Policy Institute, 1968), p. 109.

THE RELEVANCE OF PIEDMONT SMSA'S
TO APPALACHIA AND THE COASTAL PLAINS

Although the foregoing discussion has concentrated on the North Carolina Piedmont, the Piedmont Crescent is frequently defined to include not only the North Carolina SMSA's already mentioned, but also Greenville, South Carolina; and Atlanta, Columbus, and Macon, Georgia. The data in Table 13 show that population growth in each of these SMSA's has been greater than that in the Crescent as a whole. Despite their rapid growth, none of these cities has been designated by the Economic Development Administration as a growth center, though each is either in or close to Appalachia or the Coastal Plains. On the other hand, the three relevant states have fourteen multicounty districts, each having a designated economic development center. (See Table 14.)

With the exception of Atlanta, two of the Piedmont Crescent SMSA's had 1960 populations of somewhat over 250,000 (Greenville, 255,806; and Charlotte, 316,781). The rest varied between 111,000 and 246,000. Thus, most of the SMSA's in the Crescent would have been able to qualify as development centers; with the exception of Atlanta, any of them would be able to qualify with only a relatively small change in the 250,000 population limitation set by the Public Works and Economic Development Act of 1965. Evidence that they are, in fact, relatively efficient growth centers—in the sense of providing jobs for residents of lagging areas—is given in Table 15.

The migration estimates presented in the third row of Table 15 pertain to the polynucleated urban region extending from Raleigh to Greenville. This core area, the Piedmont Industrial Crescent, is an intermediate urban area in the sense employed earlier. The total population of the SMSA's in this region is not much above that of the combined EDA development centers in the three states under discussion. However, the Industrial Crescent SMSA's are providing substantially more jobs to Appalachian and Coastal Plains residents. In relation to their own population, the Industrial Crescent SMSA's are providing 51.1 jobs per 1000 inhabitants, whereas the comparable value for the EDA development centers is only 25.7. If the Georgia SMSA's of Columbus and Macon are included, the SMSA value is still a relatively high 42.0, which is approximately the same as that for Atlanta.

The average income estimates shown in Table 16 indicate that the greatest gains were made by migrants to Atlanta. In this case, the increase was 86 per cent, as compared with 69 per cent for the EDA development centers and 57 per cent for the other SMSA's, irrespective of whether Columbus and Macon are included. These gains, of course, reflect increases over time, as well as differences attributable to location; however, differences in percentage change values are reflections of locational differences. Excluding Atlanta, it should be noted that the 1965 values (Column 10) are not very different for SMSA's and the development centers. The higher rate of increase for the migrants to development centers is primarily related to their lower incomes in 1960.

In general, then, an efficient growth center strategy would put greater emphasis on relating problems in the lagging areas under discussion to job

TABLE 13

Growth in Population of the Piedmont Crescent and Crescent SMSA's, 1940-66

Area	Population		Per Cent Increase
	1940	1966	
Piedmont Crescent	4,099,000	6,081,000	48.4
Charlotte, N.C.[a]	151,826	325,717	114.5
Durham, N.C.	80,244	121,179	51.0
Greensboro and High Point, N.C.	153,916	271,665	76.5
Raleigh, N.C.	109,544	200,362	82.9
Winston-Salem, N.C.	126,475	214,811	69.8
Greenville, S.C.[b]	136,580	233,800	71.2
Atlanta, Ga.	558,842	1,261,700	125.8
Columbus, Ga.[c]	75,494	158,100	109.4
Macon, Ga.[d]	83,783	147,800	76.4

[a] Excludes Union County, N.C.

[b] Excludes Pickens County, S.C.

[c] Excludes Russell County, Ala.

[d] Excludes Houston County, Ga.

Source: James G. Maddox, ed., *Growth Prospects of the Piedmont Crescent* (Raleigh: North Carolina State University Agricultural Policy Institute, 1968), p. 15.

TABLE 14

Economic Development Centers in
Georgia, South Carolina, and North Carolina

EDA District	Number of Counties	Economic Development Centers[a]
Central Savannah River	13	Augusta-Swainsboro, Ga.
Coastal	6	Brunswick-Hinesville, Ga.
Coastal Plain	9	Valdosta-Tifton, Ga.
Georgia Mountains	14	Gainesville-Toccoa, Ga.
Heart of Georgia	9	Dublin, Ga.
Northeast	9	Athens, Ga.
Oconee	7	Milledgeville, Ga.
Slash Pine	9	Waycross, Ga.
Southwest	13	Albany-Bainbridge, Ga.
West Central	8	Americus, Ga.
Southeastern	10	Wilmington-Fayetteville, N.C.
Savannah	4	Aiken, S.C.
Pee Dee	6	Florence-Darlington, S.C.
Upper Savannah	6	Greenwood, S.C.

[a] This list includes all relevant centers designated through March, 1969.

Source: Data supplied by the Economic Development Administration.

TABLE 15

Estimated Migration from Appalachia and the Coastal Plains to SMSA's in the Piedmont Crescent and to EDA Economic Development Centers in Georgia, South Carolina, and North Carolina, 1960-65

Area	(1) Population in 1960 (thousands)	(2) Migrants from Appalachia	(3) (2)÷(1)	(4) Migrants from Coastal Plains	(5) (4)÷(1)	(6) (2)+(4)	(7) (6)÷(1)
Atlanta	1,017	24,000	23.6	19,500	19.2	43,500	42.8
Other Piedmont SMSA's	1,556	35,000	22.5	30,400	19.5	65,400	42.0
Other Piedmont SMSA's, Excluding Macon and Columbus	1,157	32,600	28.2	26,500	22.9	59,100	51.1
EDA Development Centers	1,075	10,900	10.1	18,700	17.4	29,600	27.5

Sources: Column 1: U.S. Bureau of the Census, *County and City Data Book, 1967;* Columns 2-7: Estimates based on 1 per cent Social Security sample data (see Appendix).

118

TABLE 16

Estimated Average Income Change for Migrants from Appalachia and the Coastal Plains to SMSA's in the Piedmont Crescent and to EDA Economic Development Centers in Georgia, South Carolina, and North Carolina, 1960-65

SENDING AREAS (1950)

RECEIVING AREAS (1965)	Appalachia				Coastal Plains				Appalachia and Coastal Plains			
	(1) 1960 Income	(2) 1965 Income	(3) Change	(4) Per Cent Change	(5) 1960 Income	(6) 1965 Income	(7) Change	(8) Per Cent Change	(9) 1960 Income	(10) 1965 Income	(11) Change	(12) Per Cent Change
Atlanta	2,180	4,147	1,967	93.0	2,317	4,188	1,871	80.8	2,241	4,165	1,924	85.9
Other Piedmont SMSA's	2,619	4,114	1,495	57.1	2,252	3,549	1,297	57.6	2,448	3,851	1,403	57.3
Other Piedmont SMSA's, Excluding Macon and Columbus	2,664	4,143	1,479	55.5	2,238	3,581	1,343	60.0	2,473	3,891	1,418	57.3
EDA Development Centers	2,798	4,512	1,714	61.3	2,050	3,585	1,535	74.9	2,325	3,926	1,601	68.9

Source: Estimates based on 1 per cent Social Security sample data (see Appendix).

opportunities in the Piedmont Crescent. While there does not appear to be any income advantage for migrants going from lagging regions to Piedmont Crescent SMSA's relative to those going to EDA development centers (unless Atlanta were to be included for policy purposes), there are many more jobs for migrants in the Crescent SMSA's.

In addition to comparing the Piedmont SMSA's to EDA growth centers, it is also useful for policy purposes to compare them to other SMSA's. Their performance in this regard may be evaluated in large measure in light of the data presented in Tables 17 and 18, which list SMSA's with potential relevance to Appalachia and the Coastal Plains, respectively.

The rankings given in these tables were made by N. Dann Milne in a report prepared for the Economic Development Administration.[17] They are not derived from any simplistic formula but are based on informed judgment concerning the observations in the tables. Because of the subjective element, the reader may find the data more important than the rankings. Nevertheless, any attempt to improve Milne's rankings should consider the factors which went into his analysis.

A growth center is defined as a place which generates new employment. However, to be useful for policy purposes, it should have strong ties to the target hinterland population. In analyzing new job creation and its significance for migrants from lagging areas, the following variables were used: employment growth, migration from lagging region to the center, migration in relation to center population, percentage employment change, and the unemployment rate.

The migrant per population of center ratio was used to show the relative attraction of a city abstracting from city size. Absolute migration was also considered as a lesser measure of this impact.

The variables studied with respect to migrants' incomes were salary increase of migrants and SMSA mean income. Because realization of a potentially high salary requires that an individual obtain employment, these variables were used only in differentiating between centers that were closely comparable (i.e., they had little weight in the selection process).

This method considers employment creation as the most significant characteristic for determining growth centers, though this growth should be creating jobs for the people of lagging regions. Also, to be considered as a growth center, employment had to be growing at least as fast as the national average, which was 19.6 per cent for the five-year period 1962-67.

The selection process was restricted to SMSA's, though non-SMSA counties were considered. The non-SMSA counties generally do not possess the qualities needed by a growth center. They lack a broad range of services, externalities, and opportunities for economies of scale and agglomeration. Only eleven counties throughout the United States, when related to regional commission areas (these include Appalachia, the Coastal Plains, the Four Corners, the Ozarks, and the Upper Great Lakes; South Texas also is included though it has no regional commission), were having as great an attractive force on migrants as Milne's selections, and they generally were not creating the same number of new jobs as the SMSA's. Non-SMSA counties also generate relatively few spread effects, and they have lower median per capita incomes. Of the nine

TABLE 17

Growth Centers for the Appalachian Region

Ranking[a]	Migrant/ Population (x 100)	City	(1) Per Cent Employment Change 1962-67	(2) Employment Increase 1962-67	(3) Mean Per Capita Income[b] 1966	(4) Migrants from Region 1960-65	(5) Per Cent Income Increase of Migrants
1.	5.54	Knoxville, Tenn.[c]	19.93	17,087	$2,557	20,600	28.7
2.	5.40	Harrisburg, Pa.	23.52	21,983	$2,872	20,100	65.0
3.	4.57	Greenville, S.C.	36.57	28,188	$2,778	11,700	77.8
	4.46	Charleston, W. Va.	[18.15]	11,246	$2,861	11,300	50.3
4.	4.41	Huntsville, Ala.	119.37	29,112	$2,421	6,800	75.4
5.	2.88	Lexington, Ky.	50.21	18,598	$2,992	3,800	49.9
	2.86	Steubenville-Weirtown, O.-W. Va.	[8.13]	3,805	$2,854	4,800	59.4
6.	2.71	Sullivan [County], Tenn.[c, d]	28.44	20,072		3,100	90.4
9.	2.47	Gadsden, Ala.	28.15	[5,057]	$2,305	2,400	53.6
	2.38	Asheville, N.C.	33.24	11,234	$2,483	3,100	76.2
7.	2.36	Atlanta, Ga.	38.63	125,760	$3,247	24,000	90.2
8.	2.24	Raleigh, N.C.	38.97	16,050	$2,709	3,800	33.0
11.	2.11	Chattanooga, Tenn.	29.83	23,924	$2,788	6,000	52.5
13.	2.10	Spartanburg [County], S.C.[e]	31.89	13,157		3,300	48.5
14.	2.10	Montgomery, Ala.	27.88	10,177	$2,310	4,200	33.8
10.	2.04	Nashville, Tenn.	33.26	43,631	$2,807	9,500	53.7

(continued)

TABLE 17 (continued)

Ranking[a]	Migrant/ Population (x 100)	City	(1) Per Cent Employment Change 1962-67	(2) Employment Increase 1962-67	(3) Mean Per Capita Income[b] 1966	(4) Migrants from Region 1960-65	(5) Per Cent Income Increase of Migrants
15.	2.01	Roanoke, Va.	28.60	12,809	$2,855	3,200	3.2
	2.01	Tuscaloosa, Ala.	[14.61]	2,712	$1,850	2,200	76.8
	2.00	Huntington-Ashland, W. Va.-Ky.-O.	[16.37]	9,050	$2,561	5,100	51.0
	1.97	Binghamton, N.Y.-Pa.	[17.14]	13,104	$3,097	5,600	105.1
	1.89	Altoona, Pa.[c]	23.01	[6,304]	$2,465	2,600	82.9
12.	1.84	Greensboro-High Point-Winson Salem, N.C.	20.71	37,533	$2,975	9,600	60.8
	1.84	Wilkes Barre-Hazleton, Pa.	[16.33]	13,652	$2,318	6,400	49.3
16.	1.83	Charlotte, N.C.	30.36	34,445	$3,158	5,800	37.5
	1.63	Erie, Pa.	23.37	77,932	$3,005	4,100	43.2
	1.58	Jackson, Miss.	26.49	13,744	$2,497	3,500	92.2
	1.57	Scranton, Pa.	[9.74]	4,968	$2,533	3,700	29.0

[a]Ranked by migrants per population ratio. The condemning statistic in the selection process is shown in brackets. Subsequent choices are shown but not numbered in most cases.

[b]National SMSA mean per capita income for the period (1966) was $2,968.

[c]EDA growth center.

[d]Contains Bristol-Kingsport-Johnson City, Tennessee.

[e]Contains Spartanburg, S.C.

Sources: Columns 1 and 2, U.S. Department of Commerce, Office of Business Economics, County Business Patterns, U.S. Summary 1962-67; column 3, U.S. Department of Commerce, Office of Business Economics, U.S. Department of Commerce News, August 26, 1968; columns 4 and 5, 1 per cent Social Security sample data (see Appendix).

TABLE 18

Growth Centers for the Coastal Plains Region

Ranking[a]	Migrant/ Population (x 100)	City	(1) Per Cent Employment Change 1962-67	(2) Employment Increase 1962-67	(3) Mean Per Capita Income[b] 1966	(4) Migrants from Region 1960-65	(5) Per Cent Income Increase of Migrants
1.	3.72	Raleigh, N.C.	38.97	16,050	$2,709	6,300	82.9
	3.30	Albany, Ga.[c]	31.26	4,790	$2,409	2,700	60.1
4.	2.50	Durham, N.C.	31.42	11,938	$2,364	2,800	89.2
3.	2.30	Columbia, S.C.	32.17	17,147	$2,565	6,000	42.7
2.	2.14	Charlotte, N.C.	30.36	34,445	$3,158	6,800	45.5
	2.06	Wilmington, N.C.[c]	25.05 [18.10]	4,942	$2,251	1,900	62.8
	1.96	Savannah, Ga.	38.63	7,338	$2,481	3,700	57.3
	1.92	Atlanta, Ga.	38.63	125,760	$3,247	19,500	80.7
	1.66	Augusta, Ga.-S.C.	40.70	18,817	$2,604	3,600	76.3

[a] Ranked by migrants per population ratio. The condemning statistic in the selection process is shown in brackets. Subsequent choices are shown but not numbered in most cases.

[b] National SMSA mean per capita income for the period (1966) was $2,968.

[c] EDA growth center.

Sources: Columns 1 and 2, U.S. Department of Commerce, Office of Business Economics, *County Business Patterns*, U.S. Summary 1962-67; column 3, U.S. Department of Commerce, Office of Business Economics, *U.S. Department of Commerce News*, August 26, 1968; columns 4 and 5, 1 per cent Social Security sample data (see Appendix).

counties that were attracting more migrants from the Appalachian Region than the lowest of the fourteen selected SMSA's shown in Table 17, only two were creating as many jobs as the lowest selected SMSA. Because Sullivan County, Tennessee (creating 20,072 jobs), and Spartanburg County, South Carolina (creating 13,197 jobs), met all of the criteria of migration, growth rates, and job creation, they were given consideration as potential growth centers even though they were not SMSA's. However, with these two exceptions, other non-SMSA areas related to Appalachia did not have the attributes of a growth center.

The rankings in Tables 17 and 18 show that Piedmont SMSA's are highly relevant to Appalachia, as well as to the Coastal Plains. Raleigh, Charlotte, and Atlanta are making a significant contribution to people from *both* regions, though the rankings in the respective tables do not take account of this dual role.

SUMMARY AND CONCLUSIONS

The SMSA's of the Piedmont Crescent represent promising growth centers with relevance to the people of Appalachia and the Coastal Plains. Unfortunately, the potential opportunities offered by these cities are not being fully exploited because federal policy is focused on programs to promote growth in the lagging regions on either side. Both the Appalachian and the Coastal Plains Regional Commissions are working to upgrade the quality of human resources in their respective areas, but there are no systematic efforts to assist migration to opportunities in the Piedmont. Yet there is ample evidence that migration streams can be rechanneled away from northern cities toward the Piedmont and that assisted migration can play an important role in reducing poverty among the poor in the lagging regions.

NOTES

1. Wilbur R. Thompson, *A Preface to Urban Economics* (Baltimore: The Johns Hopkins Press, 1965), p. 34.

2. *Ibid.*, p. 35.

3. U.S. Bureau of the Census, "Projections of the Population of Metropolitan Areas: 1975," *Current Population Reports*, Series P-25, No. 415 (Washington, D.C.: Government Printing Office, 1969), pp. 15-18.

4. Truman Hartshorn, "Toward a Factorial Ecology of the Southeast: The Spatial Structure of Socio-Economic Development, 1950-1960" (unpublished paper).

5. Ralph W. Pfouts, "Patterns of Economic Interaction in the Crescent," in F. Stuart Chapin, Jr., and Shirley F. Weiss, eds., *Urban Growth Dynamics in a Regional Cluster of Cities* (New York: John Wiley & Sons, 1962), pp. 31-58; F. Stuart Chapin, Jr., "Policy Implications of Research Findings," in Chapin and Weiss, eds., *op. cit.*, pp. 463-64.

6. *Ibid.*, pp. 464-65.

7. John Gulick, Charles E. Bowerman, and Kurt W. Back, "Newcomer Enculturation in the City: Attitudes and Participation," in Chapin and Weiss, eds., *op. cit.*, p. 356.

8. *Ibid.*, p. 357.

9. Rupert B. Vance, *Human Geography of the South* (Chapel Hill: University of North Carolina Press, 1932), p. 507.

10. F. Stuart Chapin, Jr., "Introduction," in Chapin and Weiss, eds., *op. cit.*, p. 18.

11. C. E. Bishop, "City and Countryside: An Interdependent Future," *Appalachia*, Vol. 1, No. 8 (April, 1968), 11.

12. Charles K. Fairchild, "Rural Disadvantaged Mobility," *Labor Law Journal*, Vol. 20, No. 8 (August, 1969) 461-73.

13. *Ibid.*, p. 473.

14. Winfred L. Godwin, "The Educational Establishment in the Piedmont Crescent," in James G. Maddox, ed., *Growth Prospects of the Piedmont Crescent* (Raleigh: North Carolina State University Agricultural Policy Institute, 1968), p. 30.

15. *Ibid.*, pp. 30-31 and 38-39.

16. C. E. Bishop and F. A. Mangum, "The Crescent's Human Resources," in Maddox, *op. cit.*, pp. 26-27.

17. N. Dann Milne, "Selecting Growth Centers," Program on the Role of Growth Centers in Regional Economic Development Discussion Paper No. 6 (Austin: University of Texas Center for Economic Development, 1970).

7

As originally designated by the Secretary of Commerce on March 2, 1966, the Ozarks Region consisted of forty-four counties each in Arkansas and Missouri and thirty-seven counties in Oklahoma. On September 22, 1967, the Secretary of Commerce granted a request by the Governor of Kansas to include 9 counties in the southeastern corner of that state in the region, making a total of 134 (see Map 4). The 1960 population of the area was 2,700,000, with a large proportion still living in rural areas. In fact, only 40 per cent of the region's people lived in towns of 2500 or more, compared to a national proportion of 70 per cent.

Per capita income in 1960 in the Ozarks Region was $1,260, 68 per cent of the national average. Of the families in the Ozarks Region, 44 per cent had incomes of less than $3,000, the frequently used poverty level of income. The corresponding figure for the nation was 21 per cent. Not one county in the Ozarks Region had less than the national norm. The county closest to the national average, Pulaski County, Arkansas, had 26 per cent of its families with incomes of less than $3,000. In the same year, only 5 per cent of the Ozarks families had incomes greater than $10,000, compared to a national figure of 15 per cent.[1]

The low levels of income and development in the Ozarks Region are explained, in large measure, by its economic structure. The data in Table 19 show that agriculture continues to dominate the economy; 13.4 per cent of the area's labor force was in agriculture in 1960, compared to 6 per cent for the United States as a whole. Manufacturing employment in 1960 was dominated by such slow-growth, low-wage industry groups as lumber and furniture, textiles, and apparel. The ten-year change from 1950 shows little improvement in this respect. Projections for 1975 indicate that the industrial structure will become somewhat more diversified, but the region will continue to be dominated by slowly growing industries.

126

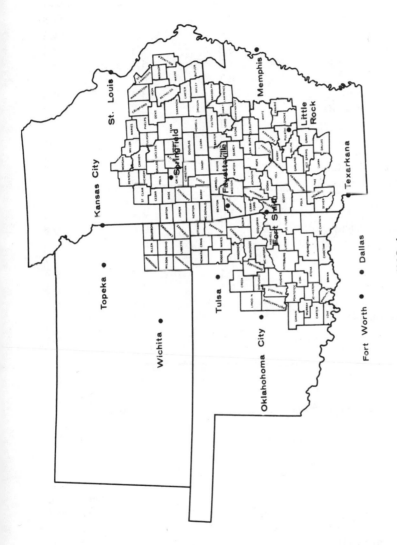

MAP 4

THE OZARKS REGION

TABLE 19

Employment in the Ozarks Region, 1950-75, by Type of Industry

Type of Industry	1950	1960	1975[a]
Trade, Wholesale and Retail	17.9	19.4	27.8
Services	13.8	15.7	19.3
Civilian Government	8.8	11.3	14.1
Miscellaneous Manufacturing	3.7	5.5	5.1
Construction	6.1	6.4	5.1
Agriculture	28.2	13.4	4.6
Finance-Insurance-Real Estate	1.9	2.9	3.5
Food Products	2.1	3.2	3.4
Armed Forces	0.2	3.8	3.2
Lumber and Furniture	4.3	4.0	3.0
Fabricated Textile Products	1.1	1.9	2.4
Transportation-Warehousing	4.6	3.9	2.1
Machinery	0.5	1.3	1.5
Mining	3.2	2.4	1.0
Aircraft, Ship, RR Equipment	0.1	0.6	0.8
Chemicals	0.4	0.6	0.8
Printing and Publishing	0.8	1.1	0.7
Utilities	1.1	1.3	0.6
Communications	1.1	1.0	0.5
Motor Vehicles	0.1	0.3	0.4
Textile Mill Products	0.1	0.2	0.1
	100.1[b]	100.2[b]	100.2[b]

[a] Projected.

[b] Components do not necessarily add to totals due to rounding.

Source: Ozarks Regional Commission, *Ozarks Region, An Opportunity for Growth*, 1967.

The underdevelopment of the Ozarks is also reflected in demographic data. In 1960, persons under five years of age accounted for 9.5 per cent of the total population while 13 per cent of the population was sixty-five years of age or older. The comparable national percentages were 11.3 per cent and 9.2 per cent.[2] Contributing to this unusual age structure was a net outmigration between 1950 and 1960 of 400,000 persons, a large percentage of whom were in the most productive age groups.

Low levels of educational attainment are among the region's greatest problems. In only 27 of the 134 counties was the median level of school years completed in 1960 more than nine years.[3] The comparable figure for the entire region was 9.3, reflecting the large gap in attainment levels between the few urban counties and the rural counties. The corresponding national figure was 10.6 years.

With respect to transportation facilities, the Ozarks Region has many deficiencies, though when completed, the Arkansas River Navigational System will undoubtedly bring about major improvements. The Interstate Highway System provides four-lane, limited-access service to only 35 of the 134 designated counties. The bypassed areas are served by an inadequate secondary road system and estimates of the costs of improving it are staggering.[4] The lack of rail transportation in many upland areas compounds the problems of the inadequate highway system. Limited commercial airline service is yet another problem; only four cities (Little Rock, Hot Springs, Fort Smith, and Springfield) are served by trunkline air routes, and only eleven cities and towns by regional airlines.[5]

Migration trends in the Ozarks also reflect the underdevelopment of the area. From 1960 to 1965, an estimated 185,000 persons moved from counties in the Ozarks Region. Of this total, 123,500 persons, or 66.7 per cent, migrated to counties outside the area.[6]

Tables 20 and 21 break down outmigration from the Ozarks region according to age and industry classifications, respectively. The selectivity of the movement out of the area is obvious. Of those leaving, 69.9 per cent are in the "under forty-five" category, indicating a severe loss of workers in their most productive years. Likewise, the types of jobs secured by these persons in their new places of residence suggest that they tend to be the more talented or skilled.

TABLE 20

Migrants from the Ozarks Region, 1960-65, by Age and Sex

Sex	Under 25 (Per Cent)	25 - 44 (Per Cent)	Over 45 (Per Cent)	Not Reported (Per Cent)	Total (Per Cent)
Male	11.7	36.4	18.5	—	66.6
Female	6.6	15.2	7.4	—	29.2
Not Reported	—	—	—	4.0	4.0
Total	18.3	51.6	25.9	4.0	99.8[a]

[a]Components do not add to 100 per cent due to rounding.

Source: Compiled from a 1 per cent sample of workers covered by the Social Security Administration (see Appendix).

TABLE 21

**Migrants from the Ozarks Region, 1960-65,
by Sector of Employment, 1965**

Sector	Percentage
Agriculture	3.2
Mining	2.1
Construction	7.9
Manufacturing	25.5
Transportation	6.3
Trade	23.9
Finance	3.4
Service	18.2
Government	5.3
Not Reported	4.0
Total	99.8[a]

[a]Components do not add to 100 per cent due to rounding.

Source: Compiled from a 1 per cent sample of workers covered by the Social Security Administration (see Appendix).

GROWTH CENTER POLICY IN THE OZARKS

In attacking the development problems of the Ozarks region, the Economic Development Administration has designated nine economic development centers in the region. These nine centers, which are shown in Table 22, are located within designated economic development districts. The Ozarks Regional Commission has a more elaborate designation procedure. It intends to "avoid the mistakes of the 'worst-first' policy, the shortsightedness of certain designatory practices, and probably generate the maximum amount of local, county, and regional support for all our programs."[7] All areas within

TABLE 22

EDA Growth Centers in the Ozarks, 1968

State	County	Urban Place
Arkansas	Boone	Harrison
	Crawford	Van Buren
	Garland	Hot Springs
	Pope	Russellville
	Sebastian	Fort Smith
	Washington	Fayetteville Springdale
Oklahoma	Creek	Sapulpa
Missouri	Butler Howell	Poplar Bluff West Plains
Kansas	—	—

Source: Data supplied by the Economic Development Administration.

the region have been classified by the Commission as either IMPACS (Immediate Project Absorptive Capability Areas) or HIPACS (High Project Absorptive Capability Areas). The Commission notes that HIPACS (growth centers) will tend to have larger populations, higher per capita incomes, and fewer problems of underdevelopment and underemployment than the surrounding areas. The Commission emphasizes, however, that the other areas are not ignored by its programs, functions, and objectives. Thus, it designates all remaining areas as IMPACS. If development opportunities appear in these areas, attempts will be made to exploit them.

The Ozarks Commission had designated thirty-three growth centers as of September, 1968. They were chosen by a procedure in which each county was evaluated according to nine characteristics. If the county scored in four or more categories, it was designated a growth center.* The designated counties and their respective principal urban places are listed in Table 23.

*The following characteristics were used by the Ozarks Regional Commission in arriving at its growth centers: (1) 10 per cent or more population increase, 1960-65; (2) basic trading area—same as chief city; (3) total employment increase between 1950 and 1960; (4) principal city over 5,000; (5) seventy-five or more Ranally retail sales units; (6) 25 per cent or more projected employment increase, 1960-70; (7) fifty or more Ranally manufacturing units; (8) 50 per cent or more projected personal income increase, 1960-70; and (9) $5 million or more increase in bank deposits, 1960-64.

TABLE 23

Growth Centers Designated by the Ozarks Regional Commission

State	County	Urban Place
Arkansas	Benton	Rogers
	Boone	Harrison
	Clark	Arkadelphia
	Crawford	Van Buren
	Faulkner	Conway
	Garland	Hot Springs
	Hot Springs	Malvern
	Pope	Russellville
	Pulaski	Little Rock
	Saline	Benton
	Sebastian	Fort Smith
	Washington	Fayetteville
	White	Searcy
Oklahoma	Carter	Ardmore
	Creek	Sapulpa
	Garvin	Pauls Valley
	Mayes	Pryor
	Muskogee	Muskogee
	Okmulgee	Okmulgee
	Ottawa	Miami
	Pittsburg	McAlester
	Pontotoc	Ada
	Rogers	Claremore
Missouri	Greene	Springfield
	Howell	West Plains
	Jasper	Jasper
	Miller	Eldon
	Newton	Neosho
	Phelps	Rolla
Kansas	Allen	Iola
	Crawford	Pittsburg
	Labette	Parsons
	Montgomery	Coffeyville

Source: Data supplied by the Ozarks Regional Commission.

Thus, there are thirty-four growth centers designated by EDA and the Ozarks Regional Commission (Butler County, Missouri, is the only EDA-designated center not likewise designated by the Ozarks Commission). These centers serve as the focus of public investment policy for the development of the Ozarks area. Table 24 presents population and employment growth data for the selected centers. One of their most striking characteristics is their relatively small size. Only two of the counties had a population of more than 100,000 in 1960, and only six had a population of more than 50,000. With these exceptions, the growth centers are basically rural, with only limited agglomeration economies and amenities. It should also be noted that six of the counties declined in population, and only nine had average yearly rates of increase of more than 2 per cent. Eleven centers had negative net migration. In general, growth potential is scarcely in evidence in these areas if population change is a critical evaluative factor.

Employment growth patterns for the period 1962-67 present a somewhat better picture. Although two counties exhibited negative employment changes, most of the counties showed reasonable employment increases. However, with the exception of Pulaski, Sebastian, and Greene counties, the large percentage increases represent only small absolute increases.

It is also interesting to analyze the manufacturing bases of these centers. Table 25 breaks down manufacturing employment according to fast-growth and slow-growth industries for 1967.[8] With only a few exceptions, manufacturing employment of the growth centers is weighted *heavily* toward slow-growth manufactures. Thus, past experience indicates that these areas are attracting those slow-growth, low-wage industries not conducive to rapid economic growth.

The tertiary sector (trade, finance, insurance, real estate, general government, and personal, professional, business, and repair services) has been the source of nearly all the net growth in employment in the United States since World War II. Table 26 gives the percentage of the total reported employment in such sectors for each growth center. It should be noted that this percentage overstates the percentage of total employment concentrated in the tertiary sector, since all but a few of these counties are basically rural, and farm workers are not included in reported employment. In only ten of the centers does the tertiary sector account for more than 50 per cent of the reported employment. With their relatively large urban populations, it would be expected that Pulaski and Greene counties would have a relatively high proportion of their total employment in the tertiary sector.

In general, the industrial composition of the growth centers chosen by EDA and the Ozarks Regional Commission has not been favorable to rapid future growth. With only rare exceptions, slow-growth sectors dominate the economic bases of these areas.

The interaction of an area with its surrounding hinterland is another important criterion by which to judge any potential growth center. Table 27 shows this interaction in terms of migration. It lists the twenty SMSA's and counties receiving the most migrants from the Ozarks Region. Most of the places exerting a large influence upon the Ozarks area, in terms of migrants received, lie outside the region or at its fringe. Only seven of the twenty top recipients are in the region and fifteen of the twenty are SMSA's.

TABLE 24

Growth Characteristics of EDA and Ozarks Regional Commission Growth Centers

State	County	Population 1960	Population 1966	Per Cent Change	Net Migration Change	Employment 1962	Employment 1967	Per Cent Change
Arkansas	Benton	36,272	43,800	20.8	6,000	6,912	10,921	58.0
	Boone	16,116	17,200	7.0	300	3,056	4,488	46.9
	Clark	20,950	22,800	9.0	800	3,249	4,219	30.0
	Crawford	21,318	24,200	13.6	1,300	1,903	2,011	5.7
	Faulkner	24,303	32,100	32.0	5,900	4,932	4,519	− 8.4
	Garland	46,697	51,300	9.8	3,200	11,625	14,171	21.9
	Hot Springs	21,893	22,300	2.1	− 700	3,905	3,694	− 5.4
	Pope	21,777	26,400	24.4	3,600	3,749	4,655	24.2
	Pulaski	242,980	280,000	15.2	11,800	63,145	84,181	33.3
	Saline	28,956	32,100	10.7	1,000	4,518	6,710	48.5
	Sebastian	66,685	73,600	10.3	a	21,892	29,046	32.7
	Washington	55,797	72,600	30.0	12,000[b]	10,970	16,808	53.2
	White	32,745	38,700	18.3	4,000	4,105	5,655	37.8
Oklahoma	Carter	39,044	37,800	− 3.3	− 2,800	6,950	8,200	18.0
	Creek	40,495	43,200	6.7	1,000	5,627	6,242	10.9
	Garvin	28,290	27,500	− 2.7	− 2,000	3,770	4,076	8.1
	Mayes	20,073	22,800	13.8	1,900	2,403	2,698	12.3
	Muskogee	61,866	62,100	0.3	− 2,500	10,456	11,664	11.6
	Okmulgee	36,945	36,500	− 1.2	− 1,700	5,612	6,325	12.7
	Ottawa	28,301	30,200	6.8	1,300	5,142	6,118	19.0
	Pittsburg	34,360	39,900	16.2	4,400	4,022	5,740	42.7
	Pontotoc	28,089	25,900	− 7.7	− 3,100	4,919	5,204	5.8
	Rogers	20,614	24,600	19.5	2,900	1,555	1,877	20.7

Missouri	Butler	34,656	35,500	2.3	- 500	2,998	4,059	35.4
	Greene	126,276	140,700	11.4	7,100[b]	30,429	39,804	30.8
	Howell	22,027	22,600	2.8	- 100	2,998	4,509	35.4
	Jasper	78,863	81,200	3.0	a	19,427	23,500	21.0
	Miller	13,800	14,700	6.6	300	2,129	2,213	3.9
	Newton	30,093	33,600	11.8	2,100	4,332	4,848	11.9
	Phelps	25,396	26,800	5.7	- 400	3,300	4,034	22.2
Kansas	Allen	16,369	15,300	- 6.8	- 1,300	2,498	2,634	5.4
	Crawford	37,032	40,000	8.0	2,600	6,034	7,363	22.0
	Labette	26,805	28,000	4.7	800	3,590	4,484	24.9
	Montgomery	45,007	40,300	-10.4	- 5,400	9,012	10,175	12.9

[a] Less than 50.

[b] Reflects changes in college population.

Sources: U.S. Bureau of the Census, *Current Population Reports*, Series P-25, No. 401, August 28, 1968, and No. 407, October 10, 1968; U.S. Bureau of the Census, *County Business Patterns*, 1962 and 1967.

TABLE 25

**Manufacturing Employment in Fast-Growth and
Slow-Growth Firms in Designated Growth Centers**

State	County	Per Cent of Manufacturing Employment in Fast-Growth Firms[a]	Per Cent of Manufacturing Employment in Slow-Growth Firms[a]
Arkansas	Benton	13.2	72.6
	Boone	.0	89.2
	Clark	10.6	63.9
	Crawford	.0	97.3
	Faulkner	22.8	52.6
	Garland	.0	67.2+[b]
	Hot Springs	.0	76.0
	Pope	.0	90.1
	Pulaski	32.1+[b]	46.7
	Saline	36.1+[b]	16.4
	Sebastian	26.9	63.4+[b]
	Washington	7.5	71.6
	White	43.2+[b]	53.5
Oklahoma	Carter	70.6	23.7
	Creek	.0	85.7
	Garvin	46.8	42.2
	Mayes	31.3	29.3
	Muskogee	16.1	73.6
	Okmulgee	7.5	84.9
	Ottawa	17.0	27.0
	Pittsburg	15.7	81.3
	Pontotoc	.0	98.6
	Rogers	.0	100.0
Missouri	Butler	.0	75.5
	Greene	17.9	60.6
	Howell	.0	90.5
	Jasper	22.4	61.8
	Miller	.0	88.1
	Newton	.0	55.3
	Phelps	.0	95.7
Kansas	Allen	21.3	85.9
	Crawford	22.7	79.9
	Labette	27.2	32.9
	Montgomery	49.2	47.3

[a] Only the number of reporting units in particular employee-size categories—not the exact number of employees—are available. Thus, the number of employees for each reporting unit is assumed to be the average for that particular employee-size category.

[b] Included here are reporting units of the category "500 or more."

Source: Compiled from U.S. Bureau of the Census, *County Business Patterns*, 1967.

TABLE 26

Tertiary Employment in Designated Growth Centers

State	County	Total Reported Employment 1967	Total in Tertiary Sector 1967	Per Cent of Total in Tertiary Sector
Arkansas	Benton	10,921	3,615	33.1
	Boone	4,488	1,926	43.0
	Clark	4,219	1,849	43.8
	Crawford	2,011	1,022	49.8
	Faulkner	4,519	2,052	45.4
	Garland	14,171	9,177	64.8
	Hot Springs	3,694	996	27.0
	Pope	4,655	1,888	40.6
	Pulaski	84,181	48,684	57.8
	Saline	6,710	1,492	22.2
	Sebastian	29,046	11,964	41.2
	Washington	16,808	7,507	44.7
	White	5,655	2,786	49.3
Oklahoma	Carter	8,200	3,992	48.7
	Creek	6,242	2,593	41.5
	Garvin	4,076	1,909	46.8
	Mayes	2,698	1,398	51.8
	Muskogee	11,664	5,761	49.4
	Okmulgee	6,325	2,711	42.9
	Ottawa	6,118	2,371	38.8
	Pittsburg	5,740	3,091	53.9
	Pontotoc	5,204	2,788	53.6
	Rogers	1,877	1,190	63.4
Missouri	Butler	5,425	3,594	66.2
	Greene	39,894	22,085	55.5
	Howell	4,049	1,862	46.0
	Jasper	23,500	10,649	45.4
	Miller	2,213	930	42.0
	Newton	4,848	2,082	43.0
	Phelps	4,034	2,437	60.4
Kansas	Allen	2,634	1,301	49.1
	Crawford	7,363	3,872	52.6
	Labette	4,484	2,094	46.7
	Montgomery	10,175	4,495	44.2

Source: Compiled from U.S. Bureau of the Census, *County Business Patterns*, 1967.

TABLE 27

Migration from the Ozarks to Highest-Ranking SMSA and County Receiving Areas, 1960-65

SMSA or County	Migrants
Oklahoma City, Okla.	10,900
Kansas City, Kan.	8,500
St. Louis, Mo.	7,500
Tulsa, Okla.	6,700
Little Rock, Ark.	6,200
Dallas, Tex.	3,900
Los Angeles, Calif.	3,200
Wichita, Kan.	2,800
Fort Smith, Ark.	2,500
Springfield, Mo.	2,400
Washington County, Ark.	1,800
Chicago, Ill.	1,700
Houston, Tex.	1,600
New Orleans, La.	1,600
Jasper County, Mo.	1,600
Jefferson County, Ark.	1,400
Denver, Colo.	1,300
Garland County, Ark.	1,300
Benton County, Ark.	1,300
Memphis, Tenn.	1,200

Source: Compiled from a 1 per cent sample of employees covered by the Social Security Administration (see Appendix).

ALTERNATIVE STRATEGIES FOR THE OZARKS

This section reviews and evaluates three alternative approaches to present growth center policy for the Ozarks.

The approach of John Kuehn and Lloyd Bender[9] accepts the legislative assumption that viable growth centers exist within economically lagging areas and are identifiable, or else that they can be created. The authors point out that they were not concerned with the issue of whether or not economic development centers within distressed areas would, in fact, contribute substantially to the growth of the entire region.

Kuehn and Bender begin by assuming that growth centers are atypical places in relation to neighboring areas and that apparently some change in their competitive advantage due to exogenous forces is occurring—or else they exhibit growth potential because they have reached a stage of development where externalities attract new economic activity. However, their objective "was clearly limited to designation of sites which offered potential for employment increases given the infrastructure already in place and the changing employment structure."[10] Their method of identifying potential growth centers is essentially shift-share analysis, which permits a description and comparison of the changing employment structure of geographic areas. Their key assumption is that "evidence of internal shifts in industrial composition of an area from a past traditional structure to different structures indicates emerging growth impetus."[11] Why internal employment shifts necessarily imply movement away from a "traditional structure" and why this necessarily implies favorable growth potential is not made clear.

After analyzing the competitive and composition components of employment change for each industry sector in each county, the authors computed an index value for each county based on similarity of change among counties. On the basis of this value, they selected the eighteen potential growth centers shown by rank in Table 28.

While Kuehn and Bender did identify some rapidly growing counties, their approach clearly illustrates the problems of focusing growth center strategy only on lagging regions. The mean growth rate in employment from 1962 to 1967 in their centers was 30 per cent; during the same period there were ninety-three other counties in Arkansas, Oklahoma, and Missouri with higher rates of growth. Moreover, a number of SMSA's near the region have been providing more opportunities for migrants moving out of Ozark counties. Their role has been examined by Eldon Nosari and by Milne.[12]

The SMSA's listed in Table 29 was examined by Nosari in relation to the Ozarks.[13] St. Louis and Kansas City were eliminated from consideration because they were regarded as congested. They had slow rates of population growth between 1960 and 1966; Kansas City had only a small amount of net inmigration, while the net migration figure for St. Louis was negative. In contrast, the Dallas-Fort Worth area shows vigorous employment growth, having a positive net migration value of 104,000. Nosari finds that because of its rapid growth and the benefits accruing from existing agglomeration

TABLE 28

**A Profile of Kuehn and Bender's Potential
Economic Development Centers in the Ozarks Region**

1950-60 Index Rank County & State	1960 Population (thousands)	Per Cent Urban	Migration Rate	Percentage of 1960 Civilian Labor Force in			Select[b] Major Functions
				Agriculture	Manufacturing	Trade, Service[a]	
1. Pulaski, Mo.	47	–	+247	7	11	32	M1
2. Pulaski, Ark.	243	82	+ 3	2	16	22	P,MS
3. Greene, Mo.	126	77	+ 8	4	20	24	P,MS
4. Garland, Ark.	47	61	- 10	2	14	38	R
5. Phelps, Mo.	25	44	+ 1	7	11	23	E
6. Saline, Ark.	29	36	+ 5	2	3	16	PLC,Mi
7. Jasper, Mo.	79	70	- 8	5	24	24	MS,Mi
8. Okmulgee, Okla.	37	60	- 25	6	24	20	C
9. Camden, Mo.	9	–	+ 10	14	10	35	R
10. Seminole, Okla.	28	62	- 37	6	9	22	O
11. Sebastian, Ark.	67	80	- 14	2	22	25	MS
12. Taney, Mo.	10	–	- 5	12	8	24	R
13. Baxter, Ark.	10	–	- 22	16	9	30	R
14. Muskogee, Okla.	62	62	- 14	7	14	23	MS
15. St. Francois, Mo.	37	37	- 7	4	15	20	PLC,Mi
16. Ottawa, Okla.	28	55	- 19	8	23	22	R
17. Washington, Ark.	56	54	- 2	13	18	21	PLC,E
18. Rogers, Okla.	21	32	- 6	11	14	22	C
Ozark Region Medians	12	22	- 21	18	17	20	

[a]Includes retail trade, other personal services, repair services, recreation, and amusement.

[b]Codes are as follows: P-provincial City; MS-major local service center; PLC-potential linear city; Mi-mining; Ml-military; R-recreation; E-education; C-commuting; and O-oil.

Source: John Kuehn and Lloyd Bender, "An Empirical Identification of Growth Centers," *Land Economics*, Vol. 45, No. 4 (November, 1969), 442.

TABLE 29

Growth Characteristics of Potential Growth Centers

SMSA	Population			Net Migration Change	Employment		
	1960	1966	Per Cent Change		1962	1967	Per Cent Change
Dallas, Tex.	1,119,460	1,366,500	22.1	104.000	372,324	511,405	37.3
Fort Smith, Ark.	135,110	151,500	12.1	10,000	21,892	34,854	59.2
Fort Worth, Tex.	573,215	638,300	11.4	9,000	154,381	197,914	28.2
Kansas City, Kan.	1,092,545	1,260,200	9.9	9,000	330,025	409,592	24.1
Little Rock, Ark.	271,936	312,100	14.7	14,000	62,043	90,891	46.5
Memphis, Tenn.-Ark.	674,583	748,200	10.9	5,000	157,091	207,034	31.8
Oklahoma City, Okla.	511,833	586,500	14.6	27,000	132,040	160,475	21.5
St. Louis, Mo.	2,104,669	2,267,800	7.8	- 3,000	597,878	743,476	24.4
Shreveport, La.	281,481	286,900	2.0	-17,000	56,256	65,649	16.7
Springfield, Mo.	126,276	140,700	11.4	7,000	30,429	39,804	30.8
Texarkana, Tex.-Ark.	91,657	100,000	9.1	4,000	14,556	23,590	62.1
Topeka, Kan.	141,286	150,800	6.7	- 5,000	32,177	38,438	19.5
Tulsa, Okla.	418,974	441,974	5.3	-12,000	114,732	147,386	28.5
Wichita, Kan.	381,626	393,700	3.1	-25,000	100,442	130,673	30.1

Sources: U.S. Bureau of the Census, *Current Population Reports*, Series P-25, No. 401, August 28, 1968, and No. 407, October 10, 1968; U.S. Bureau of the Census, *County Business Patterns*, 1962 and 1967.

economies and amenities, public investment in Dallas-Fort Worth to accelerate growth is not necessary.

Fort Smith, Little Rock, Springfield, Oklahoma City, and Texarkana exhibit vigorous growth. All possess high rates of population increase, large employment increases, and significant net inmigration. Memphis exhibits meager net inmigration but a healthy increase in employment in the period of 1962-67. This small net inmigration can be partially explained by the substantial loss of population due to outmigration from Crittenden County, Arkansas, which is part of the Memphis SMSA.

On the basis of these criteria, Nosari finds that Shreveport, Topeka, Tulsa, and Wichita have less desirable growth center possibilities. All of these SMSA's have slow rates of population growth, somewhat slower rates of employment increase (except in the case of Oklahoma City), and substantial net outmigration. Large net outmigration figures are indicative of the inability of these SMSA's to create employment opportunities at a rate sufficient to retain growing populations and to attract a substantial number of migrants. The case of Wichita can be explained by its heavy reliance upon the aircraft industry. These 1960-66 migration figures, of course, miss part of the effect of the Vietnam War, and in all probability, this condition has changed somewhat (note the 30.1 per cent increase in employment from 1962 to 1967).

The manufacturing bases of the potential growth centers are presented in Table 30. These SMSA's show a much better balance between fast-growth industries and slow-growth industries than did the smaller growth centers evaluated earlier. This is no doubt a result of direct relationship between size and diversification of the manufacturing base. The exceptions are Fort Smith and Springfield, both relatively small and located in the heart of the Ozarks Region. These two SMSA's have a large proportion of their manufacturing employment in the food, apparel, lumber, and furniture industries, activities common to the Ozarks region. Again, Wichita's heavily skewed distribution is due to the aircraft industry, which was classified as slow-growth during the early 1960's.

Table 31 presents the importance of the tertiary sector in each SMSA's economic base. The percentages in this table actually understate the importance of the tertiary sector because government employment and self-employment are not reported in *County Business Patterns*. These two sectors play an important part in the employment pattern of large urban centers. Even disregarding this fact, and with perhaps Wichita and Fort Smith excepted, the importance of the vigorously growing tertiary sector in these centers is quite evident.

The data in Table 32 indicate the attractive power of the possible growth centers on migrants from the Ozarks. Only Texarkana, Shreveport, and Topeka show an inability to affect appreciably the Ozarks region in this respect. The importance of the tertiary sector as an attractive force is also clear.

After considering all criteria, Nosari's analysis eliminates Wichita from the list of potential growth centers. The economic base of this SMSA depends heavily upon the aircraft industry, and past experience indicates that in consequence, employment fluctuations are too unpredictable. Net outmigration of 25,000 between 1960 and 1966 illustrates the problem. Moreover,

TABLE 30

Manufacturing Bases of Potential Growth Centers

SMSA	Percentage of Manufacturing Employment in Fast-Growing Firms[a]	Percentage of Manufacturing Employment in Slow-Growing Firms[a]
Fort Smith, Ark.	20.4+[b]	67.5+[b]
Little Rock, Ark.	32.8+[b]	41.9
Memphis, Tenn.	27.8+[b]	53.6+[b]
Oklahoma City, Okla.	27.8+[b]	34.8
Shreveport, La	22.0+[b]	51.4
Springfield, Mo.	17.7	62.5
Texarkana, Tex.-Ark.	9.7	15.8
Topeka, Kan.	24.1	35.3
Tulsa, Okla.	19.8	36.3
Wichita, Kan.	10.8	82.7

[a] Only the number of reporting units in particular employee-size categories—not the exact number of employees—are available. Thus, the number of employees for each reporting unit is assumed to be the average for that particular employee-size category.

[b] Included here are reporting units of the category "500 or more."

Source: Compiled from U.S. Bureau of the Census, County Business Patterns, 1967.

Wichita's distance from the Ozarks has a negative influence on its ability to attract potential migrants.

The Texarkana-Shreveport urban area also was eliminated, in part because of its dependence on the Red River Arsenal, an insecure base for economic growth. The tertiary sector of Texarkana is also relatively small, and the attraction of this SMSA to persons of the Ozarks region is insignificant. Shreveport's economy shows no vigor whatsoever. It exhibits the least increase in population and employment during the periods studied of any of the

TABLE 31

Tertiary Sectors of Potential Growth Centers

SMSA	Total Reported Employment 1967	Total in Tertiary Sector 1967	Percentage of Total in Tertiary Sector
Fort Smith, Ark.	34,854	14,869	42.7
Little Rock, Ark.	90,891	50,176	55.2
Memphis, Tenn.	207,034	116,073	56.1
Oklahoma City, Okla.	160,475	97,605	60.8
Shreveport, La.	65,849	37,246	56.7
Springfield, Mo.	39,804	22,085	55.5
Texarkana, Tex.-Ark.	23,590	11,386	48.3
Topeka, Kan.	38,438	24,412	63.5
Tulsa, Okla.	147,386	71,073	48.2
Wichita, Kan.	130,673	57,709	44.2

Source: Compiled from U.S. Bureau of the Census, *County Business Patterns*, 1967.

potential centers and the least ability to attract persons from the region. The elimination of Topeka is justified on essentially the same terms. Topeka, along with being quite distant from the region, possesses a weak growth potential and has had little effect on the Ozarks region in terms of migration.

The growth centers Nosari recommends are Fort Smith, Little Rock, Memphis, Oklahoma City, Springfield, and Tulsa. Each of these SMSA's has experienced rapid growth of population and employment. Tulsa shows the least growth potential, but it possesses a favorable industrial mix and ability to exert an influence on the Ozarks region. Springfield and Fort Smith possess a vigorous past growth pattern and exert a strong influence upon the area, though they have an industrial mix which is unfavorable. However, these SMSA's have been able to attract a more than proportionate share of the slow-growth sectors, and consequently have been able to experience rapid growth. Little Rock, Memphis, and Oklahoma City are desirable in every respect. In conclusion, Nosari points out:

TABLE 32

Migrants from the Ozarks to Potential Growth Centers, 1960-65

SMSA	Number of Migrants
Fort Smith, Ark.	2,500
Little Rock, Ark.	6,200
Memphis, Tenn.	1,200
Oklahoma City, Okla.	10,900
Shreveport, La.	500
Springfield, Mo.	2,400
Texarkana, Tex.-Ark.	700
Topeka, Kan.	900
Tulsa, Okla.	6,700
Wichita, Kan.	2,800

Source: Based on a 1 per cent sample of employees covered by the Social Security Administration (see Appendix).

An attempt to initiate and then accelerate the growth rate in rural areas or small urban places is contrary to the market forces of our dynamic economy. Such a program is not only inefficient in an economic sense, but the public investment required for such a plan would be staggering. However, this is exactly the program offered by EDA and the Ozarks Regional Commission in their effort to develop the Ozarks.

I have suggested an alternative to that plan, one based upon intermediate-sized urban centers offering both growth potential and an ability to spread their influence to the depressed hinterland. Three of these centers are located outside the Region, two on the fringe, and one inside. Public investment in these centers would accelerate a growth which is already present and would serve to encourage outmigration from the hinterland areas experiencing the greatest underdevelopment. Human resource development should be the

TABLE 33

Growth Centers for the Ozarks

Ranking	Migrant/ Population (x 100)	SMSA	(1) Per Cent Employment Change 1962-67	(2) Employment Increase 1962-67	(3) Mean Per Capita Income 1966	(4) Migrants from Region 1960-65	(5) Per Cent Income Increase of Migrants
1.	2.55	Little Rock, Ark.	34.32	23,228	2,740	6,200	69.7
2.	2.12	Oklahoma City, Okla.	21.54	28,435	2,837	10,900	80.8
5.	1.90	Springfield, Mo.	30.81	9,375	2,451	2,400	49.0
4.	1.85	Fort Smith, Ark.-Okla.[a]	31.87	8,424	1,955	2,500	39.3
3.	1.57	Tulsa, Okla.	28.46	32,654	3,142	6,700	63.4
	.77	Kansas City, Mo.	22.80	76,051	3,275	8,500	95.3
	.76	Texarkana, Ark.-Tex.[a]	62.06	9,034	2,235	700	76.6
	.73	Wichita, Kan.	30.10	30,231	3,197	2,800	63.3
	.63	Topeka, Kan.	[19.46]	6,261	2,988	900	124.6
	.35	Dallas, Tex.	36.17	135,405	3,201	3,900	81.0

[a] EDA Growth Center.

Sources: Columns 1 and 2, U.S. Department of Commerce, Office of Business Economics, County Business Patterns, U.S. Summary 1962-67; column 3, U.S. Department of Commerce, Office of Business Economics, U.S. Department of Commerce News, August 26, 1968; columns 4 and 5, 1 per cent Social Security sample data (see Appendix).

thrust of investment funds in this hinterland area. Investment of this nature will facilitiate outmigration while making it evident to the people of the Ozarks that they are the important element in the development process.[14]

Milne, on the basis of criteria discussed in the previous chapter (see pp. 120-24), has ranked the growth center potential of SMSA's relevant to the Ozarks as shown in Table 33. The five centers which he selects correspond to the centers selected by Nosari on largely different grounds, though Nosari adds Memphis whereas Milne leaves it out of consideration because the inmigrant to population ratio was too low. In any case, these analyses both indicate that the most feasible growth centers for the Ozarks are intermediate-size cities which have considerable attraction for the residents of the lagging region.

SUMMARY AND CONCLUSIONS

Despite efforts of the Economic Development Administration and the Ozarks Regional Commission to implement growth center policies based on a relatively large number of centers, usually small cities, the present study indicates that Fort Smith, Little Rock, Oklahoma City, Tulsa, and Springfield would constitute the core of an efficient growth center strategy for the Ozarks.

Nevertheless, preliminary results from the 1970 census indicate relatively rapid population growth in an eleven-county area corresponding approximately to the Tulsa-Fayetteville-Fort Smith triangle. This entire area may have a promising future, but more detailed analysis is necessary when the relevant data become available. Similarly, Grant and Faulkner Counties, Arkansas, have experienced rapid growth and may be considered as part of the Pulaski County (Little Rock) growth area. With these qualifications, the preliminary census results do not seem to warrant any significant change in the proposed growth center designations. While a few isolated counties with small populations have experienced relatively rapid population growth, they are not places capable of altering the problems confronting the region as a whole. Once again the evidence suggests that growth center investments should be more concentrated than is now the case and that investments in hinterland areas should be focused primarily on human resources.

NOTES

1. "Ozarks Region, An Opportunity for Growth" (Little Rock, Ark.: Ozarks Regional Commission, 1967), pp. 2 and 35. This excludes the ten counties in Kansas; however, the figures would be altered only slightly.

2. *Ibid.*, p. 11.

3. *Ibid.*, pp. 42-44.

4. U.S. Congress, Senate, Committe on Public Works, *Hearings on Ozarks-Four Corners Regional Development Commissions,* 90th Congress, 1st Session, 1967, p. 94.

5. "Ozarks Region, An Opportunity for Growth," *op. cit.,* p. 20.

6. Data based on a 1 per cent sample of workers covered by the Social Security Administration (see Appendix).

7. "Report of September, 1968" (Little Rock, Ark.: Ozarks Regional Commission, 1968).

8. The data used in this classification are found in Bureau of the Census, U.S. Department of Commerce, *Long Term Economic Growth, 1860-1965* (Washington, D.C.: Government Printing Office, 1966), pp. 92-96. In this publication, growth rates of value added for each manufacturing group are computed with the compound interest rate formula using averages of annual data for the 1957-60 business cycle and the period 1960-65. Industry groups possessing a rate of more than the average for all manufacturing were classified as fast growth and those possessing a rate lower than the average were classified as slow growth.

9. John A. Kuehn and Lloyd D. Bender, "Empirical Identification of Growth Centers," *Land Economics,* Vol. 45, No. 1 (November, 1969), 435-43.

10. *Ibid.*, p. 436.

11. *Ibid.,* p. 437.

12. Eldon Nosari, "The Ozark Region: A Growth Center Strategy" (unpublished manuscript).

13. *Ibid.*

14. *Ibid.*

8

THE
MEXICAN AMERICANS
OF
SOUTH TEXAS

Spanish-surnamed Americans are the nation's second largest minority group. However, because most—about 6.5 million—reside in the Southwest, they have tended to receive relatively meager attention in national affairs.[1] Although economic and social difficulties are widespread among the Mexican-American population, they are particularly great in South Texas.

This chapter examines the economic conditions of the Mexican Americans in Texas, focusing on twenty South Texas redevelopment area counties, that is, they have been designated as eligible for assistance from the Economic Development Administration (see Map 5). The Mexican Americans in this area face all of the problems usually present in lagging regions: poverty, high unemployment and underemployment levels, low levels of health and education, ethnic discrimination, and cultural isolation. A growth center strategy is developed in relation to these problems, taking account of the area's unique geographic situation (it is relatively far from major economic centers and its economy is greatly influenced by the relatively poor conditions prevailing on the Mexican side of the border) and evidence concerning the locational preferences of the population in question.

THE CURRENT SITUATION

Income and Employment Levels

The median income for Mexican-American urban males in Texas in 1959 was only $2,339, almost 33 per cent less than the $3,278 median in the "next best" southwestern state, New Mexico.[2] This value was only slightly over half

Map 5

SOUTH TEXAS

Fort Worth ● ● Dallas

El Paso

● San Angelo

Austin ●

San Antonio

Houston

Del Rio

Victoria

REDEVELOPMENT
AREA COUNTIES

Corpus Christi

Laredo

HEAVY LINES INDICATE BOUNDARIES
OF ECONOMIC DEVELOPMENT DISTRICTS

Harlingen

McAllen-Edinburg

Brownsville

the comparable Anglo median. Of the approximately 270,000 Mexican-American families in Texas in 1960, 51 per cent had incomes less than the frequently cited poverty level of $3,000; 58 per cent of the nonwhite and 21 per cent of the Anglo families fell into this category.[3] In South Texas, Mexican-American family incomes were even less than the average for the state as a whole.[4]

Low income levels are directly related to the types of occupations that Mexican Americans have. These, in turn, are a function of educational attainment. The data in Table 34 show that Mexican-American males in Texas are heavily concentrated in the "farm laborers" and "other laborers" categories, while the Anglos show nearly four times the concentration of the

TABLE 34

Percentage of Male Labor Force of Texas in Major
Occupational Categories, by Anglo and Spanish-Surname Groups, 1960

Occupational Category	Anglo	Spanish-Surname
Professional and Technical	11.5	3.1
Farmers	7.1	2.6
Managers	14.5	4.6
Clerical and Sales	14.9	8.2
Craftsmen	20.5	15.9
Operatives	16.9	21.8
Private Households	0.04	0.2
Service Workers	3.8	7.4
Farm Laborers	2.2	16.2
Other Laborers	4.2	15.8
Not Reported	4.4	4.3
TOTAL	100.0	100.0
Absolute Total	1,752,514	277,639

Source: H. L. Browning and S. D. McLemore, A Statistical Profile of the Spanish-Surname Population of Texas (Austin: Bureau of Business Research, University of Texas, 1964), p. 41.

Mexican Americans in the "professional and technical" occupational category. Table 35 points out in another way the employment problems of the Mexican Americans. Their employment is relatively high, compared to Anglos, in the lagging "agriculture, forestry, and fisheries" sector, whereas it is conspicuously low in "professional and related services," as well as in "finance, insurance, and real estate." It is not surprising, given the occupational structure of Mexican-American employment, to find unemployment rates in South Texas two to three times the national average, or to see subemployment estimates as high as 42 to 47 per cent for Mexican Americans living in urban slums.[5]

Education

There is considerable evidence that educational attainment is closely associated with variation in personal income and that "the relative income of the Mexican Americans, by state, appears to depend upon their relative schooling compared to that of the Anglo population."[6] Although educational achievement is varied for the Mexican Americans, Joan Moore maintains that "the reality of educational deprivation for Mexican Americans is unmistakable. Mexican American leaders without exception consider educational disadvantage an outstanding handicap."[7] As with income, it appears that the average educational attainment of Mexican Americans falls as one moves from the national level to Texas and finally to South Texas. In 1960, 22.9 per cent of the Mexican Americans twenty-five years old or older residing in Texas had *no* formal training. Only 1.1 per cent of the Anglos and 5.4 per cent of the nonwhites of Texas fell into this category.[8] For the same year, the median number of school years completed was 6.1 for Mexican Americans but 8.1 and 11.1 for nonwhites and Anglos, respectively.[9] In many of the South Texas counties, the median number of school years completed was much lower; fourteen were in the 2.5 to 5 year range.[10]

Evidence suggests that this bleak picture of Mexican-American education is changing. Enrollment figures for the age group from five to thirty-four show Mexican Americans running only a shade below Anglos in every state except Texas.[11] In sharp contrast to the group twenty-five years and over, 80.2 per cent of the Spanish-surname population aged five to fifteen years currently has been enrolled in school in Texas.[12] Moore has demonstrated that poor rural education standards force rural Mexican Americans into a cycle of low educational attainment.[13] In 1960, however, about 71 per cent of the Mexican Americans in South Texas lived in the region's three SMSA's. Data compiled by H. L. Browning and S. D. McLemore reveal that the urban Mexican American attains relatively higher levels of education compared to those in rural areas.[14]

There can be no doubt that education pays off for the Mexican American, especially since discrimination is much less a problem than in the case of the Negro population. However, the increasing level of education of the nation's population as a whole and structural changes in the labor market make it imperative that educational opportunities for Mexican Americans be increased so that they may realize their economic potential. This is especially true in the case of South Texas.

TABLE 35

**Percentage of Employed Population of Texas in Major
Industrial Categories by Anglo and Spanish-Surname Groups, 1960**

Industrial Category	Anglo	Spanish-Surname
Agriculture, Forestry, and Fisheries	7.6	17.4
Mining	3.8	0.9
Construction	7.6	9.1
Manufacturing, Durable	8.1	4.9
Manufacturing, Nondurable	9.3	8.8
Transportation, Communication	7.9	6.0
Wholesale and Retail Trade	21.8	22.6
Finance, Insurance, and Real Estate	5.0	1.7
Business and Repair Services	2.9	2.5
Personal Services	4.5	9.6
Entertainment and Recreational Services	0.7	0.8
Professional and Related Services	12.0	6.1
Public Administration	5.2	5.8
Industry Not Reported	3.7	3.8
TOTAL	100.0	100.0
Absolute Total	2,534,629	381,222

Source: H. L. Browning and S. D. McLemore, *A Statistical Profile of the Spanish-Surname Population of Texas* (Austin: Bureau of Business Research, University of Texas, 1964), p. 17.

Migration from South Texas

In response to widespread poverty and unemployment in South Texas, there has been large and selective outmigration. The major stream of migration from South Texas in the past was directed toward California, with a lesser flow toward the other southwestern states. In the early decades of this century, Texas had an overwhelming proportion of the Mexican-born population in the United States,[15] but recently it has lost much of its attractive force for Mexicans entering the United States. In the first quarter of this century, most Mexicans gave Texas as their intended place of residence. Now, more than half name California as their intended residence.[16] Thus, whereas 65 per cent of the Mexicans living in the United States in 1900 resided in Texas, only 35 per cent lived there in 1960.[17] For the 1950-60 decade, Browning and McLemore estimate Mexican-American outmigration from Texas at 48,957.[18]

A recent estimate of labor force migration from South Texas suggests that although California still ranks high as a receiver of Texas Mexican Americans, Texas itself absorbs a greater proportion of migrants from its southern counties. Between 1960 and 1965, estimated outmigration of the labor force from South Texas was 44,600; 56 per cent of the migrants went to SMSA's. Moreover, total outmigration would be greater than the indicated figure because the estimate was based on a sample only of those persons covered by the Social Security Administration. Twenty-two states received migrants from South Texas. However, Texas and California accounted for 59 per cent and 20 per cent, respectively, of the total migration. It is evident that many Mexican Americans from South Texas are migrating to the larger cities in Texas.[19]

The causes and consequences of outmigration are complex. Education and health standards are frequently relatively low in lagging areas, and the inhabitants often do not gain the skills necessary to operate in an urban-industrial environment. Thus, the most skilled and best educated (i.e., the most productive) members of these populations are best able to reap the benefits that result from migration to economically healthy areas. Outmigration, therefore, tends to be selective. It tends to draw off the potential leaders and the most productive members of the populations of lagging regions. Dale Hathaway notes that outmigration does not increase income levels in the lagging region because the least productive members are left behind; productivity drops with a resultant depressing effect on per capita income.[20]

The selective nature of outmigration from South Texas is seen in the data presented in Table 36. Of the 25,100 migrants who went to SMSA's, 42.2 per cent were males in the twenty-five to forty-four age gruop. Of all migrants, 72 percent were males, and 57.7 per cent were in the twenty-five to forty-four age category.

Over time, one would expect a population experiencing selective outmigration to become skewed toward females, the old, and the young.[21] Although no data are available to verify this for South Texas, the data in Table 37 do show the age structure for the Mexican-American population of all Texas

TABLE 36

Outmigration from South Texas, 1960-65, by Age and Sex

Sex	Per Cent Under 25	Per Cent 25-44	Per Cent Over 45	Total (Per Cent)
Male	14.7	42.2	15.1	72.0
Female	8.4	15.5	4.0	27.9
Total	23.1	57.7	19.1	99.9[a]

[a] Components do not add to 100 per cent due to rounding.

Source: Compiled from a 1 per cent sample of employees covered by the Social Security Administration (see Appendix).

TABLE 37

Age Characteristics of Anglo and Spanish-Surname Groups in Texas, 1950 and 1960

Sex	Percentage in Age Groups			Dependency Ratio[a]
	14 and Under	15-64	65 and Over	
Anglo				
1950	27.3	65.5	7.2	.526
1960	30.1	61.2	8.7	.634
Spanish-Surname				
1950	41.0	55.6	3.4	.800
1960	44.4	51.7	3.8	.933

[a] The dependency ratio is the population in the 14-and-under and 65-and-older age groups divided by the population in the 15-64 age group.

Source: H. L. Browning and S. D. McLemore, *A Statistical Profile of the Spanish-Surname Population of Texas* (Austin: Bureau of Business Research, The University of Texas, 1964), p. 20.

for a period during which the state was experiencing heavy Mexican-American outmigration. Compared to the Anglo group, the Spanish-surname population does show a skewness toward the young age group. Furthermore, the data show a significantly higher dependency ratio for the Spanish-surname group compared to the Anglo group. Those who do not migrate inherit the burden of supporting a larger and larger proportion of nonworkers.

The Border Problem

South Texas is relatively distant from the major urban-industrial zones of the United States. Eight of the counties in the region lie on the Mexican-American border, and the region's economy is closely interrelated with that of northern Mexico. Employment opportunities in South Texas tend to attract migrants from other parts of Mexico into Mexico's northern border cities, increasing immigration and commuting of Mexican labor into South Texas cities.[22] This tends to depress wages and increase unemployment of Mexican Americans.

On the other hand, workers from Mexico are also consumers, and they account in many cases for a significant percentage of retail purchases in the American border cities.[23] Although much opposition has been generated against Mexican commuters by labor unions and Mexican-American leadership in the area, it would be difficult to cut off the flow of laborers without also cutting off the flow of consumers from Mexico to American border cities. Though the following abstracts from complex political and economic problems of this border relationship, its importance should not be forgotten.

GROWTH CENTERS FOR SOUTH TEXAS

A major problem in selecting growth centers for South Texas is that some cities, particularly those in or near the region, have unfavorable population growth and net migration patterns, although several have rapidly growing employment. The data in Table 38 indicate that the two largest and most dynamic Texas cities—Houston and Dallas—dwarf all others in population and employment growth. These cities have attracted large numbers of migrants from South Texas, and they probably will continue to do so. However, because of their extremely large size and their distance from the region, they are not considered here as growth centers for South Texas.

Several other Texas cities are dropped from consideration as growth centers because of their slow or negative growth in employment. They are Amarillo, Galveston, Wichita Falls, and Abilene. El Paso, which is quite distant from the region and has had heavy net outmigration, is also dropped. Other cities with negative net outmigration, but which lie in or near the region, will be considered in more detail later.

Table 39 shows SMSA's that have attracted a large number of migrants from South Texas. Although California still receives large numbers of migrants from the region, cities in Texas are much more significant as points of

TABLE 38

Growth Characteristics of Selected SMSA's in Texas

SMSA[a]	Population			Net Migration	Employment		Per Cent Change
	1960	1965	Per Cent Change		1962	1967	
Houston	1,418,323	1,696,000	19.6	139,000	380,996	568,291	49.16
Dallas	1,083,601	1,289,000	18.9	104,000	372,374	511,405	37.34
San Antonio	716,168	808,000	12.8	16,000	130,415	161,914	24.15
Fort Worth	573,215	627,000	9.4	9,000	154,381	197,914	28.20
El Paso	314,070	344,000	9.6	- 22,00	60,507	72,817	20.34
Corpus Christi	266,594	286,000	7.2	-11,000	44,512	62,521	40.46
Austin	212,136	247,000	16.2	14,000	42,947	56,901	32.49
McAllen-Pharr-Edinburg	180,904	202,000	11.5	- 5,000	20,377	24,362	19.56
Lubbock	156,271	185,000	18.2	8,000	35,375	42,230	19.38
Brownsville-Harlingen-San Benito	151,098	151,000	- 0.1	-20,000	21,612	25,445	17.74
Amarillo	149,493	168,000	12.1	3,000	32,323	36,967	14.37
Galveston-Texas City	140,364	157,000	12.2	6,000	35,241	37,879	7.49
Wichita Falls	129,638	130,000	0.1	-11,000	27,025	26,401	- 2.31
Abilene	120,377	126,000	4.9	- 5,000	26,870	25,386	- 5.52
Texarkana	91,657	100,000	9.5	4,000	14,556	23,590	62.06
Tyler	86,350	93,000	8.2	1,000	19,944	25,914	29.93
Laredo	64,791	76,000	16.9	- 1,000	8,257	11,652	41.12
San Angelo	64,630	73,000	13.3	3,000	13,042	16,121	23.61

[a]Texas SMSA's not listed here are Midland, Odessa, Waco, Sherman-Denison, Beaumont-Port, and Arthur-Orange.

Sources: U.S. Bureau of the Census, *County Business Patterns,* 1962 and 1967; U.S. Bureau of the Census, *Current Population Reports,* Series P-25, No. 371.

TABLE 39

Estimated Inmigration to Selected SMSA's from South Texas, 1960-65

SMSA	Estimated Inmigration[a]	Distance[b]	1960 Population[c]
Houston, Tex.	3,400	250	1,418,323
San Antonio, Tex.	2,300	80	716,668
Dallas, Tex.	1,800	330	1,083,601
Brownsville, Tex.	1,600	180	151,098
Corpus Christi, Tex.	1,600	120	266,594
Chicago, Ill.	1,500	1,130	6,220,913
San Bernardino, Calif.	1,100	1,120	809,782
Los Angeles, Calif.	1,000	1,190	6,038,771
Austin, Tex.	900	160	212,136
Fresno, Calif.	700	1,320	365,945
McAllen, Tex.	700	160	180,904
New Orleans, La.	700	560	907,123
Fort Worth, Tex.	500	320	573,215
Anaheim, Calif.	400	1,150	703,925
Galveston, Tex.	400	270	140,364
Salinas, Calif.	400	1,420	198,351
San Jose, Calif.	400	1,440	642,315
Bakersfield, Calif.	300	1,240	291,984
Laredo, Tex.	300	60	64,791
Phoenix, Ariz.	300	830	663,510
Santa Barbara, Calif.	300	1,170	168,892
Waco, Tex.	300	250	150,091

Sources: [a]Compiled from a 1 per cent sample of employees covered by the Social Security Administration (see Appendix); [b]air travel distance from the geographic center of the South Texas region of the SMSA; [c]compiled from U.S. Bureau of the Census, Current Population Reports, Series P-25, No. 371.

destination. Because of the importance of migration patterns in selecting potential growth centers, it is instructive to examine the determinants of migration in terms of the following regression equation:

$$Y = 10.478 - 0.267 D_a + .002 P_{60} - .057 S$$
$$(.083) \qquad (.00026) \quad (.022)$$

where Y = inmigration, D_a = air travel distance from South Texas to the SMSA, P_{60} = population of the SMSA in 1960, and S = percentage change in

Spanish-surname population, 1950-60. The values in parentheses are the standard errors of the regression coefficients. The F test is significant at the .01 level; D_a at the .01 level; P_{60} at the .001 level; and S at the .05 level. The equation has an adjusted $R^2 = .83$.

These three variables then "account for" a large part of the variation in migration from South Texas to Texas SMSA's. The coefficient of partial correlation, r^2. for D_a, P_{60}, and S are .312, .826, and .178, respectively. Immediately evident is the importance of the size of the SMSA (P_{60}) as an "explanatory" factor of the migration patterns. The r^2 for the distance variable (D_a) is negative as expected, but its magnitude suggests that incremental distances may not be a major determinant of variation in migration. Although the r^2 value for S is not very large, the evidence indicates that present migration patterns are inversely related to where migrants have gone in the past.

Only three counties in South Texas are of any significant size. They are Cameron, Hidalgo, and Webb, which contain the only SMSA's in the region, Brownsville-Harlingen-San Benito, McAllen-Pharr-Edinburg, and Laredo. The other seventeen counties are rural and of little consequence as places of commerce or employment. Thus, the SMSA's should provide central points for migration and employment for the rural population of the region. The data in Table 39 show that they did receive a substantial amount of inmigration for the period 1960 to 1965. However, if the points of origin of this inmigration are examined, it is not at all clear that these cities have much influence on the region with respect of migration. First, *all* of the sample migration into Cameron County originated in the contiguous SMSA, Hidalgo County. Further, *all* of the sample migration into Hidalgo came from Cameron County. Finally, 66 per cent of the sample inmigration to Webb County originated in Cameron and Hidalgo Counties. What appears to be happening is a reshuffling of residents among the SMSA's, with a minimal influx of migrants from rural parts of the region. One cannot say, then, that these cities act as a polarizing force on the region's migration flows. Moreover, the data in Table 38 show that the SMSA's in question have been experiencing outmigration. Thus, not only do the region's major cities fail to act as migration and employment centers, but they too add to the flow of migrants out of the region. By way of illustration, from 1960 to 1965, Houston received 1,800 migrants from Cameron County, 1,300 from Hidalgo, and 100 from Webb. Corpus Christi received 800, 500, and 100, respectively; Dallas received 800, 600, and 200; and San Antonio, 500, 200, and 400. In general, then, the migration patterns of the region suggest that the growth centers for the area lie outside South Texas.

Other definitions of areas of influence may be used to supplement the migration analysis. To the extent that these areas and their centers agree with the migration analysis, the case for selecting growth centers outside the region is enhanced. Table 40 presents three separate delineations of areas of economic influence in South Texas. The relationships are based, for the most part, on labor commuting patterns and consumer shopping patterns. All delineations show the three or four counties (Table 40, Area 1) in the southeastern part of the region to be dominated by Brownsville-Harlingen-San Benito and McAllen-Pharr-Edinburg, the two SMSA's in that area. However, except for this

TABLE 40

Three Delineations of Economic Regions in South Texas[a]

A		B		C	
RAND McNALLY		OFFICE OF BUSINESS ECONOMICS		ECONOMIC DEVELOPMENT ADMINISTRATION	
Basic Trading Areas (Counties)	Trading Center (Cities)	OBE Districts (Counties)	Metropolitan Center (Cities)	EDA Districts (Counties)	Potential Growth Center (Cities)
1 Starr Hildalgo Willacy Cameron	Brownsville McAllen Harlingen	1 Starr Hildalgo Willacy Cameron	Brownsville Harlingen San Benito	1 Hidalgo Willacy Cameron	Brownsville Harlingen McAllen
2 Dimmit Frio Gonzales Karnes Kinney LaSalle Maverick Medina Real Uvalde Val Verde Zavala	San Antonio	2 Frio Goliad Gonzales Karnes Kinney Maverick Medina Real Uvalde Val Verde Zavala	San Antonio	2 Dimmit Frio Jim Hogg Kinney LaSalle Maverick Medina Real Starr Uvalde Val Verde Webb Zapata Zavala	Uvalde Laredo
3 Jim Hogg	Corpus Christi	3 Dimmit Jim Hogg LaSalle Webb Zapata	Corpus Christi	3 Goliad Gonzales Karnes	Corpus Christi
4 Goliad	Victoria				
5 Webb Zapata	Laredo				

[a]Those counties in the trading areas or OBE districts but not in the group of EDA-designated counties have been excluded from the table.

Sources: Compiled from the *Rand McNally Commercial Atlas and Marketing Guide* (Chicago: Rand McNally Co., 1968); OBE Economic Areas, Office of Business Economics, U.S. Department of Commerce, January, 1969; data supplied by the Economic Development Administration.

four-county area, the rest of the region is shown to be related to cities on the fringe of South Texas. The largest subregion includes more than half of the counties. Rand McNally and OBE definitions show these counties to be influenced by San Antonio, but EDA has many of the same counties economically related to and dependent on Uvalde and Laredo. Uvalde is indeed growing so far as employment is concerned, but it is not much larger in employment, sales, or manufacturing than several of the other rural counties in the region. Moreover, because of its small size (1960 population: 10,293), it does not have the agglomeration economies or urban services necessary for rapid future growth. The same criticism applies to Victoria (Table 40, Area 4), which may indeed be the commercial center for one South Texas county but is too small (1960 population: 36,500) and too distant from the problem areas to represent a relevant growth center. This leaves the following cities for consideration: Brownsville, McAllen, San Antonio, Corpus Christi, and Laredo.

Further analysis of the growth potential of Laredo, Brownsville, and McAllen—all EDA development centers—reveals their weakness as potential growth centers. Although Laredo has experienced a rapid increase in employment in the last several years, over 40 per cent of the increase has been in the government sector.[24] Also, the Laredo Air Force Base is an important economic element in the county.[25] Thus, the increased military activity of the last decade has given Laredo a temporary economic stimulus. Only four manufacturing firms have been established in Webb County since 1960 and only six were established between 1950 and 1960. The county had thirty-eight manufacturing establishments in 1967 with only three of these employing more than 100 persons, while seventeen had fewer than 8 employees.[26] Laredo's environment is not that of a dynamic urban economy, and it is not likely to attract large, fast-growing firms.

Some discrepancy exists as to the population and migration data for the period 1960 to 1965 for McAllen. The Bureau of the Census estimates shown in Table 38 for McAllen indicate a more favorable trend than do data published by the University of Texas, which indicate a 300-person decrease in population between 1960 and 1967, as well as net outmigration of 27,000 between 1960 and 1965.[27] Agriculture is the most important source of income and employment in Hidalgo County, and it has the largest seasonal fluctuation in jobs of any of the border counties.[28] Employment varied from 48,130 in October to 61,420 in April, 1967.[29] Outside of food processing and other agriculturally oriented manufacturing only two relatively large-scale operations are located in the county; they are both manufacturers of men's work wear employing over 100 employees.[30] Thus, Hidalgo County also seems to lack the dynamic economic base necessary for future growth.

Cameron County displays a more varied economic base than the other two SMSA's. Although it, too, is dominated by agriculture and food processing, Brownsville, the major city in Cameron, has an advantage in being a port. Some manufacturing establishments in Brownsville are tied to its port activities, giving the city a source of income and employment not available in Webb and Hidalgo Counties. However, Cameron County has experienced an accelerated rate of outmigration, and three military bases in the county were closed during the early 1960's.[31] Military population declined by about 3,000 which undoubtedly led, via the multiplier process, to further declines in employment and income in the civilian sector. Finally, large outmigration and lack of population growth suggest that employment is not increasing at a rate sufficient to maintain the current population base. Nevertheless, of the three SMSA's in the region, Brownsville may have the best chance of future growth because of its diverse economic base.

In general, Houston has the most dynamic growth qualities of any city within several hundred miles of South Texas, and it will undoubtedly continue to provide employment opportunities for migrants from South Texas. However, its size and its distance from the region are not conducive to making it a growth center for policy purposes. Dallas stands in a very similar situation.

For a growth center policy, special attention should be given to Corpus Christi and San Antonio because of their proximity to the target region. Corpus Christi has experienced relatively rapid growth in service employment (27.7 per cent between 1964 and 1967), but much of this expansion has been associated with military activities whose future is uncertain. Tourism and recreation often are the last cry of a declining or stagnating area, but the Padre Island National Seashore gives the Corpus Christi area considerable potential in this regard. Creation of a more active tourist trade in the area would provide many jobs for Mexican Americans. However, if more tourists are to be attracted, it will be necessary to construct more first-rate accommodations. A government loan of $410,000 made possible the recent construction of a marina inn, which has provided nearly 100 jobs at or above the minimum wage for Mexican Americans who otherwise would have been unemployed.

An $830,000 grant from EDA (Corpus Christi is an EDA-designated growth center) has permitted preliminary work to begin on a new city, based on tourism and recreation, on the northern end of Padre Island. The city is expected eventually to have a population of 45,000. The city of Corpus Christi plans to go out into EDA redevelopment areas in rural South Texas and recruit Mexican Americans for employment in new jobs resulting from the project. The recruiting will be done in the depressed counties by running advertisements in local newspapers and posting notices in post offices, high schools, and similar places. Special programs have also been instituted to train Mexican Americans for employment in the fishing industry at Aransas Pass, which is part of the Corpus Christi growth center. The main difficulty with providing employment to migrants in Corpus Christi is housing. To help overcome this difficulty, a fairly complex plan is being considered which would utilize the bond-issuing power of local housing authorities, federal subsidies, and a nonprofit developer-sponsor. The housing would be made available on a nondiscriminatory basis to lower-income families, and the units would be available on a scattered site basis to avoid the stigma of "public housing." Unfortunately, housing difficulties and many other problems of the city have been compounded by the disastrous hurricane of July, 1970.

On the basis of the evidence presented in this chapter, the place which most closely fulfills the criteria for a growth center is San Antonio. With the exception of Houston, it is attracting more migrants from South Texas than any SMSA in the country. In terms of Rand McNally basic trading areas and OBE regional delineations, it clearly has a wider sphere of influence in South

Texas than any other city. It also has a relatively high proportion of service activity and relatively rapid growth in this sector. However, because San Antonio has one of the largest concentrations of military activity in the nation, the government sector weighs large in the city's economy. In 1960, military payrolls, including payments to civilians, accounted for about 46 per cent of local wage and salary income. Military payrolls exceeded San Antonio's manufacturing payroll by over 300 per cent.[32] A recent analysis of the city's economy concludes that "since federal military expenditures are subject to variable policy directives which San Antonio can little influence, the city's continued intemperate reliance upon these expenditures appears hazardous. Thus, manufacturing must receive primary attention in San Antonio's prospective economic expansion."[33] Howard Davis has demonstrated that a large number of manufacturing activities not now found in San Antonio could be located there efficiently. Examples include metal products, machine products, electronic components, paper and allied products, petroleum refining, and chemicals. In general, Davis shows how adapting a general locational framework to the unique requirements of San Antonio "provides an expedient, thorough, and clear plan for the future expansion of an underdeveloped city."[34]

Any policies which involve migration of Mexican Americans to San Antonio must of course take account of the problems already existing in the city. San Antonio's largest slum area comprises 29,000 families, over 80 per cent of whom are Mexican Americans. A special household survey by the Department of Labor in this area in November, 1966, revealed that the unemployment rate was 8 per cent in contrast to a rate of 4.2 per cent for the San Antonio SMSA as a whole.[35] However, when account was taken of all of the negative employment factors in the area, it was estimated that the subemployment rate was 47.4 per cent. The survey found that unemployment and subemployment in the area were largely related to personal, rather than economic, conditions. "The problem is less one of inadequate opportunity than of inability, under existing conditions, to use opportunity. Unemployment in these areas is primarily a story of inferior education, no skills, discrimination, fatherless children, unnecessarily rigid hiring practices and hopelessness." Nevertheless, many of the persons contacted in the survey indicated a willingness to take concrete steps to improve their chances for employment. Seventy-five per cent said they would be willing to take on-the-job training, and over 50 per cent said they would be willing to return to school for training if necessary. Despite the gravity of the problems encountered in the slums, the survey report concludes that "though the percentages involved here are deplorably high, the number of people involved is comparatively small. The barriers to their useful employment are serious, but they are removable barriers. The problem is clearly of manageable proportions."

Although Mexican-American migrants to San Antonio may encounter difficulties related to slum neighborhoods, there is evidence that they are among the best, if not the best, adapted urban residents to have migrated from lagging rural areas. A study directed by Daniel Price for the Office of Economic Opportunity contains a great deal of valuable information on the kinds of people who are better off because they have moved from a rural to an urban area.[36] The population studied was composed of Negro migrants from Yazoo County, Mississippi, to Chicago; Anglo migrants from Butler County, Kentucky, to Louisville and Indianapolis; and Mexican-American migrants from South Texas to San Antonio and Chicago. The Mexican-American migrants were from Maverick, Dimmitt, and Zavala Counties, all in the "South Texas" area discussed in this chapter. Interviews were conducted with both migrants from these rural areas and residents of the same areas.

Of the migrant groups, Mexican Americans had the lowest levels of educational attainment. For all groups, it is noteworthy that there was no association between migrants' being above or below the poverty line and levels of education, a phenomenon which may be explained by the quality of education available in the migrants' home areas.

Most of the rural residents were not interested in moving from their home communities. For those who did migrate, little thought was given to alternative destinations; rather, the place to which they moved was chosen because of friends or relatives living there. Indeed, nearly all of the migrants spent their first night in the city with friends or relatives. The primary reason for moving was better economic opportunity in the city, and the migrants were, in fact, better off financially than the nonmigrants. The Mexican-American migrants had a median individual income of $2,500 in South Texas, whereas those in Chicago had a median of $5,545 and those in San Antonio a median of $4,167. However, compared to the median income of the total population in each city, the San Antonio figure was relatively better. Because higher incomes in large cities are usually offset by higher living costs, the migrants were asked if they thought they were better off financially as a consequence of moving. *All* of the Mexican-American migrants to San Antonio stated that they were making more money, were better off financially, and were happier than they were in South Texas. (Of the Mexican-American migrants to Chicago, 98 per cent stated that they were making more money, 97 per cent stated that they were financially better off, but only 86 per cent indicated that they were happier than in South Texas.)

Of the migrant groups, the Mexican Americans apparently were the happiest and least frustrated in urban areas; the Negroes were the most disappointed, even though they made the largest economic advance. When asked under what conditions they would consider moving back, 42 per cent of the Mexican Americans in San Antonio and 27 per cent of the Mexican Americans in Chicago indicated they would never go back. These were the *highest* percentages found among *any* group, and the San Antonio figure is clearly much above that for Chicago. Similarly, 60 per cent of the Chicago Mexican Americans stated they would return to South Texas if the proper econonic conditions prevailed, whereas only 42 per cent of the San Antonio Mexican Americans gave this response. Finally, while about 50 per cent of the Chicago group had considered returning to South Texas, only 14 per cent of the San Antonio group had ever considered going back.

Another aspect of the study dealt with the migrants' attitudes toward city people:

The urban migrants were asked a series of questions about their opinions of people in the city as compared to those in the rural areas, and, in general, they indicated that the urban dwellers were less helpful, more selfish, and less trustworthy. The Mexican Americans in San Antonio were the one exception, indicating in general that they preferred urban residence to rural residence. This might be explained on the basis of the high proportion of Mexican Americans living in San Antonio, although the Negroes in Chicago tend to live in almost entirely black neighborhoods.[37]

The successful adaptation of Mexican-American migrants to San Antonio does not, of course, tell us very much about the extent to which San Antonio is a relevant center for the population still living in South Texas. To shed more light on this issue, a survey was made of the locational preferences of potentially mobile Mexican Americans in South Texas.

LOCATIONAL PREFERENCES OF MEXICAN AMERICANS IN SOUTH TEXAS

The analysis of the locational preferences of the target population was carried out in a manner similar to that involving high school seniors in Eastern Kentucky (see pp. 98-105) though the problems involved in South Texas were more complex than those encountered in Eastern Kentucky.

Before deciding who would be interviewed and the exact nature of the questions to be posed, the author met with government and school officials in South Texas to establish what places would have relevance to interviewees in the region. There was a clear consensus that Mexican Americans in South Texas are very attached to their area and that few would be likely to want to leave, even when moving would improve their economic opportunities. This was held to be true even for high school juniors and seniors and young adults who wanted to leave the migrant farm labor stream for employment in a fixed place. Nevertheless, it was decided to interview persons in these two categories, since they would be among those with at least relatively high-mobility potential.

In the case of Eastern Kentucky, the respondents' familiarity with Lexington and Louisville and with certain northern metropolitan areas was well established. To find comparable urban alternatives for the South Texas Mexican Americans was not so easy. In particular, the preliminary interviews pointed up differences between the Laredo area and the Lower Rio Grande Valley (hereinafter termed "the Valley"). It was generally felt that Laredo area residents were relatively more mobile. There was nearly universal agreement that potential migration destinations for Valley residents were limited largely to Texas, with San Antonio and Corpus Christi being relevant cities which are intermediate in size and location in comparison with the large metropolitan areas of Dallas and Houston, farther to the north. On the other hand, it was felt that Chicago (and, to a lesser extent, Detroit) was familiar to most potential interviewees in Laredo and that San Antonio, Corpus Christi, Dallas, and Houston all represented intermediate centers in relation to Chicago. These opinions formed the basis for the location alternatives listed on the interview schedules.

The interviews were made during the summer of 1970. High school juniors and seniors in the Valley were in Neighborhood Youth Corps programs in the following cities and towns: Brownsville, Los Fresnos, San Benito, La Feria, Port Isabel, Harlingen, and Raymondville. Another group of Valley junior and seniors who were interviewed were in the Migrant Cultural Enrichment Program in Rio Grande City.

Valley adult interviewees were enrolled in MDTA or Adult Basic Education programs in Edinburg, Peñitas, Mercedes, and Weslaco. Another group was enrolled in the Communications Skill Center of the Texas State Technical Institute in Harlingen. The vast majority of these persons were in their twenties or early thirties.

In Laredo, the high school interviewees were in the Migrant Cultural Enrichment Program and the adults were taking MDTA training.

In all, 1,043 persons were interviewed. They included 347 Valley adults, 463 Valley high school students, 31 Laredo adults, and 207 Laredo high school students.

The data in Table 41 show the locational preferences of all respondents under various wage rate assumptions. (The eight relative wage structures are the same as those presented to the Eastern Kentucky respondents.) With the wage rate the same in all locations (Case I) over 75 per cent of the respondents would stay in South Texas, but only a relatively small wage advantage outside South Texas (Case II) would make over 50 per cent of the respondents prefer to leave for larger Texas cities. As the wage differential between South Texas and Dallas or Houston increases, with the wage in San Antonio or Corpus Christi being in between (Cases II, III, IV, VII, VIII), there is a consistent shift out of South Texas to the northern Texas cities; the proportion who would go to the intermediate cities remains relatively constant. On the other hand, a comparison of Cases VI and VII, which reverse the wage rates in the two sets of alternatives outside of South Texas (with South Texas held constant), shows that there is virtually no difference in the attractive power of the cities outside of South Texas.

Table 42 breaks down the preference patterns according to high school and adult groups. The ordering of preferences by each group is nearly the same as in Table 41, but differences between the groups are quite evident. Compared to the totals in Table 41, it is clear in each case that the high school students prefer to leave South Texas much more often than do the adults. In Case II, for example, about 75 per cent of the high school students would *leave* South Texas, while about 66 per cent of the adults would *stay*. Whether this simply reflects the usual inverse relationship between migration and age or whether there is also a shift over time in favor of outmigration within age groups cannot be ascertained from the evidence here. However, the wide disparity between these groups and the fact that most of the adults are young suggest the possibility of a shift.

The values shown in Table 43 indicate clearly that females prefer to leave South Texas more often than do males. Only in Case VIII, where the wages outside of South Texas depart the most from the wage in South Texas, are the male and female patterns nearly the same. The females are relatively more attracted by Dallas and Houston, but a comparison of Cases VI and VII

TABLE 41

Locational Preferences of Mexican Americans in South Texas Under Differing Wage Structure Assumptions, All Respondents

Place	Wage	Relative Frequency of Preferences	Place	Wage	Relative Frequency of Preferences
Case I			*Case V*		
South Texas	$1.50	77	South Texas	$3.50	84
San Antonio,			San Antonio,		
Corpus Christi	1.50	10	Corpus Christi	2.50	8
Dallas, Houston	1.50	13	Dallas, Houston	1.50	7
Case II			*Case VI*		
South Texas	1.50	47	South Texas	1.50	31
San Antonio,			San Antonio,		
Corpus Christi	1.75	13	Corpus Christi	3.50	58
Dallas, Houston	2.00	40	Dallas, Houston	2.50	12
Case III			*Case VII*		
South Texas	1.50	38	South Texas	1.50	29
San Antonio,			San Antonio,		
Corpus Christi	2.00	15	Corpus Christi	2.50	13
Dallas, Houston	2.50	47	Dallas, Houston	3.50	59
Case IV			*Case VIII*		
South Texas	1.50	30	South Texas	1.50	23
San Antonio,			San Antonio,		
Corpus Christi	2.25	13	Corpus Christi	3.50	13
Dallas, Houston	3.00	57	Dallas, Houston	5.50	65

TABLE 42

Locational Preferences of Mexican Americans in South Texas Under Differing Wage Structure Assumptions, by High School and Adult Groups

Place	Wage	Relative Frequency of Preferences	
		High School	Adult
Case I			
South Texas	$1.50	67	84
San Antonio, Corpus Christi	1.50	12	9
Dallas, Houston	1.50	21	7
Case II			
South Texas	1.50	26	64
San Antonio, Corpus Christi	1.75	17	11
Dallas, Houston	2.00	57	25
Case III			
South Texas	1.50	18	55
San Antonio, Corpus Christi	2.00	19	11
Dallas, Houston	2.50	63	34
Case IV			
South Texas	1.50	15	43
San Antonio, Corpus Christi	2.25	15	11
Dallas, Houston	3.00	70	46

Place	Wage	Relative Frequency of Preferences	
		High School	Adult
Case V			
South Texas	$3.50	77	90
San Antonio, Corpus Christi	2.50	11	6
Dallas, Houston	1.50	12	3
Case VI			
South Texas	1.50	17	42
San Antonio, Corpus Christi	3.50	65	52
Dallas, Houston	2.50	18	6
Case VII			
South Texas	1.50	16	40
San Antonio, Corpus Christi	2.50	15	10
Dallas, Houston	3.50	69	50
Case VIII			
South Texas	1.50	13	30
San Antonio, Corpus Christi	3.50	14	12
Dallas, Houston	5.50	73	58

TABLE 43

Locational Preferences of Mexican Americans in South Texas Under Differing Wage Structure Assumptions, by Male and Female Groups

Place	Wage	Relative Frequency of Preferences	
		Male	Female
Case I			
South Texas	$1.50	83	68
San Antonio, Corpus Christi	1.50	7	14
Dallas, Houston	1.5C	10	18
Case II			
South Texas	1.50	56	34
San Antonio, Corpus Christi	1.75	12	16
Dallas, Houston	2.00	32	51
Case III			
South Texas	1.50	44	30
San Antonio, Corpus Christi	2.00	14	16
Dallas, Houston	2.50	42	54
Case IV			
South Texas	1.50	33	26
San Antonio, Corpus Christi	2.25	12	14
Dallas, Houston	3.00	55	59
Case V			
South Texas	$3.50	88	79
San Antonio, Corpus Christi	2.50	7	11
Dallas, Houston	1.50	6	10
Case VI			
South Texas	1.50	33	27
San Antonio, Corpus Christi	3.50	56	59
Dallas, Houston	2.50	10	14
Case VII			
South Texas	1.50	31	25
San Antonio, Corpus Christi	2.50	11	14
Dallas, Houston	3.50	57	61
Case VIII			
South Texas	1.50	23	22
San Antonio, Corpus Christi	3.50	12	13
Dallas, Houston	5.50	66	65

indicates almost no difference in the attractive power of San Antonio and Corpus Christi, on the one hand, and Dallas and Houston, on the other.

The response shown in Table 44 were obtained only from 666 high school students and young adults. The patterns for both those persons expecting to go to college and those not going on to school are quite similar to the responses of high school students shown in Table 42.

Table 45 presents a breakdown of preferences according to whether the respondents reside in the Laredo area or in the Valley. As in the earlier tables, there is considerable responsiveness to relative wage changes, though the Laredo respondents are notably less attached to their area than are the Valley respondents. This supports the opinions encountered in preliminary interviews. Of course, a bias is introduced by the fact that the Laredo group includes a relatively high proportion of relatively mobile high school students. However, when Laredo and Valley high school students were compared, it was found that the Laredo students were more mobile. For example, of the three alternatives shown in Table 41, with a wage structure as in Case IV, 21 per cent of the Valley students would stay home but only 12 per cent of the Laredo students; with a wage structure as in Case V, the comparable values are 22 per cent and 9 per cent, respectively. It is pertinent to note that in Case VII, where the South Texas wage is highest, 82 per cent of the Laredo students would stay home but only 75 per cent of those in the Valley. In other words, Laredo students react more to money incentives, whether they favor the home area or some other place.

The responses shown in Table 46 refer to the same areas as Table 41, except that Chicago and Detroit are substituted for Dallas and Houston. These responses were obtained only from 413 Laredo and Valley (Rio Grande City) former migrant farm workers, so they are not strictly comparable to Table 41. Nevertheless, there is a striking contrast between, first, the number of persons who would leave South Texas and second, the number of persons who would go to intermediate cities (San Antonio or Corpus Christi) rather than large, northern metropolitan areas. In Table 46, it is seen that in every case (except Case V where the relative frequencies are the same) a higher proportion would prefer to leave South Texas than in Table 41. However, there is now a definite tendency to prefer the intermediate Texas cities. For example, in Case VII, the northern city ($3.50) is preferred by 43 per cent and San Antonio or Corpus Christi ($2.50) by 37 per cent. With these rates reversed and that in South Texas held constant ($1.50), the *northern city* is preferred by *4 per cent only*, whereas *San Antonio or Corpus Christi* is preferred by *76 per cent*. (It will be recalled that reversing these rates in Table 41 showed that apparently the respondents were indifferent between San Antonio and Corpus Christi, on the one hand, and Dallas and Houston, on the other. This was also true for the various subgroups.) The marked preference for the Texas cities also shows up in the various subgroups, as seen in Table 46.

In general, the results indicate that under present conditions, the migration potential of high school graduates and many younger adults is greater than is believed or admitted by many, and probably most, of the Mexican-American leadership in South Texas. (Many Anglos also maintain that even young Mexican Americans are deeply attached to South Texas, though

TABLE 44

Locational Preferences of Mexican Americans in South Texas Under Differing Wage Structure Assumptions, by College-Bound (CB) and Non-College-Bound (NCB) Groups

Place	Wage	Relative Frequency of Preferences	
		CB	NCB
Case I			
South Texas	$1.50	69	65
San Antonio, Corpus Christi	1.50	13	15
Dallas, Houston	1.50	18	20
Case II			
South Texas	1.50	30	34
San Antonio, Corpus Christi	1.75	16	21
Dallas, Houston	2.00	54	45
Case III			
South Texas	1.50	22	23
San Antonio, Corpus Christi	2.00	18	22
Dallas, Houston	2.50	60	55
Case IV			
South Texas	1.50	18	19
San Antonio, Corpus Christi	2.25	15	19
Dallas, Houston	3.00	66	62

Place	Wage	Relative Frequency of Preferences	
		CB	NCB
Case V			
South Texas	$3.50	79	78
San Antonio, Corpus Christi	2.50	11	11
Dallas, Houston	1.50	10	12
Case VI			
South Texas	1.50	19	23
San Antonio, Corpus Christi	3.50	66	64
Dallas, Houston	2.50	16	13
Case VII			
South Texas	1.50	18	19
San Antonio, Corpus Christi	2.50	15	19
Dallas, Houston	3.50	67	62
Case VIII			
South Texas	1.50	12	19
San Antonio, Corpus Christi	3.50	14	16
Dallas, Houston	5.50	75	65

171

TABLE 45

Locational Preferences of Mexican Americans in South Texas Under Differing Wage Structure Assumptions, by Laredo Area and Lower Valley Groups

Place	Wage	Relative Frequency of Preferences	
		Laredo	Valley
Case I			
South Texas	$1.50	71	78
San Antonio, Corpus Christi	1.50	14	9
Dallas, Houston	1.50	15	13
Case II			
South Texas	1.50	28	53
San Antonio, Corpus Christi	1.75	18	12
Dallas, Houston	2.00	55	35
Case III			
South Texas	1.50	17	45
San Antonio, Corpus Christi	2.00	22	13
Dallas, Houston	2.50	61	43
Case IV			
South Texas	1.50	12	36
San Antonio, Corpus Christi	2.25	16	12
Dallas, Houston	3.00	72	52

Place	Wage	Relative Frequency of Preferences	
		Laredo	Valley
Case V			
South Texas	$3.50	82	85
San Antonio, Corpus Christi	2.50	9	8
Dallas, Houston	1.50	8	7
Case VI			
South Texas	1.50	13	36
San Antonio, Corpus Christi	3.50	71	53
Dallas, Houston	2.50	16	10
Case VII			
South Texas	1.50	10	34
San Antonio, Corpus Christi	2.50	17	11
Dallas, Houston	3.50	73	54
Case VIII			
South Texas	1.50	9	27
San Antonio, Corpus Christi	3.50	15	12
Dallas, Houston	5.50	76	61

TABLE 46

Relative Frequency of Locational Preferences of Mexican Americans
in South Texas for South Texas, San Antonio or Corpus Christi,
and Chicago or Detroit, by Selected Groups

	Wage Rate	All Respondents	High School	Adult	Male	Female	College-Bound	Non-College-Bound	Laredo	Valley
Case I										
South Texas	$1.50	75	72	79	82	68	75	74	73	78
San Antonio,										
Corpus Christi	1.50	15	16	14	12	18	15	14	15	14
Chicago, Detroit	1.50	10	12	8	6	14	10	12	11	9
Case II										
South Texas	1.50	42	36	48	52	31	42	41	37	48
San Antonio,										
Corpus Christi	1.75	23	23	23	20	25	21	28	25	20
Chicago, Detroit	2.00	35	41	29	27	43	37	31	38	32
Case III										
South Texas	1.50	31	24	37	37	25	30	30	25	38
San Antonio,										
Corpus Christi	2.00	34	37	32	37	32	33	41	38	29
Chicago, Detroit	2.50	35	39	31	27	43	37	30	36	33
Case IV										
South Texas	1.50	21	16	27	24	19	21	21	17	28
San Antonio,										
Corpus Christi	2.25	38	36	40	41	35	37	40	38	37
Chicago, Detroit	3.00	41	48	34	35	47	42	39	45	36
Case V										
South Texas	3.50	84	87	81	86	81	85	81	86	81
San Antonio,										
Corpus Christi	2.50	11	9	13	9	13	10	13	10	13
Chicago, Detroit	1.50	5	5	5	4	6	5	6	4	6
Case VI										
South Texas	1.50	20	15	25	24	16	20	20	16	25
San Antonio,										
Corpus Christi	3.50	76	80	72	73	79	76	76	80	71
Chicago, Detroit	2.50	4	5	3	3	5	4	4	5	3
Case VII										
South Texas	1.50	20	14	27	22	18	21	18	15	28
San Antonio,										
Corpus Christi	2.50	37	37	37	42	32	34	46	39	34
Chicago, Detroit	3.50	43	49	37	36	50	45	37	46	38
Case VIII										
South Texas	1.50	14	11	16	14	13	14	13	12	16
San Antonio,										
Corpus Christi	3.50	30	32	28	33	27	27	39	34	25
Chicago, Detroit	5.50	56	57	56	53	59	60	48	54	60

TABLE 47

Relative Frequency of Locational Preferences of Mexican Americans in South Texas for South Texas, San Antonio or Corpus Christi, and Dallas or Houston, if There Were a Government Relocation Aid Program, by Selected Groups

	Wage Rate	All Respondents	High School	Adult	Male	Female	College-Bound	Non-College-Bound	Laredo	Valley
Case I										
South Texas	$1.50	57	52	62	63	50	56	58	53	62
San Antonio,										
Corpus Christi	1.50	19	19	19	16	21	16	27	20	17
Dallas, Houston	1.50	24	29	20	21	28	28	15	27	21
Case II										
South Texas	1.50	16	11	21	18	13	15	17	12	22
San Antonio,										
Corpus Christi	2.50	19	19	19	21	17	17	25	21	17
Dallas, Houston	3.50	65	70	60	61	69	68	58	68	62
Case III										
South Texas	1.50	13	10	15	14	11	13	13	11	16
San Antonio,										
Corpus Christi	3.50	20	23	16	22	17	17	25	24	13
Dallas, Houston	5.50	68	67	68	63	72	70	62	65	71
Case IV										
South Texas	3.50	78	75	80	84	71	79	75	76	80
San Antonio,										
Corpus Christi	2.50	12	12	12	9	15	12	13	13	10
Dallas, Houston	1.50	10	12	8	6	14	9	13	11	9
Case V										
South Texas	1.50	16	12	19	15	16	14	16	12	20
San Antonio,										
Corpus Christi	3.50	73	75	71	76	70	75	69	76	69
Dallas, Houston	2.50	12	13	10	9	14	11	14	12	11

TABLE 48

Relative Frequency of Locational Preferences of Mexican Americans
in South Texas for South Texas, San Antonio or Corpus Christi,
and Chicago or Detroit, if There Were a Government Relocation
Aid Program, by Selected Groups

	Wage Rate	All Respondents	High School	Adult	Male	Female	College-Bound	Non-College-Bound	Laredo	Valley
Case I										
South Texas	$1.50	68	66	71	77	59	68	68	67	70
San Antonio,										
Corpus Christi	1.50	21	19	22	16	25	20	21	20	22
Chicago, Detroit	1.50	11	15	7	7	15	11	11	13	8
Case II										
South Texas	1.50	18	14	21	20	16	18	16	15	22
San Antonio,										
Corpus Christi	2.50	36	31	41	40	32	34	41	34	38
Chicago, Detroit	3.50	46	55	38	40	53	48	43	51	40
Case III										
South Texas	1.50	13	11	15	13	13	12	14	11	16
San Antonio,										
Corpus Christi	3.50	30	29	32	32	29	30	32	31	29
Chicago, Detroit	5.50	57	60	53	55	58	58	55	58	55
Case IV										
South Texas	3.50	79	76	83	86	73	81	75	77	83
San Antonio,										
Corpus Christi	2.50	14	17	11	10	19	14	15	17	10
Chicago, Detroit	1.50	6	7	6	4	8	5	10	6	7
Case V										
South Texas	1.50	17	15	19	19	15	17	17	15	20
San Antonio,										
Corpus Christi	3.50	77	78	75	77	77	78	76	79	73
Chicago, Detroit	2.50	6	7	5	4	8	6	7	6	6

often for different reasons than the Mexican-American leadership gives. Anglo viewpoints are often based on a desire, latent or overt, to exploit, whereas the Mexican-American bias often is based on feelings of pride that tend to become associated with place, as well as ethnic factors.) On the basis of preliminary interviews, it was hypothesized that those Mexican Americans who would prefer to migrate would prefer San Antonio or Corpus Christi over Dallas or Houston. However, the data indicate that all of these Texas cities have approximately equal attractiveness to potential migrants. In contrast, it is quite clear that the Texas cities are preferred to Chicago or Detroit.

The high school students and the Laredo adults were asked the question: "If there were a government program to pay your moving expenses, find you a job, help find you a place to live and help to get you settled, how much more willing than you are now would you be to leave your home town?" Of the 701 respondents, 45 per cent said they would be a lot more willing and 35 per cent stated they would be moderately more willing. None of the comparable percentages for the various subgroups varied by more than 3 percentage points from these values. Tables 47 and 48 (pages 174-75) show that many more persons would prefer to leave South Texas if there were a government program to assist in relocation. A comparison of Cases II and V in Table 47 shows that such a program would increase the number and proportion of migrants who would go to the intermediate growth centers (compare these cases with Cases VI and VII in Tables 41 through 45). In Table 48, Chicago and Detroit replace Dallas and Houston. Here the introduction of government relocation assistance does not have the same degree of influence on rechanneling migration paths. Nevertheless, in comparing Case I in Table 46 with Case I in Table 48 and Case V in Table 46 with the corresponding Case IV in Table 48, it is evident that relocation assistance would increase outmigration—and would do so in favor of San Antonio and Corpus Christi.

The respondents also were asked the question: "If you would leave the town where you live now, would your decision where to go be influenced by where friends and relatives have gone?" Of all persons responding, 47 per cent replied in the affirmative. Of this group, 33 per cent indicated that the influence of family and friends would be weak; the remainder felt it would be either moderate (43 per cent) or strong (26 per cent). The responses of the various subgroups varied from an affirmative 44 per cent from the adult group to 54 per cent for the non-college-bound group. It will be recalled that Price's study of the adaptation of migrants from rural areas to cities found that all of the migrants, including the Mexican Americans, spent their first night in the city with friends or relatives. Thus, when the time actually comes to move, more people are apparently influenced by friends and relatives than they might have believed earlier.

Finally, expected place of residence in five years for all respondents and each subgroup proportionately is shown in the table opposite. Over 50 per cent of all respondents expect to live outside of South Texas. The proportion of persons in the high school and college-bound groups who expect to reside outside of the region is particularly large, whereas the adult subgroup shows the greatest expectations of remaining. About 25 per cent of all respondents expect to live in places other than South Texas or the four Texas cities in question.

	South Texas	San Antonio or Corpus Christi	Dallas or Houston	Elsewhere
All Respondents	47	11	17	26
High School	34	13	21	32
Adult	58	9	13	20
Male	52	9	15	23
Female	39	13	19	29
College-Bound	28	14	22	35
Non-College-Bound	42	13	15	29
Laredo	38	16	20	26
Valley	49	9	16	26

Despite past tendencies for many Mexican Americans from South Texas to move to California, only 3.6 per cent of all respondents indicated that they expected to live there in five years.

SUMMARY AND CONCLUSIONS

Remoteness from major centers of the nation, poor resources, underdeveloped human resources, and pressures from Mexico have combined to make South Texas one of the country's poorest regions and one where solutions seem the most difficult. Although government policy has designated "growth centers" within South Texas, they do not have sufficient external economies to improve significantly the economic opportunities available in the region.

In contrast to the reluctance of firms to move into South Texas, there is considerable willingness, at least on the part of younger persons, to leave the region to take advantage of economic and other opportunities elsewhere. The evidence indicates that a government program to assist those who choose to move would increase outmigration from the region and that it might redirect some migration into San Antonio and Corpus Christi from other SMSA's. Such a program might be of particular benefit to females. Females express a greater desire to leave the area than males, but the Social Security Administration sample data indicate that about 75 per cent of the outmigrants from South Texas are males.

The Mexican Americans responding to the survey on locational preferences tended to prefer Texas cities to Chicago or Detroit, but they did not show any particular preference for either San Antonio and Corpus Christi, on the one hand, or Dallas and Houston, on the other. In any event, Corpus Christi and, especially, San Antonio seem to be the most feasible growth centers for the people of South Texas. They are closer to the region than Houston or Dallas and probably have fewer diseconomies. San Antonio exerts an influence over a large part of South Texas, and evidence indicates that

Mexican-American migrants from South Texas to San Antonio are the happiest and best-adjusted of all migrant groups moving from rural to urban places.

NOTES

1. Fred H. Schmidt, *Spanish Surnamed American Employment in the Southwest* (Washington, D.C.: Government Printing Office, 1970), p. 2; and *Manpower Report of the President, 1970* (Washington, D.C.: Government Printing Office, 1970), pp. 100-102.

2. Joan W. Moore, *Mexican-Americans: Problems and Prospects* (Madison: Institute for Research on Poverty, University of Wisconsin, 1967), p. 33.

3. H. L. Browning and S. D. McLemore, *A Statistical Profile of the Spanish Surname Population of Texas* (Austin: Bureau of Business Research, University of Texas, 1964), p. 50.

4. *Ibid.*, pp. 69-79.

5. Inter-Agency Committee on Mexican American Affairs, *The Mexican American, A New Focus on Opportunity* (Washington, D.C.: Government Printing Office, 1968).

6. Walter Fogel, *Mexican Americans in Southwest Labor Markets,* Mexican American Study Project, Advance Report No. 10 (Los Angeles: U.C.L.A. Graduate School of Business Administration, October, 1967), pp. 32-33.

7. Moore, *op. cit.*, p. 22.

8. Browning and McLemore, *op. cit.*, p. 29.

9. *Ibid.*, p. 30.

10. *Ibid.*, pp. 69-79.

11. Moore, *op. cit.*, p. 26.

12. Browning and McLemore, *op. cit.*, p. 35.

13. Moore, *op. cit.*, pp. 26-29.

14. Browning and McLemore, *op. cit.*, p. 35.

15. Leo Grebler, *Mexican Immigration to the United States: The Record and Its Implications*, Mexican American Study Project, Advance Report No. 2 (Los Angeles: U.C.L.A. Graduate School of Business Administration, January, 1966), p. 53.

16. *Ibid.*, p. 51.

17. Fogel, *op. cit.*, p. 107.

18. Browning and McLemore, *op. cit.*, p. 9, citied by Fogel, *op. cit.*, p. 107.

19. Data based on a 1 per cent sample of workers covered by the Social Security Administration (see Appendix).

20. Dale E. Hathaway, "Migration From Agriculture: The Historical Record and Its Meaning," *American Economic Review*, Vol. 49 (May, 1960), 385-86.

21. *Ibid.*, pp. 386-87.

22. Fogel, *op. cit.,* p. 49.

23. Grebler, *op. cit.*, p. 65.

24. Robert R. Nathan Associates, *Industrial and Employment Potential of the United States-Mexico Border*, prepared for U.S. Department of Commerce, Economic Development Administration, December, 1968, p. 254.

25. *Ibid.*

26. *Ibid.*, p. 253.

27. *Ibid.*, p. 257.

28. *Ibid.*, pp. 256-58.

29. *Ibid.*, p. 258.

30. *Ibid.*, p. 259.

31. *Ibid.*, p. 261.

32. Howard W. Davis, "A Case Study of Industrial Location," *Land Economics*, Vol. 45, No. 4 (November, 1969), 444-45.

33. *Ibid.*, p. 445.

34. *Ibid.*, p. 452.

35. U.S. Department of Labor, "Sub-Employment in the Slums of San Antonio" (unpublished document made available to the author by the Texas Employment Commission's San Antonio office).

36. *A Study of Economic Consequences of Rural to Urban Migration*, OEO Contract B 89-4594, Tracor Project 253-006 (December, 1969), Vols. 1-3.

37. *Ibid.*, Vol. 1, p. 12.

CHAPTER

9

MIGRATION,
HOUSING,
AND THE COSTS
OF GROWTH

In the preceding chapters, stress has been placed on the role of growth centers in providing economic opportunity for migrants and, to a lesser extent, on commuters from lagging hinterland areas. An important reason is that data on migration are easier to obtain than data on spread effects as a consequence of conceptual problems in analyzing spread effects. There is relatively little ambiguity in identifying a person who moves from one place to another, but it is extremely difficult to determine whether a given employment change in a hinterland area is a consequence of some causal force in the core area; despite such aids as input-output analysis, there are usually too many factors influencing economic activity in the hinterland to isolate those specifically attributable to linkages with the growth center. More important, however, such evidence as we have does not make a convincing case that growth center policies have had much success in transforming large, lagging areas into zones of prosperity.

THE MIGRATION ISSUE

So far, we have not given much attention to the difficulties involved in migration. Though the author has dealt with this issue at length elsewhere,[1] it is necessary to examine it here specifically in the context of the growth center considerations that have been developed.

In investigating the development efforts being made in numerous lagging areas of the United States and Western Europe, one is particularly struck by the negative responses of local leaders, including local officials of regional development agencies of national governments, to any suggestions involving outmigration. (Sometimes the need for outmigration is admitted privately,

181

though local pressures preclude expression of this sentiment publicly.) Before the subject was even raised, a Mexican-American leader in South Texas stated that "when we discuss the problems of our area let us please not talk about migration. We already have enough of that. What we need is jobs for our people." The same statement in virtually the same words could be heard in any lagging area. What this viewpoint misses is not only a full comprehension of the relative disadvantages of the lagging region—it is usually assumed that "somehow" jobs can be "brought" to the people of the area—but any real appreciation of the desire of people to move and the need for programs which respond to this desire. We have already seen in previous chapters that the mobility potential from lagging areas is still great. More generally, a well-known study of the geographic mobility of labor found that one out of five family heads would *prefer* to move. However, the number who actually *expected* to move within one year was only half as large, or about one in ten. The actual mobility rate was about only one in twenty per year for moves across labor market boundaries. Thus actual mobility was only about half of the expected mobility, which, in turn, was only about half of desired mobility.[2] Similarly, Harvey Perloff points out that "clearly it is not the lack of out-migration from the poorer areas, but the magnitude of out-migration required to achieve income equality (given the rate of population replacement in these areas) that is a basic difficulty facing the poorer regions of the country."[3]

It should be emphasized that the kind of growth center strategy proposed in this study in no way implies "forcing" anyone to move. In our market system, it is no more possible to compel people to leave lagging areas than it is possible to compel industry to move into them. The question is one of giving people viable alternatives and, therefore, the possibility of genuine choice. Families and individuals wanting to relocate should be offered a comprehensive program of assistance including education and health aids, vocational training, the information which could be made available from a coordinated national employment service, as well as counseling and monetary help.

Obviously not everyone in lagging areas has a desire to move, nor would they even if they were offered a broad range of assistance programs. Nevertheless, there are large numbers of nonmovers, as well as persons who have made irrational moves, who could be given improved economic opportunity through comprehensive relocation programs. It is not necessary that all efforts to attract industry to lagging areas be abolished, but the funds expended on many ill-conceived attempts in this regard would probably benefit more of the target population if devoted to relocation efforts. We are, after all, talking about marginal shifts and not movement of entire populations. It may be hoped that the nation as a whole would be willing to help the unemployed and underemployed in lagging regions who are unwilling or unable to move because of age, local responsibilities, sickness, and similar problems. But these are problems of welfare rather than investment in human resources and are outside the realm of growth center strategy.

Labor mobility demonstration programs carried out under the Manpower Development and Training Act "have clearly demonstrated that it is possible to divert migrants from the traditional tracks to cities with tight labor markets."[4] Donald Schon's analysis of these projects indicates that while they offered a combination of aids, "access to information about cities other than the traditional migrant terminals, and in particular, cities where jobs exist, seems to be of fundamental importance" and that "alternate informational systems must be developed to counteract the traditional networks if more efficient utilization of manpower requires diverting traditional migrant tracks."[5] This finding clearly accords with the locational preference studies discussed in previous chapters.

Another prominent factor influencing choice of location is the guarantee of a job in the receiving area. To obtain a firm job offer before relocation, the potential migrant must either receive a travel allowance for pre-employment interviews or else there must be a close working relationship between the agencies which are involved at both the sending and receiving ends of the migration path. A critical point also arises between the time a person decides to relocate and the time he actually moves. Many potential migrants back down from moving during this interval because of the influence of family, ownership, contract, or membership ties to the home area. Frequently attempts are made by merchants, growers, and others who have advanced money or other considerations to potential movers to prevent their relocation, even though the worker's indebtedness is likely to worsen if he stays in the lagging area. To overcome this obstacle to movement, it has been recommended that a system be established "for insuring payment of debts after the migrant relocates or for providing grants or long-term, low-interest, 'debt consolidation' loans to migrants so that their past outstanding debts may be paid prior to relocation."[6]

In addition to providing for transportation costs and for storage of household goods, the mobility projects have shown that the newly arrived migrant also requires a reception mechanism in the urban area. For example, he may need help in finding the best routes to work, aid in adjusting to new types of work conditions and in making social and organizational contacts. In the process of "getting settled" the migrant may also need assistance in arranging car pools with fellow workers, finding medical and dental care, opening a bank account, dealing with problems in his new job, and carrying out other tasks which might seem commonplace to the typical city dweller.[7]

THE HOUSING PROBLEM

Despite the catalogue of difficulties already noted, the greatest problem in labor mobility demonstration projects has been housing. This point has been emphasized in every interview the author has had with officials involved in the projects. The supply of housing available to low-income migrants in most cities is often substandard, located in neighborhoods with poor public and private services, poorly located in relation to public transportation facilities or place of employment, and often overpriced. Moreover, in strange cities, families may need help even in finding poor housing. Schon is quite correct in stating:

The importance of increasing the supply of decent housing available to low income inmigrants, as well as the housing of the urban poor in general, cannot be overemphasized, since it is a significant determinant of the success of migration in overcoming poverty and in realizing the full potential of the migrants' manpower. That is, poor housing in poor neighborhoods tends not only to perpetuate the condition of poverty, but also to be strongly work-related, in that it affects health, use of leisure time, and education. Therefore, a program concerned on a national level with increasing the probability of "success" of rural-to-urban migration must address the problem of housing supply with as much vigor as the problem of diverting migrants to cities with high labor needs.[8]

The housing secured by the imigrant depends not only on what he wants and is able to afford but also on the alternatives made available to him. These alternatives come from two sources: the standing stock and new construction. The household population within any region is, at any point in time, housed in a stock of dwellings that has been accumulating over a long period of time. During any period of time, there is movement in and out of a proportion of the units in that stock.* There are influences that operate both through demand and supply which produce the disequilibria that generate housing adjustment involving moves. If some of this movement involves "established" households indigenous to the region, units in the standing stock will be made available in the market. When the movement involves the newly formed family, the household moving in from outside, or the family forced to move because of the removal of units from the stock, there will be "excess" demand in the regional housing market. Construction will become profitable, and hence, new housing units will come onto the market as the construction industry responds to market pressures.**

How do market-supply conditions create special difficulties for the immigrant? First is the problem of overall supply, which is associated with what is usually termed the "short housing cycle."[9] Housing markets are subject to recurring periods of upswing and decline which are closely correlated with periods of "ease" and "tightness" in the residential mortgage market. The ultimate source of this instability is unevenness in the growth of the economy. Sequentially, the process starts with growth instability, which, in turn, generates exaggerated financial repercussions in the nation's residential mortgage market. These financial effects are translated into cycle-like movements in residential housing markets because of the importance of credit both to demanders and to suppliers.[10]

---

*Census mobility data indicate that one out of every five persons one year or older moves each year. (See *Current Population Reports*, Series P-20, No. 171.)

**Clues as to the relative importance of construction as a source of supply are found in data relating newly constructed units to the proportion of owner-occupied dwellings involved in real estate transactions. One survey indicated that approximately 33 per cent were newly constructed units. (See Robert M. Fisher, "Monetary Policy: Its Relation to Mortgage Lending and Land Economics," *Land Economics*, Vol. 45 (November, 1963), 418-24.)

During periods of economic "boom," when national output is at capacity levels, the residential mortgage market becomes tight, bringing about a slowdown in activity in the housing market. Slack in the economy, on the other hand, has the effect of increasing the flow of funds into residential mortgages, which in turn stimulates activity in the housing market. This process has repercussions on the housing search of the inmigrant. Presumably, families are most likely to migrate from one region to another when economic opportunities are at peak levels—that is, during periods of economic boom. But these are periods in which there is tightness in financial markets, which has the effect of reducing the overall supply of dwelling units coming onto the market. Those who search for housing during these times, including those with low incomes, will have fewer dwellings from which to choose. Their alternatives are best during periods of economic slack. But again, these are times when families have less incentive to move from one region to another.

A second way in which supply factors operate to restrict the choices available to the low-income migrant is in the response of the construction industry to the demands of those with low incomes. To the family moving into a community, this response is crucial. Newly constructed dwellings are important because of their appeal to inmigrants. There are usually many attributes that families look for in housing, and no two dwellings are alike in terms of these attributes.* Comparisons are not easily made when the units involved are highly differentiated, and the inmigrant is at a disadvantage in making such comparisons because he knows much less than do local residents about the services associated with the dwelling and its location. The most reliable information available to those moving into a community concerns those features that can be easily seen during the relatively short inspections that are feasible—features in which new units generally have a comparative advantage (e.g., up-to-date heating, plumbing facilities, and design). Reliable information about more intangible factors such as schools and neighborhood stability are more difficult to obtain. These are matters about which the inmigrant is more uncertain, and it is reasonable to suppose that he would be disposed to moving into the new rather than the old.[11]

Even so, the low-income migrant will encounter additional problems because there are clear indications that the construction industry is more responsive to the demands of those with higher incomes.[12] Moves into a community by low-income families usually involve standing stock units which have filtered down from the higher rent and value strata. This process is not simply a matter of units being held by the upper end of the income distribution filtering down to those at the lower end. Not all new construction is for those at the upper end of the income distribution, nor is income the only constraint that influences the way in which available housing units are reallocated to those entering the market. What the process does do, however, is to assign most low-income families to a previously occupied unit; this means that the low-income inmigrant tends

---

*Not only are there differences with respect to such characteristics as size and design, but there is a pervasive set of differences in terms of the location of the housing unit. In essence, each dwelling occupies a unique point in geographic space.

to have something less than the best accommodations possible in view of his circumstances.

Substandard housing is, of course, a complicated and controversial phenomenon. We do know, however, that slums are not built; rather they consist of aging units that have filtered through the housing stock to their present state of disrepair. They become substandard because of decisions owners have made with respect to upkeep. When rental units are involved, the monopoly, and hence exploitative position, of the landlord is usually emphasized as the key factor giving rise to low upkeep. Without denying that monopolistic elements in this market contribute to the end results, the poor care that some tenants take of this housing also contributes to the deterioration process. It has been demonstrated that in a market system, hard use by low-income families leads to low levels of upkeep.[13] Since some of the low-income families moving into urban growth centers come from rural areas where they lived in substandard housing,[14] it is reasonable to expect that some will behave in ways that make upkeep less profitable. By their actions, such tenants encourage landlords to cut back on upkeep, thereby accelerating the deterioration process. Moreover, the effects of deterioration tend to spread to neighboring units.[15]

If the goal of regional policy is to promote growth in lagging areas, then housing will tend to be assigned relatively low priority. Infrastructure investments will be given higher priority, and it probably will be assumed that economic revival will generate the market pressures, which, in turn, will lead to new housing construction. If, as in the case of the United States, the region is located in a nation that has a well-developed and responsive construction industry, this is probably a reasonable assumption.[16] However, if place-oriented policies fail to induce significant economic expansion, then the housing situation will not be significantly improved.

Public housing exists in many of our cities, and there are a variety of ways in which assistance is given to low-income families who choose to live in private dwelling units. However, while some difficulties with housing may be due to the meagerness of federal efforts, it is by no means clear that more subsidies are all that is required to solve these problems. In particular, racial discrimination requires special attention. Moreover, even if subsidies are necessary, the particular form which they should take is still not clear; very little rigorous analysis has been made of the relative effectiveness of rent supplements, public housing, and home-ownership subsidies.

Obviously, the housing problem of the low-income migrant will be alleviated if the housing circumstances of those now living in substandard housing are improved. However, any nonmarket effort to help minimize the housing problems of the inmigrant will involve institutions that may have a somewhat different perspective with respect to housing and housing problems than that associated with growth center policy.

If growth center policy promotes the growth of viable intermediate-size centers, there may be problems similar to those besetting the big cities, but they will be present to a lesser degree. A growth center strategy would require effective coordination between housing and regional development policies. At present, efforts to deal with substandard housing appear to be concentrated in places where the problems are most severe, that is, in the larger metropolitan areas. Under a growth center policy, housing policies should be flexible enough to benefit low-income families moving to growth centers.

DEVELOPMENTAL PROBLEMS IN
GROWTH CENTERS

Not all problems related to a growth center policy fall on the lagging hinterlands or on the migrants to growth centers. Although, in questions of community size, "bigger" is commonly associated with "better" (local responses to the results of the 1970 census are a good example), there are definite disadvantages to growth. Of course, community expansion is generally welcomed with good reason by established merchants, utilities, banks, and real property owners and realtors, but other members of the community may not be affected by growth, and still others may be hurt by it. Some long-term residents may be pushed out of their pleasant neighborhoods by the bulldozer or by urban blight. Some firms may face higher wage costs and taxes and possibly increased external diseconomies of congestion. It is also difficult to know how to count new jobs filled by inmigrants or new business opportunities that are exploited by firms coming in from other places.[17] Wilbur Thompson points out that rapid job creation and net inmigration may produce serious strains:

> Overloaded facilities deteriorate rapidly, creating urban blight; congestion, delays, and shortages raise the cost of doing business and lower living amenities in the booming place. Who would argue that the social costs of housing shortages and crowded schools do not, in the long run, inflict social costs that rival those of too-slow local growth? To be sure, there will be strong voices in the community all too ready to risk erring on the side of too-fast growth as the lesser evil. . . . But the local economy pays, as well as receives, high rents and land prices in a set of pure fiscal transfers that redistribute but do not create new wealth or income; growthmanship need not be blindly served.[18]

Although there is a dearth of studies of what is gained and lost by growth of cities, Ronald Crowley's analysis of inmigration to ninety-four American cities from 1955 to 1960 indicates that in 1960, the inmigrants imposed a median net burden of about $2,500,000. The median burden per migrant was $72 and that per city resident, $8. The magnitude of the burden was subject to wide variations, especially with respect to the region in which the central city is located, but city size did not appear to be a crucial factor. Crowley concludes that in general, "significant costs of inmigration do exist. Some of these costs may be only temporary, but they are positive and represent a subsidization of migrants by nonmigrant residents of a city for a period of time immediately following migration."[19]

To the author's knowledge, there has never been a case, in the United States or elsewhere, of a community refusing to be a "growth center" when so designated by planning officials. On the other hand, many communities have been angered by not being designated. Moreover, discussions of growth center strategies, as well as other regional development policies, often imply that regional "problems" only exist in lagging areas or in large metropolitan areas. All of these factors militate against making intermediate-size growth centers a key part of national urban policy because this approach seems, to paraphrase Scripture, to give too much to them which hath and to take too much away from them which hath not, even that which they hath. It has been argued at length in this volume that the net advantages to be found in intermediate-size growth centers are likely to be greater than those either in lagging regions or congested metropolitan areas. Here, however, it should be emphasized that the cities which would receive subsidies as growth centers would probably have greater problems than their local boosters realize. Indeed, a more reticent attitude on the part of the boosters might even make it easier for their cities to obtain subsidies. Perhaps our expectations begin to retreat from reality at this point.

Whatever the difficulties intermediate-size growth centers would experience as a consequence of accelerated growth, they still have two important advantages. First, the policy measures that have been proposed in the present study are consistent with the general urban framework (*armature urbaine*) that has evolved in the United States, largely through the operations of the market system. (The history of centrally planned economies during this century has demonstrated that it is difficult to circumvent the market; hence, recent movements have been toward various forms of market socialism.) Even if we could completely alter the largely market-determined spatial allocation of resources by various policy tools, the magnitude of the effort required would be far outside the realm of the politically feasible. In brief, then, the proposed growth center strategy is not intended to change "the system" so much as to make its functioning more rational.

Finally, the problems which accelerated growth might bring to growth centers can be ameliorated by enlightened city planning. G. M. Neutze finds that "unless the government knows which centres are going to grow it can only provide public services after the demand has appeared. If there is planned growth of a few centres they can be provided, with confidence, in advance."[20] Thus, city planning is not merely an adornment but an indispensable ingredient in growth center policy.

NOTES

1. Niles M. Hansen, *Rural Poverty and the Urban Crisis* (Bloomington: Indiana University Press, 1970).

2. John Lansing and Eva Mueller, *The Geographic Mobility of Labor* (Ann Arbor: University of Michigan Survey Research Center, 1967), p. 24.

3. Harvey Perloff, with Vera Dodds, *How a Region Grows* (New York: Committee for Economic Development, 1963), p. 134.

4. Donald Schon, "Assimilation of Migrants into Urban Centers," in President's National Advisory Commission on Rural Poverty, *Rural Poverty in the United States* (Washington, D.C.: Government Printing Office, 1968), p. 280. See also Hansen, *op. cit.*, Chapter 11.

5. Schon, *op. cit.*, p. 280.

6. *Ibid.*, p. 281.

7. *Ibid.*

8. *Ibid.* See also Labor Mobility Services Unit, U.S. Employment Service, *Moving to Work* (Washington, D.C.: U.S. Employment Service, 1968).

9. For a recent survey of both the short housing cycle and the literature that concerns it, see Alan R. Winger, "Fluctuations in Residential Construction," *The Mississippi Valley Journal of Business and Economics* (forthcoming).

10. For a more detailed discussion of the way in which credit influences our residential credit market, see Alan R. Winger, "Short-Term Activity in Residential Construction Markets: Some Regional Considerations," *Southern Economic Journal*, Vol. 36 (April, 1970), 390-403.

11. For a more detailed discussion of this point, see Alan R. Winger, "Mover Origin, Residential Construction and the Urban Form," Discussion Paper No. 26, Program on the Role of Growth Centers in Regional Economic Development (Lexington: University of Kentucky, February, 1970).

12. See Alan R. Winger, "Residential Construction and the Urban Housing Adjustments of the Migrating Household," Discussion Paper No. 25, Program on the Role of Growth Centers in Regional Economic Development (Lexington: University of Kentucky, February, 1970).

13. William R. Russell and Alan R. Winger, "A Neglected Aspect of Housing Behavior in Housing Programs for the Urban Poor," *Land Economics* (forthcoming).

14. The Report of the President's Committee on Urban Housing, "Technical Studies—Volume I," 1968, p. 11.

15. See Alvin Schorr, "Housing the Poor," in W. J. Bloomberg and H. J. Schmandt, eds., *Power, Poverty and Urban Policy* (Beverly Hills, Calif.: Sage Publications, 1968), pp. 115-50.

16. The construction industry's responsiveness to regional demand pressures shows up in Winger, *op. cit.*

17. Edgar M. Hoover, "Some Old and New Issues in Regional Development," in E. A. G. Robinson, ed., *Backward Areas in Advanced Countries* (New York: St. Martin's Press, 1969), pp. 348-49.

18. Wilbur R. Thompson, "The Economic Base of Urban Problems," in Neil W. Chamberlain, ed., *Contemporary Economic Issues* (Homewood, Ill.: Richard D. Irwin, 1969), pp. 21-22. See also Ezra J. Mishan, *The Costs of Economic Growth* (New York: Frederick A. Praeger, 1967).

19. Ronald W. Crowley, "An Empirical Investigation of Some Local Public Costs of In-Migration to Cities," *Journal of Human Resources,* Vol. 5, No. 1 (Winter, 1970), 11.

20. G. M. Neutze, *Economic Policy and the Size of Cities* (New York: Augustus M. Kelley, 1967), p. 127.

PART

III

CONCLUSIONS

10

It has been argued in this study that the market mechanism leads to the geographic concentration of economic activity and population because of the external economies of agglomeration, which accrue to firms locating in proximity to other firms; public overhead capital; and a relatively large and well-educated and well-trained labor force. However, such concentration is not necessarily desirable from a social point of view because of the external diseconomies (congestion, air pollution, noise, etc.) which are generated by crowding. Because firms internalize most of the benefits from agglomeration economies but internalize only a fraction of the diseconomies, it is probable that the free play of market forces will result in levels of concentration which exceed those which are socially desirable. Whenever the difference between the marginal social benefits of growth and the concomitant marginal costs are such that a larger net social product could be obtained in an alternative location, then a city has become too big. Of course, it is difficult to "prove" when a city has become too big because it is not possible to measure these variables with any real precision. Nevertheless, the fact that a growing number of countries have been developing policies to curb the growth of large metropolitan areas is indicative of more than rural nostalgia.

Growth center strategies have been particularly prominent among the policies that have been instituted to influence the location of economic activity. The principal problem with this approach has been an almost universal tendency to attempt to promote growth in lagging areas. As a consequence, the designated growth centers have generally remained relatively stagnant, or else the growth which has been stimulated by public policy measures has not been transmitted to the surrounding hinterland. Growth center theory has not been very helpful in this regard because, although it has analyzed the agglomeration process in terms of external economies, it has been notably weak in spelling out in detail how potentially beneficial spread effects may, in fact, actually be

193

transmitted to the hinterlands. Growth center theories and policies also have tended to focus on infrastructure investment in the narrow sense and have thereby diverted attention away from the critical health, education, and social problems which characterize most lagging regions.

The growth center strategy developed in this volume concentrates on viable urban centers, which are neither merely relatively bright spots in generally lagging areas nor large, congested, metropolitan areas. It also puts more stress on movement of people from lagging areas to growth centers than on spread effects from growth centers to lagging areas. Big cities, on the one hand, and small towns and rural areas, on the other, obviously need and will receive a great deal of public investment, but there are no persuasive reasons why they should be singled out for special favor—especially when growing intermediate-size cities offer more opportunities in terms of existing external economies than do small towns and rural areas and fewer diseconomies than the large metropolitan areas. There is evidence for believing that self-sustained growth is easier to maintain in a city of 200,000 than in smaller places. On the other hand, external diseconomies may make expansion of alternative locations desirable from an opportunity-cost viewpoint after a city passes, say, the 750,000 mark. Of course, these are rough indicators and not magic numbers, and more flexible limits might accommodate cities in the range from 50,000 to one million or somewhat more.

During the 1960's, there was an increasing tendency to believe that somehow the problems which plagued the nation as a result of shifts in population and economic activity were being ameliorated by some corrective mechanism—usually vaguely defined. *Business Week* recently put the matter this way:

> Throughout the decade, all levels of government—and the businessess that depended on them for data—accepted the belief that the great population revolution of the 1950s was abating. The westward tip of the nation's population center of gravity; the depopulation of rural areas and central core cities; the growth of suburbs and major metropolitan areas; the black migration from the South—all of these were thought to be slowing perceptibly.[1]

On the basis of preliminary counts of forty-two states and scattered counties in the states yet to be completed at this writing, there is sound reason to believe that blacks are leaving the rural South at a rate as high as that during the 1950's, when nearly 1.5 million left the region. The widespread belief that the gap between rural and urban areas was narrowing during the 1960's and that smaller metropolitan areas were growing faster than large ones now seems erroneous. Nor are the central cities holding their own against the suburbs, which for the first time have more people than either the central cities or rural areas. Most large central cities outside of the Gulf Coast and the Southwest have again lost population. Only recently, the proportion of counties expected to lose population was widely quoted to be 33 per cent, but now the figure is more likely to be 50 per cent—the same proportion as in the 1950's.[2]

These results have obvious implications for public policy. *Business Week* points out:

> The apparent juggernaut of urbanization is also a severe shock to people in the Administration and in Congress concerned about the increasing density of the large metropolitan areas. During the debates last winter on a bill to establish a Presidential Commission on Population Growth and the American Future, a good deal was made of the need to encourage a redistribution of the U.S. population as a matter of national policy. The commission, which is just getting underway, will be under considerable pressure to devise recommendations that will take the pressure off the crowded coastlines.[3]

Undoubtedly there will be a new flood of recommendations for subsidies to attract economic activity to lagging, and for the most part rural, areas. Unfortunately, policies which merely try to check migration do little service to either the nation as a whole or the individuals concerned, at least from an opportunity-cost viewpoint. Return migration, in particular, shows that the real problem of lagging regions is underinvestment in human resources rather than migration as such, which is more a symptom than a cause. There are, of course, many persons in lagging areas whose prospects for either local employment or for retraining and migration are not bright. Older workers would be especially likely to be in this situation. However, this is a question of welfare rather than of economic development. It is also misleading to recommend rural development on the ground that the only alternative is migration to big cities with severe ghetto problems. This position ignores the many rapidly growing intermediate-size cities whose problems are still relatively manageable. If there is planned growth of those intermediate-size cities with relevance to the populations of lagging regions, then these growth centers can be provided with an integrated and coherent system of public overhead capital in advance of demand. Moreover, it is not necessary that a growth center be limited to one city. A system of cities or towns linked by adequate transportation and communications might serve as well or better. Such a system could take the form of a cluster of urban centers or a development axis. In any case, public policy for lagging areas should emphasize manpower and human resource development programs linked to opportunities in intermediate-size growth centers.

A great deal of evidence indicates that large numbers of persons in lagging areas prefer to leave their regions and that they have a pronounced tendency to prefer intermediate-size growth centers not too distant from their homes. There also is clear evidence that migrants from lagging rural areas to intermediate-size growth centers tend to adapt well to their urban environments. This is shown in data presented in the case studies of this volume and also in data pertaining to relocatees who participated in labor mobility pilot projects coordinated by the Department of Labor. These demonstration projects, which unfortunately have been abandoned for lack of political support, involved twenty-two projects in nineteen states and were administered by both the Unites States Employment Service and independent agencies and institutions such as Northern Michigan

University, Tuskagee Institute, and the North Carolina Fund. Table 49 shows the proportion of relocatees reporting improved housing, community facilities, and transportation, by city size. In each case, the response pattern tends to have an inverted-"U" shape; that is, the proportion of relocatees reporting improved conditions increases with city size up to a point and then declines with increasing size. Housing has a peak in the 50,000-99,999 range, while community facilities and transportation each has a peak in the 100,000-249,999 range.

If migrants are to be given an opportunity to depart from traditional paths to the big cities, it is essential that they have more information concerning alternative locations. At present, too many rural to urban migrants act only on the basis of informal information networks, usually involving family and friends. The need for better labor market information has also been pointed out by businessmen. For example, it was demonstrated in Chapter 5 that there is considerable willingness among businessmen in Lexington and Louisville to extend employment opportunities to people from Eastern Kentucky. Firms in these cities—whether medium- or large-size, Kentucky- or non-Kentucky-based—have little or no interest in locating in Eastern Kentucky, and federal inducements only increase their reluctance. Firms also were reluctant to cooperate in government programs to bring workers to the city if these programs implied any direct government involvement with the firms, even in such matters as on-the-job training. In contrast, a great majority of the firms would cooperate in helping Eastern Kentuckians by providing information to—and using the services of—an agency concerned with interarea labor market information exchange and placement programs.

In general, then, the growth center policy proposed here essentially builds on the existing urban structure. The evidence indicates that intermediate-size growth centers could play a key role in a national urban policy with relatively little addition of government programs. What is primarily called for is greater development of human resources in lagging hinterlands and an improved labor market information system. Many businessmen who would provide job opportunities in growth centers would be cooperative on this basis alone; most have little or no interest in subsidies to themselves to locate in lagging areas or to bring workers to the cities. Of course, there are costs involved in economic growth, but a growth center policy would have the advantage of helping city planners to provide a rational system of public services in advance of demand.

In Chapter 1 attention was given to Friedmann and Miller's contention that a new element of spatial order is coming into being—the urban field—which will unify both core and periphery within a single matrix. Whatever the problems in their analysis, they correctly pointed out that

> primary responsibility for the development of urban fields will unquestionably come to rest with the states; but this is only a beginning. The federal government will have a role to play as important as that of local governments, while interstate and intercommunity cooperation in development planning will become much more common that it is at present.[4]

TABLE 49

Percentage of Pilot Demonstration Project Relocatees Reporting Improved Housing, Community Facilities, and Transportation, by City Size

	Population of Receiving City					
	Under 10,000	10,000-49,999	50,000-99,999	100,000-249,999	250,000-499,999	500,000-999,999	1,000,000 and Over
Housing Quality	40	36	45	44	39	35	38
Community Facilities	42	56	59	60	58	47	49
Transportation	24	32	37	46	43	29	34

Source: Compiled from data supplied by the U.S. Department of Labor.

Similarly, Anthony Downs maintains:

State governments are the best focal points for development of any overall strategies controlling future urban growth or even for increasing our choices among forms of future urban growth. They are the only institutions that combine metropolitanwide perspective, decisive powers to override local governments, and sufficient local knowledge and local political roots to make use of such powers acceptable.

The proper federal role in shaping future urban growth should probably be one of structuring effective financial incentives for state governments to assume major policy responsibilities, financing subsidies needed for socially and economically "balanced" new development, and continuing to sponsor innovative approaches to key urban problems.[5]

In many respects, the regional commission approach represents the most efficient framework for implementing growth center policy conforming with these principles. The "Title V" commissions, created under the Public Works and Economic Development Act of 1965, have not yet been very active in implementing projects, but the activities of the Appalachian Regional Commission, created by the Appalachian Regional Development Act of 1965, have been of sufficient scope to permit at least some preliminary evaluation.

The activities of the ARC represent not only an effort to develop a large, lagging region but, even more importantly, a novel experiment in the reform of intergovernmental relations. Ideally, its approach combines respect for national objectives and regional and local differences with broad state and local participation in formulating plans to meet state and local needs. All formal Commission decisions require the affirmative vote of the federal cochairman and a majority of the state members. Program funds are administered through federal agencies, so there is no duplication of effort in this regard by the Commission.

Before creation of the ARC, states and local communities were faced with a maze of agencies, regulations, and forms which made it extremely difficult to prepare coordinated plans. To secure federal funds, state agencies often bypassed the governors' offices by dealing directly with counterpart federal agencies. The ARDA gave the relevant governors a strong voice in establishing how and where federal funds would be spent in their respective states, and it provided a single federal official—the federal cochairman—with whom they could deal on a broad range of grant programs. Through this procedure, the states became brokers between local areas and federal agencies with program funds. With pressure for state agencies to cooperate through the governor's office it became possible to consider systematically such questions as identification of growth centers and the investments they should receive.

Appalachian experience has shown that the regional commission approach depends heavily on the quality of state planning. Since the states have responsibility for determining program and project priorities, the ARC's efforts have had least success in states that have treated it as simply another federal public works program and relied, as in the past, on uncoordinated requests from individual localities for funds. There are a number of reasons why the quality of state planning still leaves much to be desired. First, the planning capacities of existing state agencies were overestimated. Second, only portions of states (with the exception of West Virginia) have been involved in the program. There have not been enough funds in the program to hold the attention of governors faced with competing demands from other parts of their states. Third, where planning has been done by independent, or line, agencies it has been less effective than when done by an agency functioning as a staff unit in the governor's office. Fourth, failure to view the Appalachian program as a long-term operation has resulted in some states' treating it as only another grant-in-aid scheme. Finally, low pay and high personnel turnover rates in state agencies have made it difficult to develop and maintain planning expertise at the state level.

At this writing, the Nixon administration is giving careful consideration to regionalizing the United States, at least on a regionally voluntary basis, and to creating regional commissions for areas willing to cooperate in attempts to implement decentralization of many federal programs. The evidence indicates that it is difficult to make a case for splitting states, unless large metropolitan areas overlap regional boundaries. If whole states are used for planning, it will do much to overcome regional policies aimed more at places than at people. It would then be easier to relate problems of lagging hinterland areas to opportunities in viable growth centers (such centers would include, in Appalachia for example, Lexington, Louisville, and the Piedmont Crescent cities of the Carolinas). Because intrastate moves are likely to cause fewer political problems than interstate moves, the use of whole states would facilitate the implementation of human resource and manpower development programs in lagging areas, as well as comprehensive relocation assistance linked to opportunities in growth centers. However, until the United States has a comprehensive regional policy it will be difficult to define, let alone evaluate, the potentially promising role that regional commissions can play in simultaneously improving the federal system and encouraging more rational spatial resource allocation.

NOTES

1. "Surprises from the Census," *Business Week* (August 8, 1970), p. 16.

2. *Ibid.,* pp. 16-17.

3. *Ibid.,* p. 17.

4. John Friedmann and John Miller, "The Urban Field," *The Journal of the American Institute of Planners*, Vol. 31, No. 4 (November, 1965), 319.

5. Anthony Downs, "Alternative Forms of Future Urban Growth in the United States," *The Journal of the American Institute of Planners,* Vol. 36, No. 1 (January, 1970), 11.

APPENDIX

MIGRATION DATA AND THE ONE PER CENT
SOCIAL SECURITY SAMPLE

In Chapters 6 and 7, tables were presented which ranked places relevant to the Appalachian, Coastal Plains, and Ozarks regions according to the number of migrants they received from these respective areas in relation to their own populations (see, especially, Tables 17, 18, and 33). Migration data in these tables, as well as in several other places in the case studies, were obtained from a 1 per cent Social Security sample. The data were processed at the request of the author by David Hirschberg, Office of Business Economics, U.S. Department of Commerce. The ratio rankings for migration from region to population of center for South Texas, the Upper Great Lakes, and the Four Corners are presented in Appendix Tables 1, 2, and 3.

Social Security Administration (SSA) data are excellent for regional work-force and migration analysis, although several technical limitations exist. The SSA maintains, on magnetic tape, an annual 1 per cent sample of all Social Security records based on specific digits in a person's Social Security number. Because the same Social Security numbers are selected for inclusion each year, it is possible to establish a work history file for all relevant persons who worked in a given period and to determine their socio-economic characteristics for prior or subsequent years. (Before making the data available, all identification of individuals is removed by the SSA.) This file provides information on the demographic characteristics of workers, their wages, their industry, and their geographic location. Specifically, the annual file brings together information from three sources: (1) data on sex, race, and date of birth are obtained from the employee's application for a Social Security number; (2) data on industry and county are obtained from the employer's application for an identification number; and (3) quarterly data on earnings are obtained from employers' contribution reports.

Although Social Security benefits and taxes have increased substantially in recent years, there have been no major changes in the coverage provisions of the Social Security system since 1954. The SSA sample covers almost 90 per cent of persons in paid employment.

There are two types of SSA coverage: mandatory and elective. Employees in profit-making nonfarm industries, regular domestic employees, and federal employees not covered by the federal retirement system are covered on a mandatory basis. Groups covered on an elective basis, individually or jointly, include ministers, employees in nonprofit establishments, and state and local government workers. Farm employees and household workers are required to meet minimum earnings and length of employment conditions. Excluded are most federal civilian workers and railroad workers covered under the Railroad Retirement Act. Data for regular self-employed are available but were not included in this study.

The SSA sample fills an important gap in regional data for employment, migration, earnings, and work-force participation. It is important to note that a considerable amount of data needed for regional economic analysis are not readily available. Except for 1940, 1950, and 1960, no long-term, consistent, and comparable data series is available on employment by industry for regions such as Appalachia. With respect to migration, only data on net flows are available by county for the 1950-60 period, whereas the basic need is for gross flows. Moreover, little regional demographic data are available, aside from those in the decennial censuses, on employment, wages, and migration for whites and Negroes, for males and females, and for the young and old. Unlike the Social Security sample, which is longitudinal, the decennial censuses do not provide data for the same workers over time. Instead they provide data for workers in the same regional demographic category at selected periods in time.

In 1966, according to the SSA, 78.5 million civilian and military workers held approximately 127.0 million jobs. If a worker held more than one job during the year, his earnings from all jobs were combined in order to determine his total wages. However, only one place of work and one industry of employment have been assigned to each worker. For multiple jobholders, the industry and geographic location of the employer paying the highest wages were the determining factors in making this assignment.

The problem of statistical sampling errors in tabulations made from the 1 per cent sample has been examined in a number of documents. They indicate that the 1 per cent sample will yield reasonably reliable estimates of mobility, as long as the number of workers in any tabulated group is not too small. The SSA has suggested that it is reasonably safe to treat the data as random. In the following table, the chances are nineteen out of twenty that the sample value will not differ from the true value by more than the specified percentage variation:

Number of Workers in Sample	Per Cent Variation	Number of Workers in Sample	Per Cent Variation
5	87	1,000	6
10	63	2,500	4
50	28	5,000	3
100	20	10,000	2
500	9	50,000	1

Source: Values supplied by David Hirschberg, Office of Business Economics.

In the three tables that remain, a migrant is defined as anyone working in a given region in 1960 who moved between 1960 and 1965 and who worked in a specified center in 1965.

APPENDIX TABLE 1

Growth Centers for the Southwest Texas Region

Migrant/ Population (x 100)	SMSA	(1) Per Cent Employment Change 1962-67	(2) Employment Increase 1962-67	(3) Mean Per Capita Income 1966	(4) Migrants from Region 1960-65	(5) Per Cent Income Increase of Migrants
1.05	Brownsville-Harlingen-San Benito, Tex.[a]	17.74	3,833	$1,725	1,600	57.7
.60	Corpus Christi, Tex.[a]	25.23	12,598	$2,365	1,600	121.1
.46	Laredo, Tex.[a]	41.12	3,395	$1,375	300	142.9
.42	Austin, Tex.	32.49	13,954	$2,407	900	32.9
.38	McAllen-Pharr-Edinburg, Tex.[a]	19.95	3,985	$1,250	700	395.6
.32	San Antonio, Tex.[b]	20.88	27,234	$2,313	2,300	93.6
.28	Galveston-Texas City, Tex.	7.49	2,638	$2,596	400	− 46.5
.23	Houston, Tex.[c]	37.83	153,528	$2,929	3,400	60.9
.23	Tyler, Tex.	29.93	5,970	$2,502	200	316.5
.20	[Salinas-Monterey, Calif.]	38.17		$3,607	400	199.0

[a] EDA growth center.

[b] Guadalupe County excluded. Data not available.

[c] Liberty and Montgomery Counties excluded. Data not available.

Sources: Columns 1 and 2, U.S. Department of Commerce, Office of Business Economics, *County Business Patterns,* U.S. Summary 1962-67; column 3, U.S. Department of Commerce, Office of Business Economics, *U.S. Department of Commerce News,* August 26, 1968; columns 4 and 5, 1 per cent Social Security sample data (see Appendix).

APPENDIX TABLE 2

Growth Centers for the Upper Great Lakes Region

Migrant/ Population (x 100)	SMSA	(1) Per Cent Employment Change 1962-67	(2) Employment Increase 1962-67	(3) Mean Per Capita Income 1966	(4) Migrants from Region 1960-65	(5) Per Cent Income Increase of Migrants
3.24	Winnebago [County], Wisc.	21.51	7,033		3,500	49.9
1.98	Duluth-Superior, Minn.- Wisc.,[a]	15.88	8,370	$2,665	5,500	30.6
1.67	Minneapolis-St. Paul, Minn.	26.77	123,918	$3,621	24,800	84.1
1.39	Madison, Wisc.	32.24	17,540	$3,044	3,100	76.4
1.35	Green Bay, Wisc.	31.80	9,738	$2,720	1,700	113.1
.94	Fargo-Moorhead, N.D Minn.	17.49	3,976	$2,797	1,000	175.3
.90	Lansing, Mich.	36.43	24,220	$3,030	2,700	118.2
.84	Racine, Wisc.	32.57	11,894	$3,322	1,200	67.7
.74	Bay City, Mich.	40.55	7,790	$2,890	800	203.4
.69	Grand Rapids, Mich.	26.52	34,444	$3,185	3,200	146.8
.68	Saginaw, Mich.	30.90	14,689	$3,105	1,300	238.9

[a] St. Louis County, Minnesota, in the Duluth SMSA, is an EDA growth center.

Sources: Columns 1 and 2, U.S. Department of Commerce, Office of Business Economics, County Business Patterns, U.S. Summary 1962-67; column 3, U.S. Department of Commerce, Office of Business Economics, U.S. Department of Commerce News, August 26, 1968; columns 4 and 5, 1 per cent Social Security sample data (see Appendix).

APPENDIX TABLE 3

Growth Centers for the Four Corners Region

Migrant/Population (x 100)	SMSA	(1) Per Cent Employment Change 1962-67	(2) Employment Increase 1962-67	(3) Mean Per Capita Income 1966	(4) Migrants from Region 1960-65	(5) Per Cent Income Increase of Migrants
8.45	Santa Fe [County], N.M.[a]	24.00	1,733		3,800	25.6
1.83	Albuquerque, N.M.	16.74	10,127	$2,820	4,800	35.9
1.74	Salt Lake City, Utah	15.56	18,394	$2,722	7,800	61.9
1.35	Phoenix, Ariz.	29.42	62,267	$2,842	9,000	41.9
1.30	Provo-Orem, Utah	17.95	3,129	$1,874	1,400	3.1
1.21	Denver, Colo.	14.10	38,927	$3,233	11,300	50.3
1.18	Colorado Springs, Colo.	32.61	8,685	$2,779	1,700	36.1
.78	Las Vegas, Nevada	22.59	11,710	$3,816	1,000	63.8
.71	Tucson, A-iz.	9.31	5,261	$2,468	1,900	34.8
.67	Pueblo, Colo.	4.58	1,052	$2,521	800	73.8
.63	Ogden, Utah	10.49	1,950	$2,895	700	86.8

[a]EDA growth center.

Sources: Columns 1 and 2, U.S. Department of Commerce, Office of Business Economics, County Business Patterns, U.S. Summary 1962-67; column 3, U.S. Department of Commerce, Office of Business Economics, U.S. Department of Commerce News, August 26, 1968; columns 4 and 5, 1 per cent Social Security sample data (see Appendix).

ABOUT THE AUTHOR

Niles M. Hansen is Professor of Economics and Director, Center for Economic Development, at the University of Texas at Austin. He is the author of *French Regional Planning*, *France in the Modern World*, and *Rural Poverty and the Urban Crisis* and has contributed to several professional journals in economics and the social sciences. Professor Hansen is a member of the Board of Editors of *Growth and Change*, *Review of Regional Studies*, and *Regional and Urban Economics*. He served as a member of the U.N. Expert Group on Growth Centers at Geneva in 1969 and was U.S. representative at the Conference on Growth Pole Hypotheses and Policies sponsored by the U.N. Research Institute for Social Development at Madrid in 1970.

Professor Hansen holds a Ph.D. from the University of Indiana.